ELM TREE, EAST RIVER
Under this tree Rev. Jas. McGregor preached the first sermon on the East River, Oct., 1786

PICTONIANS AT HOME AND ABROAD: SKETCHES OF PROFESSIONAL MEN AND WOMENT OF PICTOU COUNTY [CANADA]-ITS HISTORY AND INSTITUTIONS

Rev. J.P. MacPhie

HERITAGE BOOKS
2008

HERITAGE BOOKS
AN IMPRINT OF HERITAGE BOOKS, INC.

Books, CDs, and more—Worldwide

For our listing of thousands of titles see our website
at
www.HeritageBooks.com

Published 2008 by
HERITAGE BOOKS, INC.
Publishing Division
100 Railroad Ave. #104
Westminster, Maryland 21157

Copyright © 1914 Rev. J.P. MacPhie

All rights reserved. No part of this book may be reproduced or transmitted in any form or by any means, electronic or mechanical, including photocopying, recording or by any information storage and retrieval system without written permission from the author, except for the inclusion of brief quotations in a review.

International Standard Book Numbers
Paperbound: 978-0-7884-4635-1
Clothbound: 978-0-7884-7076-9

FOREWORD

THE preparation of this book has been a labor of love. Although the author has been called to spend most of his life in other and distant fields, he has never wavered in his devotion to the place of his birth and the friends of his youth. It has at times been his dearest hope to repay in some measure, by some serviceable deed, the debt of gratitude which he owes to his native land.

Hence the undertaking of this book, the aim of which is to rescue from oblivion the names, the deeds, the heroism of the pioneers of Pictou, and to show how notable a contribution, in men and women, the county has made to the intellectual life and growth of the country.

No fairer scenes than Pictou County presents can be found in the land. Merely as a piece of Mother Earth it is deserving of the most enthusiastic admiration and ardent attachment. Its beautiful elm-studded valleys, its clear, winding streams, its sunlit hills with their fertile fields gently sloping toward the sea, its bonnie, happy homes, its thriving towns, its peaceful villages, its infinitely varied forests and even its rugged glens present charms which never pall.

But the county's moral claim for its people's love and loyalty is stronger than the physical. No spot in our wide Dominion, of equal size and population, has contributed so much to all that is best in our national life. Nowhere else have religion and education so effectually joined hands for the uplift of the people and the promotion of good. Nowhere have righteousness and truth been more genuinely wedded, or produced finer fruitage.

In support of these statements the evidence in this book is confidently submitted. The gathering of the evidence has been a difficult task. It is not claimed that it is either exhaustive or absolutely accurate, but the author has done his best, and he has had the hearty co-operation of many to whom he is sincerely grateful.

It has been said that Pictou is noted for coal and clergymen. Great as is the yield of coal, yet that which is Pictou's proudest product is her men and women. In less than a hundred years she has given to the church nearly three hundred clergymen. She has sent forth one hundred and ninety physicians, sixty-three lawyers, forty professors, fifteen men and eleven women missionaries, eight college presidents, four judges, two governors, two premiers and a chief justice for the Province, besides a host of journalists, politicians and business men of note and name.

There is inspiration in studying the lives of men and women. It stirs within us a deepening desire to imitate and achieve all that was best in their lives. If this book will help the youth of the land to do this, it will have accomplished the main purpose of the writer.

Our fathers have left us a precious heritage and a rare record. We owe them the debt of a grateful remembrance. "Happy are the people," says John Fiske, "that can look back upon the work of their fathers and in their heart of hearts pronounce it good."

June 1, 1914   J. P. MacPhie

TITLES OF CHAPTERS

		PAGE
I.	THE PIONEERS OF PICTOU	1
II.	THE RELIGIOUS HISTORY OF THE COUNTY	33
III.	PICTONIANS IN THE PULPIT	61
IV.	PICTONIANS IN THE MEDICAL PROFESSION	105
V.	THE BENCH AND THE BAR	123
VI.	THE STORY OF PICTOU ACADEMY	135
VII.	PICTOU EDUCATIONISTS	149
VIII.	PICTONIANS IN FOREIGN FIELDS	177
IX.	THE PRESS AND PRINTERS OF PICTOU	191
X.	PICTOU IN POLITICS	203
XI.	PICTOU IN THE BUSINESS WORLD	217

"A wise nation preserves its records, decorates the graves of its illustrious dead, repairs the great public structures, and fosters national pride and love of country by perpetual references to the sacrifices and glories of the past."—*Joseph Howe.*

LIST OF ILLUSTRATIONS

ELM TREE, EAST RIVER	*Frontispiece*
MAP OF PICTOU COUNTY	*Opp. Page* 4
LANDING OF THE HECTOR	8
HON. D. C. FRASER	24
PIONEER MINISTERS OF PICTOU	34
HON. JAMES D. McGREGOR	40
GROUP OF DECEASED MINISTERS	54
CHURCHES IN NEW GLASGOW	62
CHURCHES IN PICTOU TOWN	66
PROFESSIONAL MEN OF PICTOU	74
GROUP OF RETIRED MINISTERS	78
REV. WILLIAM FRASER, D. D.	84
GROUP OF CHURCHES	90
MINISTERS OF TODAY	94
MINISTERS OF TODAY	96
PROF. WILLIAM R. GRANT, M. D.	110
THE BENCH AND THE BAR	126
REV. THOS. McCULLOCH, D. D.	136
PICTOU ACADEMY	140
GROUP OF EDUCATIONISTS	144
SIR WILLIAM DAWSON, LL. D.	150
COLLEGE PRESIDENTS	156
FOUR STUDENTS	162
GROUP OF FOREIGN MISSIONARIES	178
GROUP OF FOREIGN MISSIONARIES	186
MISSIONARIES IN THE FOREIGN FIELD	188
GROUP OF MEN IN PUBLIC LIFE	194
MEN IN PROFESSIONAL AND PUBLIC LIFE	204
TOWN OF PICTOU	220
TOWN OF NEW GLASGOW	226

THE PIONEERS OF PICTOU

Our sires—brave hearts that crossed estranging seas,
And broke the hush of the primeval wood,
Who lit their candles in the solitude,
And met the saffron morn upon their knees—
What though their homes were void of luxuries,
Learning ne'er begged, nor altars smokeless stood,
Nor Cheer nor Friendship lacked the joys their rude,
Kind, log-heaped hearths could give,—It is to these
I bare my head! They wrought without the aid
Invention brings, ere smoke of Industry
Hung o'er these hills and vales; with care they made
This place a garden of the mind; and we,
Cradled in comfort, now bid Mem'ry hold
The fragrance of their lives in jars of gold.

Alexander L. Fraser.

THE PIONEERS OF PICTOU

Chapter I

The "Hope" People

THE beginnings of history-making in Pictou were modest; but they were highly promising if there is aught of force in the adage which says that well begun is half done. There was good augury in the very name of the brig "Hope," the first immigrant vessel which dropped anchor in the Harbor. Yet the future importance of Pictou was probably not even dreamed of by those connected with the little brig. At that time the enterprise doubtless looked hopeful mainly from a land-speculator's point of view.

The "Hope," bearing officers of the Philadelphia Company, so-called, and the families of half a dozen intending settlers, arrived at Pictou from Philadelphia, on June 10, 1767. The Company had obtained a Royal grant of 180,000 acres of land in the district. To this grant were attached the usual stringent settlement conditions. It was in compliance with those conditions that the expedition had been sent out. The families who came by the "Hope," according to Dr. Patterson, were: Dr. John Harris, agent of the Company and his wife; Robert Patterson, the Company's surveyor, his wife and five children; James McCabe, his wife and six children; John Rogers, his wife and four children; Henry Cumminger, his wife and four or five children; and a sixth family of unknown name—it may have been Hand. There is on record in the Pictou Registry, a deed to Recompense Hand of land adjoining that originally taken up by John Rogers.

Of these pioneers the only name which has remained continuously prominent in the County, is that of Harris. J. Sim. Harris, the High Sheriff, is a lineal descendant, in the fourth generation, of Dr. John Harris. He is the fourth Sheriff in succession in that family. None but a Harris has ever been Sheriff of Pictou County.

No descendant of Robert Patterson, bearing his name, is now resident within the County, although his blood runs in the veins of a number of well-known Pictou families. A few of McCabe's descendants bearing his name are to be found in the County. John Rogers gave his name to the district since known as Rogers Hill. His descendants are few, the most distinguished of them being Rev. Anderson Rogers of Halifax, late Moderator of the Presbyterian Synod of the Maritime Provinces. The Cumminger name early disappeared from the County.

The courageous little band which came in the "Hope" had to encounter the usual trials and difficulties of pioneer settlers in a densely wooded country, remote from human neighborhood. But they had plentiful supplies; were busy making improvements, and were cheered from time to time by the arrival of other families and individuals to join their settlement. Of the early followers of the "Hope" from Philadelphia the most important were Rev. James Lyon, a large shareholder of the Company, and Matthew Harris, an elder brother of Dr. John, who settled on the Davidson farm at West River, above the Saw Mill bridge.

Additional settlers came from Truro. Of these the most noteworthy was William Kennedy, who located at the mouth of what has since been known as Saw Mill Brook, where he erected, in 1769, the mill from which the stream took its name. This mill was the first frame building erected in the County.

Up to the 1st of January 1770, there had been 67 arrivals and four births at Pictou. But 36 had removed or died, and the total population was 84. The first census, then taken, sets forth that the settlement possessed 6 horses, 16 oxen, 16 cows, 16 young cattle, 37 sheep and

THE PIONEERS OF PICTOU

10 swine. Dr. Harris is credited with the ownership of a fishing boat and a small vessel, the pioneer of Pictou's subsequent extensive mercantile fleet. The settlers had that year harvested 64 bushels of wheat and 60 of oats.

The heads of families were: John Harris, Robert Patterson, Robert McFadden, Henry Cumminger, James McCabe, Nathan Smith, Rev. James Lyon, Barnabas McGee, William Kennedy, Moses Blaisdell, William Aiken, George Oughterson, Thomas Skead, Matthew Harris, Barnett McNutt, James Archibald, Charles McKay and Robert Dickey.

The "town" or centre of the settlement, was located opposite Brown's Point, at the mouth of Haliburton Creek, since generally known as the "Town Gut." This most unsuitable site had to be accepted because when the Philadelphia settlers arrived, Colonel McNutt, that notorious Nova Scotia land-grabber, had secured a grant of all the shore lands from Brown's Point to the mouth of Pictou Harbor, and thence around the coast to Cariboo Harbor. It was not until the escheating of McNutt's grant that the Harbor front was made available for settlement. After that, a village sprang up at Norway House Point. But it was only at a considerably later date that the present Town site began to be occupied.

The nearest settlement to Pictou was at the head of Cobequid Bay, near what is now, the town of Truro. It was imperative that a safe means of access to this settlement, then known as Cobequid, should be immediately opened up. Accordingly, one of the first cares of the "Hope" settlers was to have a trail laid out between the two places. This path, known as the "Cobequid Road," was in no true sense of the word a road; but it served most useful purposes. It was free from dangerous obstructions; was clear-cut and direct, and could be easily traversed on foot or horseback.

PICTONIANS AT HOME AND ABROAD

It seems rather singular that exact knowledge of the location of this most important land route should so soon have perished. Even Dr. Patterson appears to have been able to secure only vague information as to the location of parts of it. But it can be clearly traced through the land Registry office. The Cobequid Road followed the line of the present West River Road from the Town Gut to "Belmont," the Evans farm. Thence it ran along the West River "old road" to a point near Leithead's stone house. Thence it struck across the face of the hill back of Durham, following exactly the south-west line of James D. Maclellan's lands, and came out near the late Robert Patterson's house. Thence, following the same direction, it crossed Auchincairn to the Four Mile Brook Road, a short distance from the house of the late Thomas Rogers, Postmaster. Thence it followed the present Brook Roads to Mount Thom, over the top of which it passed, and thence down the Salmon River to Cobequid, now Lower Truro. The complete oblivion into which the very existence of this road had fallen, even among the grand-children of the settlers to whom it had been so important, was curiously illustrated some forty years ago when a rusted cannon ball was picked up in the woods at Auchincairn. There was much speculation in the district at the time, as to how this old round shot could possibly have come there. It was not until long afterwards that recovered knowledge of the actual course of the Cobequid Road suggested a partial, but only a partial, explanation of the mystery. By whom or for what purpose such a piece of property as a cannon ball was being transported through the woods between Truro and Pictou, over the Cobequid Road, and how it came to be dropped in such a spot, cannot even be guessed. The Cobequid Road is said to have been laid out by Thomas Archibald and John Otterson of Truro assisted by John Rogers.

The "Hope" pioneers with the exception of Rogers'

MAP OF PICTOU COUNTY

THE PIONEERS OF PICTOU

family, and possibly one other family, were all located along the north side of the West River estuary, from the Town Gut to the "Harbor Head," when the ship "Hector" with her contingent arrived.

The Truro settlers had been advised of the coming of the "Hope," and had sent a delegation to meet and welcome those on board. The delegation consisted of Samuel Archibald, father of the afterwards famous S. G. W. Archibald, John Otterson, Thomas Troop and Ephraim Howard. Tradition says that the two last-mentioned bestowed their names as they passed on the outstanding hills still known as Mount Thom and Mount Ephraim.

The whole County was densely wooded at that time. On the shores of the Harbor, extending up the river valleys and clothing the hills were magnificent growths of pine, almost every tree a gigantic model of its kind. The grove which covered the present site of the town is said to have been notably fine. To the north, more particularly around the shores of Cariboo, there were splendid stretches of oakland. The coast-waters and streams were overflowing with fish, the woods with game. With shelter, fuel and food thus at hand in richest abundance, the original pioneer band and the succeeding parties of settlers can scarcely have suffered the harrowing experiences which later imaginations have conjured up. No doubt they endured certain trials, and privations, like all pioneers. But they were young and vigorous; and their healthy joys must have far more than counterbalanced their troubles. The physical delights of pioneering are too often overlooked in listening to the reminiscences of old men and women regarding their youthful days in the wilds.

One thing is certain—the children of the pioneers never ceased to regret the good old times, "the golden age" of their youth, when they and their neighbors' young folk gathered in the evenings, around blazing wood fires in wide, hospitable, log-cabin chimney places, and when social intercourse had a peculiar freedom and charm, which was sadly missed in later and supposedly more happy years, of greater seeming comfort.

The "Hope" settlers had completed the political organization of the Pictou district, and their members had been materially increased from other sources before the next large band of immigrants joined them, six years later. These are facts which should be duly kept in mind, because they suggest a very different idea of the relative importance of the two first bands of pioneers than that generally entertained. They also shed valuable light on the real condition of the Pictou settlement when the ship "Hector" arrived in 1773.

Effective municipal government had, at that date, been established. The following is a list of its officials in February, 1775:

John Harris...................... Clerk of District
Robert Meresom
John Harris...................... Overseers of Poor
James Fulton
Moses Blaisdale
William Kennedy.............. Surveyors of Lumber
William Aiken........................... Constable
James Fulton..................... Clerk of Market
Abraham Slater..................... Culler of Fish

Before the "Hector" arrived, McNutt's grant had been, in 1770, escheated to the Crown. The whole Harbor front and Cariboo shore were thus thrown open to settlement. The "Hector" reached Pictou on September 15, 1773. Some forty or more years ago this date was arbitrarily selected as Pictou's "Natal Day," a selection made for purely temporary purposes, which has been largely responsible for the popular modern belief that the real history of Pictou began with the coming of the "Hector." But the truth is, that September 15 was chosen because

THE PIONEERS OF PICTOU

June 10, the "Hope" day was past at the time when it became desirable to hold a public picnic for a charitable purpose.

THE "HECTOR" PEOPLE

Those who reached Pictou by the "Hector," on September 15, 1773, numbered, according to one statement, 189; according to another, 179. On January 1, 1770, there were 84 in the Pictou settlement. Probably a good many others had arrived in the intervening three years; so that had the whole "Hector"contingent remained in the County they would scarcely have outnumbered those already in the settlement. But it appears from the list given by Dr. Patterson, which was compiled by William Mackenzie, who ultimately settled at Loch Broom, and was admittedly the only specially educated member of the party, that of 57 heads of families or single men who came by the "Hector," only 27 remained in Pictou. Thirty almost immediately left for other parts of the Province. Even of the 27 who found ultimate resting-place in Pictou several at first went elsewhere; and they or their children only returned at later dates, when the settlement had been very materially increased by immigration from various other sources. These facts indicate that the "Hope" settlement was far from being submerged or eclipsed by the "Hector" party. It seems unlikely that those from the "Hector" who actually settled in the County numbered as many as the "Hope" people whom they found in original possession. Moreover, the "Hector" element was much weakened in influence by two special causes.

With the exception of William MacKenzie, Alexander Cameron, George McConnell, Alexander Fraser and John Patterson, not many of its members could speak English at all fluently; and they scattered themselves over the County, while the "Hope" people were compactly settled together on the Harbor front. It was the descendants of the

PICTONIANS AT HOME AND ABROAD

"Hector" people rather than the first-comers of them who made their influence felt in the District. But there were certain marked exceptions to this which will be duly noted. The party had been recruited from many parts of the North of Scotland. Of those who shipped at Glasgow, John Patterson settled at Pictou; and George McConnell, great-grandfather of the late Robert McConnell, the well-known journalist, at West River. Of those from Invernesshire, William McKay settled on the East River, near Stellarton along with Roderick McKay, Colin McKay, Donald Cameron and Donald McKay; Hugh Fraser settled at McLennan's Brook; Donald McDonald at Middle River; Colin Douglas at Middle River; Hugh Fraser at Twelve Mile House, West River; Alexander Fraser, at Middle River; James Grant, settled first in King's County but returned to upper East River; Alexander Cameron settled at Loch Broom; Alexander Ross, at Middle River; Colin McKenzie at East River, near New Glasgow; William MacKenzie at Loch Broom; John McLennan at the mouth of McLennan's Brook; William McLennan, his relative on the east side of West River; above Durham; Alexander Falconer, near Hopewell. Of those from Southerlandshire, Kenneth Fraser, after first settling at Londonderry returned and settled at Middle River, back of Green Hill; Walter Murray settled at Merigomish; James McLeod, at Middle River; Hugh McLeod at West River; William Matheson settled first at Londonderry, but returned to Rogers Hill. Of those above-named, the following impressed themselves specially on the history of the County:—

William McKay, who settled at East River became a Justice of the Peace; and exercised much influence in his day. One of his sons, William, prepared a map of Nova Scotia, which was published in London and was regarded as authoritative for many years. Another son, Alexander, owned the town site of New Glasgow.

LANDING OF THE HECTOR

THE PIONEERS OF PICTOU

Roderick McKay of Beauly, Invernesshire, also settled at East River. One of his daughters was married to Rev. Dr. McGregor, the pioneer Presbyterian clergyman of the County, and was the grandmother of James D. McGregor the present Lieutenant Governor of Nova Scotia. Another of Roderick McKay's daughters was the mother of the late J. D. B. Fraser, of Pictou, who, besides being prominent in business, was a distinguished leader in the early temperance movement. R. P. Fraser, Esq., Collector of Customs at Pictou, is his son. Roderick McKay's son, the late Robert McKay, Esq., was long Keeper of the Rolls of the County. His grandson, John U. Ross, K. C., is Chairman of the Nova Scotia Public Utilities Commission.

Alexander Cameron settled at Loch Broom which was so named because of its resemblance, from the Harbor approaches, to Loch Broom in Invernesshire. He was of notable family, being a near relative of Cameron of Lochiel, who figured so prominently at the battle of Culloden, which young Alexander Cameron witnessed as a runaway boy of fifteen. Many distinguished Pictou County names are in his line of descent. Among them, Rev. Alexander Blaikie, D. D., long a leading clergyman of Boston; Thomas Fraser, a Californian Senator, and Alexander Fraser, his brother who constructed the first ship railway across the Isthmus of Panama; the late E. M. Macdonald, M.P., a prominent journalist and at the time of his death Collector of Customs at Halifax; his brother A. C. Macdonald of Pictou, barrister, at one time Speaker of the Nova Scotia House of Assembly and father of the late C. D. Macdonald, barrister, of Arthur C. Macdonald, a prominent Consulting Engineer and capitalist of London, England, and of Mrs. James Primrose of Pictou; John D. Macdonald, late Treasurer of the County of Pictou and his sons, E. M. Macdonald, K. C., M. P., barrister, at present representing the County in the Dominion Parliament, Rev. Peter M. Macdonald, a leading clergyman and literary man of Toronto, and John D. Macdonald, editor and proprietor of the Pictou "Advocate"; the late Hon. W. D. R. Cameron, formerly of Durham, Member for Guysborough County of the Legislative Council of Nova Scotia; William Cameron, ex-M. P. P., at present Municipal Treasurer of the County, and Mrs. W. E. Maclellan of Halifax. This partial list of Alexander Cameron's better-known descendants furnishes striking evidence of the possible value of one good settler to a new country.

Alexander Fraser, settled at Middle River. He also was of excellent birth. He was an immediate descendant of the Frasers, Lords Lovat. Along with the noble head of that House he was deeply involved in the "Forty-Five." Two of his brothers were slain at Culloden. His wife was Marion Campbell, youngest daughter of the Laird of Skreigh, Invernesshire, who had raised a troop for Prince Charlie, and was wounded at Culloden. A son of this couple was the first native-born Pictonian. From them descended the Rocklin Frasers, so prominent in the industrial life of the County. John Fraser of Hopewell, is a grandson. His son, Thomas, the "Beachcomber" of the Morning Chronicle and formerly editor of the Halifax "Daily Echo," is at present a leading citizen of Saskatoon. Mrs. J. P. Esdaile of Halifax is Alexander Fraser's great granddaughter. Dr. Patterson states that Fraser was in most "comfortable circumstances" when he left Scotland.

William MacKenzie ultimately settled at Loch Broom, beside his particular friend and associate, Alexander Cameron, after having spent some years at Liverpool, Nova Scotia, where he married a daughter of one of the pioneer settlers of that place, a lineal descendant of one of the "Pilgrim Fathers," who came to Massachusetts Bay in the "Mayflower," in 1621. William MacKenzie also was of good family. His father was a gentleman of title and a scion of the Seaforth MacKenzie family. Young MacKenzie was a student of eighteen, when he left Scot-

THE PIONEERS OF PICTOU

land. He engaged himself as schoolmaster to the "Hector" party in a spirit of youthful adventure, but pressed also, no doubt, by the necessities of the times. The party broke up at Pictou, and he was never required to exercise his assumed vocation; but he became, which was of much more importance, the historian of the party. It was from his memoranda and diaries that Dr. Patterson obtained most of his definite authentic information concerning the "Hector" party. He had only one son, and nearly all of his grandchildren removed to the United States where, without exception, they prospered in business or industry. Only two of his lineal descendants are now in Nova Scotia —Mrs. W. E. Maclellan of Halifax and Mrs. John Carson of Pictou.

He was known in his day as the "Peacemaker." It was he who donated the site of the first church erected in Pictou County, which was situated at Loch Broom, close to the east shore of the West River estuary, on lands latterly owned by the late Duncan McCabe.

John Patterson, grandfather of the late Rev. Dr. Patterson, the painstaking and talented historian of the County, settled near the future town, where he became a prosperous business man, a Justice of the Peace and a leading citizen. Several of his descendants, besides the late Dr. Patterson have been prominent as public and business men in Colchester and other counties of the Province. His Honor, Judge Patterson, of the County Court, New Glasgow, is a son of Dr. Patterson and a great grandson of John Patterson of the "Hector".

Alexander Falconer, who settled near Hopewell, was the grandfather of the late Rev. Dr. Falconer, a few years ago Moderator of the General Assembly of the Presbyterian Church in Canada, whose two talented and highly distinguished sons are Dr. R. A. Falconer, President of the University of Toronto, and Dr. James W. Falconer, of the Presbyterian College, Halifax,

PICTONIANS AT HOME AND ABROAD

William Matheson who settled at Rogers Hill was the father of the late William Matheson, of Durham, grandfather of the late David Matheson, barrister of Pictou, and great grandfather of E. S. Matheson Town Engineer, Yarmouth.

Should it seem surprising to any that so many men of good birth came to Pictou among the pioneers, it is only necessary to point out that the same thing is now happening in the Northwest. Sons of some of the best families in the United Kingdom are at present homesteaders and working farmers on the Canadian prairies. A few years ago the titled head of one of the oldest Baronetcies in Ireland died as a billiard-marker in a Winnipeg Saloon; and he was no scapegrace. He had gone to the West in the hope of restoring the fallen family fortunes, and had accepted the first employment available. It was only after his death that his identity was disclosed, although without proclaiming his title he had not changed his name.

Speaking of the times when Pictou was first settled, in connection with the fact that a noble Lord, a member of the Scottish House of Peers and the representative of one of the oldest families in Scotland was a glover in Edinburgh, Burke, compiler of "Burke's Peerage" and "Landed Gentry", in his "Vicissitudes of Families" states that a Nobleman, one of whose family afterwards settled in Pictou County, "used to stand for years in the Old Town, Edinburgh, selling gloves to those present; for, according to the fashion of the time, a new pair was required for every dance. The only occasion in which he was absent from his post was at the ball following the election of a representative Peer, when he appeared in full dress, and joined with those present in the dance. It may be added that sons of the best families in Scotland are often found at trades in these times, arising from the difficulty of being provided for."

THE PIONEERS OF PICTOU

The great disadvantage under which most of the "Hector" settlers labored was lack of means. The fact that they were able to emigrate at all, at their own charge in those days of "hard times" is proof positive that they were the most prosperous and enterprising of their contemporaries, and that they were much better off than the average of their countrymen at that time. Scotland was then in a state of extreme financial and industrial depression. With reference to that period the latter half of the eighteenth century—Lord Rosebery, in addressing the annual meeting of the Edinburgh Savings Bank, in 1909, stated that "there was not then more than two or three hundred thousand pounds of current money in all Scotland," whereas at the date of his speech there were "over fourteen million pounds of deposits in the two savings Banks of Edinburgh and Glasgow alone." Lord Rosebery said, and his words are well worth pondering by all who would form just conceptions of the character of the "Hector" settlers in Pictou,—"Our great grandfathers—my great grandfather, at any rate—was living at that time. Our great grandfathers did great things in those days on a mess of pottage—they had no more, but with it they helped to mould the Empire. They maintained their poor without legal compulsion. They sought nothing from external help; and they laid, in their nakedness, and barrenness, the foundations of the prosperity which reigns in Scotland at this moment. None of us would care to live as they did. Some of the poorest in our country at present would shrink from the manner of life which was endured by some of the noblest in those days. We should not care to share their privations; but we should not be unwilling to be convinced that we possess their independence, their self-reliance, their self-respect; and I regard that as the greatest blessing resulting out of thrift—independence of character. Whether Scottish pride arose out of Scottish thrift, or whether Scottish thrift arose out of Scottish pride, I really cannot decide; but they are closely intertwined so closely that you cannot perhaps separate them. But, at any rate, the combination produced a character which has governed the country."

These are striking facts, vouched for by a very great and reliable man. Dr. Patterson's invaluable history of Pictou County makes it clear beyond dispute that the "Hector" settlers possessed "the thrift" and "the pride" of their country in the highest degree. The subsequent lives of them and their descendants have demonstrated beyond question that they possessed also the "governing character."

At the close of 1773, there were thus in Pictou County, two very distinct pioneer strains, almost equal in numbers—the "Hope" settlers of mixed American, English, South of Scotland and North of Ireland origin, who had been some years in the country, and the "Hector" settlers, of north of Scotland extraction, newly arrived and, for the immediate time being, a charge rather than a help to the struggling settlement, although they contributed so materially to its development and progress in later years.

The South of Scotland People

A year and a half after the arrival of the "Hector" came the third and last band of those who may properly be called the pioneers of Pictou. These were the south of Scotland people, sometimes erroneously spoken of as the "Dumfries Settlers."

Their party was organized to take up lands in Prince Edward Island. They chartered their own vessel; sailed from the port of Annan, in Dumfriesshire, and arrived at Georgetown in the spring of 1773. Although exceptionally well outfitted, they were immediately overtaken by bad luck.

A great plague of mice destroyed their first season's crop. The following spring they procured seed from Nova

Scotia, and re-planted; but the mice ate the very seed in the ground. That autumn, to crown their misfortunes, supplies which they had brought from Scotland and stored at Georgetown Harbor were plundered by riotous New England sailors and fishermen, who were ashore on a drunken orgie on the eve of sailing for their homes. The settlers were left in dire straits for food; and suffered intensely during the succeeding winter. In the following spring, 1775, they removed in a body to Pictou. There were thirteen families and one single man in the party. With one exception they settled permanently in Pictou County.

Seven of the party located at West River. These were Anthony Maclellan, William Clark, David Stewart, William Smith, Joseph Richards, John McLean and Charles Blaikie. Four settled on the Middle River, namely, John Crockett, Robert Marshall, Robert Brydone and John Smith. Two, Thomas Turnbull and Anthony Culton, went to the East River. One, Wellwood Waugh, remained in Pictou for a time, but later removed to Colchester County where he gave his name to Waugh's River. His half brother, William Campbell, the bachelor of the party, settled at the Beaches, a mile below the present Town of Pictou.

The members of this party added a new and specially valuable element to the primitive Pictou settlement. They came from one of the best agricultural districts in Scotland. They had been closely associated with the land all their lives. Several of them were sons of landowners; others had been tenant farmers. They knew how best to deal with the soil, and they had the means to enable them to put their knowledge into practice. They lost no time in getting to work. Most of them prospered from the beginning. This party, more than any of its predecessors, directly and indirectly influenced the future of Pictou. They seem to have been well satisfied with their new home; and at once, by means of letters to those whom they had left behind, became the most effective of immigration agents. Through their representations their relatives and acquaintances in the South of Scotland were directed to Pictou; and continued coming in increasing numbers, for many years.

The original members of the party were mostly from Galloway, that famous, old Principality in the extreme southwest of Scotland, made up of the Shires of Kirkcudbright and Wigton; but a few of them were from Dumfriesshire and Ayr, or had connections in those counties. A glance at the names of those most prominent in the early commercial, industrial and political life of Pictou will show that a large proportion of them were from one or other of the south Scottish counties above mentioned. The monuments in the old Cemetery of Pictou, and the still older Durham Cemetery reveal an overwhelming preponderance of Galloway, Dumfries and Ayrshire names.

These south of Scotland settlers imported live-stock, seeds and fruit-trees from the land of their birth. At West River traces of the famous black cattle of Galloway were distinctly discernible not many years ago; and quite possibly are yet to be found. The sturdy Galloway breed of horses, too, left its mark in the county. But the Galloway people made a far deeper and infinitely more valuable impress on the social life of the county. From them, to mention an outstanding name, came Rev. Thomas McCulloch, the founder of Pictou Academy, who, although himself a native of Renfrewshire, was the descendant of one of the oldest and most honorable of the baronial families of Kirkcudbrightshire, with a history dating back almost to the Norman invasion. The names of Thomas, Michael and William McCulloch, so familiar in Pictou history, are distinctly traceable through hundreds of years of the annals of Galloway. John Dawson, another of Pictou's worthy early settlers, who, following the southern pioneers, came

THE PIONEERS OF PICTOU

to Pictou in 1791, and whose great grandson Mr. Bonar Law is now leader of the Conservative party in Great Britain, was also a Galloway man, a native of the Parish of Irongray in Kirkcudbrightshire.

Of the members of the south of Scotland party, Wellwood Waugh, as already stated, did not remain long in Pictou. He was of the Waughs, Lairds of Barnbarroch, Kirkcudbrightshire. His father had married a daughter of Dr. Wellwood, of London, hence the name "Wellwood." After the death of her first husband, Mrs. Waugh married a Mr. Campbell, and had a son, William Campbell, who came to Pictou with his half-brother Waugh, and settled at the Beaches. His sons, in after years, went to Tatamagouche where they entered into commercial and shipbuilding enterprises, and became prominently identified with the public life of Colchester County. Mrs. Patterson and Mrs. John S. Maclean of Halifax are William Campbell's granddaughters, as was also the late Mrs. Howard Primrose, Pictou.

Of the two members of this party, Thomas Turnbull, and Anthony Culton, who settled on the East River, there are few descendants bearing their names in the County. Dr. Albert Culton of Cumberland County is a great grandson of Anthony Culton.

Of the four who settled on the Middle River, John Smith early lost his life by drowning. His descendants if any are unknown. John Crockett's descendants are still to be found on the Middle River and a number of them in Upper Stewiacke, Colchester County, to which place one of his sons removed. Most of Robert Marshall's descendants bearing his name, have removed to the United States. David Marshall and Robert Brown, merchants of Pictou, are his great grandsons. There are few of the Brydone name now left in the County, but a large number of Robert Brydone's descendants remain; among them have been two clergymen, three lawyers and four physicians.

Of those who went to the West River, Anthony Maclellan settled at Durham where he purchased a large block of land on the west side of the River. In addition, he owned lands purchased from one of the Blaikies on the east-side of the River opposite Durham, which were reconveyed by his son Anthony Maclellan, junior, to James Blaikie by deed dated February 23, 1800. It was out of this lot that Anthony Maclellan set aside the site of the old West River Church and of the older part of the West River Cemetery in which he was the first man buried, in the year 1786. A Mrs. Gerard was interred there a year earlier. With this exception, Anthony Maclellan's is the oldest marked grave in Pictou County.

His eldest son James, was killed in 1793, by falling from a building which was being erected near the Ten Mile bridge. His remaining son, Anthony, succeeded to his property. Of his three daughters, Ann, was married first to William Smith and after his death to Donald McLeod; Catherine, to Joseph Richards, grandfather of the late Rev. John Richards; and Janet to John Collie, whose grandson is Dr. J. R. Collie, of River John and great grandson Dr. J. R. M. Collie of London, England. A somewhat striking incident, in this connection, was the marriage, at the same place and date, of the widowed Mrs. Smith and her daughter to Donald McLeod and his son, who by these marriages became respectively the forefathers of Judge John D. McLeod of Pictou and Rev. John M. McLeod, formerly of Charlottetown, and later of Vancouver, B. C.

Anthony Maclellan was of the Maclellans of Bombie, Hereditary Sheriffs of Galloway. He was born in 1720 and was fifty-three years of age when he left Scotland. In the list of his descendants are to be found the names of thirteen clergymen, six barristers, seven physicians, one member of the Dominion Parliament, many successful business men, among them the late John S. Maclean of

THE PIONEERS OF PICTOU

Halifax, the late Daniel Macdonald, Collector of Customs, Pictou, the late Robert McConnell of the Finance Department, Ottawa, W. E. Maclellan of Halifax, Post Office Inspector for Nova Scotia, and, last but not least, Robert Maclellan, LL.D., the present honored Principal of Pictou Academy.

On the east side of the River, opposite to Anthony Maclellan settled Charles Blaikie. His lands were extensive, including at one time or another all those now or lately occupied by his descendants on Green Hill, and all of the David Matheson farm, opposite Durham, now owned by Mr. Hamblin. Charles Blaikie, too, was in very comfortable circumstances on his arrival. He was a skillful farmer, and the family have always been prosperous. One of his early descendants was the late Rev. Alexander Blaikie, D.D., long a prominent Clergyman in Boston. Another is Mr. Blaikie of Londonderry, a wealthy retired merchant, at one time a business partner of the late A. W. McLelan, Lieutenant Governor of Nova Scotia.

Next above Anthony Maclellan, on the west side of the River, settled William Clark on lands all of which have ever since been continuously held by his descendants. No farmers in the County have been more enterprising and successful than they. Among the descendants of William Clark have been three clergymen of the Presbyterian Church.

Next above William Clark settled David Stewart on lands which are now in the possession of his great grandson, Robert Stewart. The Stewart name has at all times been synonymous with integrity. Among Robert Stewart's descendants are the two Drs. Collie above named.

Next above Robert Stewart settled William Smith, where his grandson Wilson Smith, now resides. He was descended from a Dumfriesshire land-owning family, members of which had borne titles of honor. He too was possessed of considerable means. A milling industry was early established at his place, which proved highly successful and was of great benefit to the surrounding country. His son, the late Anthony Smith, father of Wilson Smith and grandfather of James W. Smith of Pictou, head of the Atlantic Milling Company, was long a prominent and active member of the old Court of Sessions for Pictou County. This family too, has contributed most generously to the professional as well as to the business life of the Province. Among William Smith's descendants have been one member of the Dominion Parliament, six clergymen and three prominent barristers.

Next above William Smith settled Joseph Richards, on the lands occupied by his descendants until Robert Richards removed some thirty years ago to Manitoba, where he and his family now reside. A brother of his, Rev. John Richards, a Presbyterian clergyman, was called to Ontario, where he passed his life.

Above Joseph Richards settled John Maclean, the farthest south of the members of this party. He was of Dumfriesshire family. Rev. John Maclean of Richibucto, N. B., the father of the late John S. Maclean of Halifax, was his grandson. John Maclean, arriving in July, 1775, was one of the first-chosen elders of the first Presbyterian congregation organized in Pictou County, to which Rev. Dr. McGregor was called to minister in the autumn of 1786. The family have ever since been prominent in Church work. The late Howard Maclean, of Halifax, one of the most promising young barristers in Nova Scotia when his untimely death occurred was a great grandson of John Maclean, as was also the late J. J. Maclean of Hopewell. Mrs. George Arthur Bayne of Winnipeg is a great granddaughter.

With such settlers on its banks it is not surprising that the West River should so long have been the ecclesiastical and educational centre of the County. To Durham was early moved the first Presbyterian Church, located originally at Loch Broom. Durham did not receive its present name until the time of the late Lord Durham in Canada. The name was the suggestion of the late William Graham, merchant, and was confirmed at a public meeting held for the purpose. The late Miss Margaret Cameron of Durham distinctly remembered the meeting, and that it was on Mr. Graham's motion that the name Durham was chosen. At the West River church all those settled around the Harbor, including the people of the Town, continued to worship until Rev. Thomas McCulloch arrived in 1803 when a separate congregation was organized in Pictou. In Durham Cemetery most of the pioneer settlers of West Pictou are buried. To Durham, at a later date, the Presbyterian Theological Seminary for Nova Scotia was removed, and there established and conducted for a number of years.

But Durham, as a village, did not start until 1822. The first lot was sold on March 19, of that year, by Anthony Maclellan, junior, to John Henderson, shoemaker. It was the half-acre lot, at the lower end of the village, on which Waller's blacksmith shop stands. The price paid was 14 pounds, 10 shillings—not a bad price for a beginning. But on April 13, 1824, two years later, Henderson bought the adjacent half-acre lot, for which he paid 25 pounds. Henderson must have been prospering, for on June 14, 1826, he bought 30 acres of land in the rear of his first two purchases for which he paid 100 pounds. Durham seems to have been experiencing a "boom" at this time. On May 16, 1830, Alexander MacDonald blacksmith, bought an acre lot adjoining Henderson's lots,— price 50 pounds. Two years later, on August 15, 1832, a large lot, in the southern angle of the Rogers Hill road was sold for 125 pounds. The following day it was resold to J. R. Ritchie for 175 pounds.

From this time on, during a number of years, Durham grew and prospered greatly, owing to the development of the timber trade of which it was a large purchasing centre. At one time it had four inns—three of them "licensed," and many places of general business. It had mechanical establishments of almost every kind; two churches, and the Presbyterian Seminary. In 1849, Durham Post Office ranked fifth in the Province in revenue collected, being, in this respect, at that time ahead of New Glasgow. The Post Offices, with a larger revenue than that of Durham were Halifax, Yarmouth, Truro and Pictou. With the decay of the timber trade Durham fell into rapid decline. But the surrounding country has lost none of its solid and long-established prosperity.

The Early Settlers of the East River

The East River is well known for the variety and the beauty of its scenery. On its banks are Springville, Bridgeville, and Sunny Brae, villages of abundant peace and plenty. It is well known for its rich deposits of iron and lime; its vales and hills, its towering elms and winding river, but it is still more famous for the men and women it has produced; for the district from Churchville to Kerrowgare, a distance of about fifteen miles, has given thirty-five clergymen to the Presbyterian Church, a Governor, a Chief Justice and a Premier to the Province.

What a community produces along educational and religious lines depends not a little upon its antecedents. The early settlers of the East River were a sturdy stock, a sober, stalwart worshipping set of men and women, with iron in their blood, and a burning love in their hearts for the Church and the School. They yoked education and religion together, and the combination produced a fine type of men and moralities. The writer, thirty years ago, taught the Shorter Catechism in the public school at Sunny Brae.

As far as can be ascertained, the first settler in Churchville was John Robertson. He emigrated from the Highlands of Scotland and arrived in 1784, in Pictou. He was a brother-in-law of Roderick McKay, who was one of the first settlers on the East River. The first clearing Robertson made in Churchville was where John Robertson, miller, once resided.

John Fraser was among the first settlers of Springville. To distinguish him from others of the same clan he was called Iain Ruaidh, or Red John. He settled about 140 years ago on the place now known as the Holmes Farm, where he built the first frame house in Springville. It is still standing. Later, the property was bought by Senator Holmes and here he always lived and ended his days. The house is low, but comfortable, reminding one of "the lowroofed house of Socrates." Here the Hon. Simon H. Holmes, once Premier of the Province, was born and bred.

John Fraser, Red, had three sons James, Donald and William who settled in the community. One of his daughters married Simon Fraser, Basin: she was the mother of Thomas Fraser, Foreman, and consequently, grandmother of Graham Fraser, the Iron King of New Glasgow. Another daughter, married Mr. Fraser of McLennans Mountain and was the mother of William Fraser, Postmaster, New Glasgow.

James, his eldest son, always called Seumas Iain Ruaidh, was a devout man and well known for his honesty. He raised a large family, who were all of an intellectual turn. It was James Fraser who gave the name Springville to the place from the many sparkling streams in the vicinity.

John Fraser, eldest son of James Fraser, who went always by the name of "Catach" was quite a celebrity in his day. His second son, Donald was the geologist of the East River. His second daughter was mother of James A. Fraser, Editor of the Eastern Chronicle.

James Iain Ruaidh and David McLean were near neighbors and each had an inexhaustible lime quarry on his farm. In 1836, three thousand bushels of lime were manufactured and sold at the Albion Mines. In the same year twenty-five hundred tons of square timber were rafted down the river by the athletic sons of Sunny Brae—the Chisholms, Kennedys, Thomsons, McDonalds and McIntoshes. David McLean was the father of the Rev. James Maclean D. D., and Dr. Duncan Maclean, both settled for a long time in Shubenacadie, N. S.

James Grant, one of the passengers on the Hector settled first in King's Co., N. S. He came from Glen Urquhart, Scotland. He was married and some of his children were born in the old country. He moved from King's Co. to Cariboo, Pictou Co., and lived there for some years. Before coming to this country he gained some knowledge of milling. By this time the Upper Settlement people began to raise considerable quantities of grain, especially wheat, but they had no mill to convert it into flour. So they persuaded James Grant to leave Cariboo and move to the East River. This he did, and settled at Millstream in 1790. He erected a mill on a stream issuing from Grant's Lake, on a site some twenty rods further down than the one now occupied by Grant's Mill. This was the first regular gristmill on the East River.

James Grant died in February, 1822, age ninety-seven. He is described as a quiet, peaceful man. He lived for some years before his death on a farm subsequently owned by Duncan McPhie. When James Grant died, there were twelve families in Millstream and Lime Brook: Duncan Grant, James Grant, dyer, Alexander Grant, miller, Robert Grant, elder, John Fraser, James Fraser, David McLean, Donald Fraser, Duncan McPhie, Donald Mor Fraser, David McIntosh, and Donald Cameron.

James Grant had four sons and two or three daughters. One of his sons, Duncan, died in 1847 and was buried at Springville Bridge, and was either the first or one of the first buried there. He once owned the farm on which the Rev. Angus McGillivray lived and died.

HON. D. C. FRASER
LATE LIEUTENANT GOVERNOR OF THE PROVINCE

His sons, Alexander and Robert were men of influence and note and had much to do with the making of the life and the growth of the community. They succeeded their father in the milling business and were leaders in the Church and the State. Alexander Grant was married to Nellie McKay. The Rev. Robert Grant, the historian of the East River was their son. James, eldest son of Alexander Grant and Nellie McKay, was known as the Dyer. He owned woolen mills near Springville. His sons Alexander, John Walter, Hugh and Robert succeeded him.

Robert Grant was married to Mary, daughter of James Robertson. He had three sons; James, who owned a saw mill at the head of Grant's Lake and was for many years an elder under the Rev. Mr. McGillivray; Alexander Robert, who owned a gristmill on Millstream; and Dr. William R. Grant, a distinguished professor in Pennsylvania Medical College. One of his daughters, married John Fraser, Basin. Another was the wife of Colin Robertson, Churchville.

In 1784, a settlement of disbanded soldiers was made further up the river. They came to Pictou at the close of the American War. They were, originally, from the Highlands of Scotland.

The first who came was James Fraser, Big James, who in company with Donald McKay, elder, settled on the intervale a little below where St. Paul's Church now stands. He and fifteen others took up a tract of over three thousand acres, extending up to Samuel Cameron's on the east side of the river, and to James Fraser's, Culloden, on the west side. They were a sober and industrious class of people and endured great hardship. But they endured it with characteristic Scottish tenacity and in the belief that the future had much in store for them. A few years rolled by and they had made homes for their families and laid the foundations for a God-fearing and prosperous community. To ponder over the hazards and hardships they faced with such optimistic heroism, is but to admire and pay them a justly earned tribute.

The names of these first settlers were: Donald Cameron, his brothers Samuel and Finlay, Alexander Cameron, Robert Clark, Peter Grant, first elder in the settlement, James McDonald, Hugh McDonald on the east side of the river. James Fraser, Duncan McDonald, John McDonald, brother of James, John Chisholm, drowned at the Narrows with Finlay Cameron, John McDonald, 2d, John Chisholm, Jr.

John McDonald was born at Glen Urquhart and belonged to the Glencoe McDonalds. At the time of the Glencoe Massacre, 1692, one of the McDonalds fled to Glen Urquhart and settled there. John McDonald was a grandson or great grandson of that man. He was about eight years in the Royal Highland Emigrant Regiment, and three of his sons fought with him in the Revolutionary War on the Loyalists' side. He was married twice. By his first wife he had Duncan, Alexander, Mary and Christy. By his second wife, Margaret Grant, he had James, Ewen, Ann and Ellen. Ann was married to Thomas Fraser, Basin. Ellen was married to James Robertson. The well known Deacon Robertson, Churchville, was their son. Duncan, eldest son of John McDonald, was married to Catherine Fraser. James, their third son, was born about 1759. He was a Corporal in the 84th regiment. He married about 1782, Mary Forbes, by whom he had Alexander, Edward and other sons.

He left East River about 1834, and settled in Upper Canada where he died in 1857. He was an elder under Dr. McGregor and a very prominent man on the East River in his day. Alexander McDonald, his fifth son, settled near Bridgeville and was the father of Hon. James McDonald, Chief Justice of Nova Scotia.

Edward, second son of James McDonald, had a son John A. McDonald, who left the East River and settled in Ontario. John A. was the father of James A. Macdonald, LL.D., editor of the Toronto Globe and one of the ablest political writers in Canada. He is a Presbyterian minister and still preaches occasionally. Ontario claims the honor of being his birthplace, but the East River is entitled to some recognition in any reference to his parentage for both his parents were born there.

James Fraser, Culloden, married Ann Robertson, Churchville, and had John, Catherine, Margaret, Alexander and James. Alexander married Catherine Rankine, of Merigomish. The late Rev. James W. Fraser, of Scotsburn, was their son.

Alexander Cameron settled on the first lot above Culloden. Donald Cameron with his brother Samuel were natives of Glen Urquhart. Donald served eight years in the army. He was settled on the saddle lot. It is said that the price given for it was a saddle. Thomas Fraser, who lived in Springville, purchased it from Donald Cameron and settled on it about 1815. He married Janet Fraser, widow of Hector Thompson. He left the lot to Simon and Donald Thompson, sons of his wife by her first husband. Duncan, son of Donald Cameron, was an elder in Dr. McGregor's time.

John Campbell, son of James and Elizabeth Campbell was born at Garabeg, Glen Urquhart, July 24, 1790. He entered the army in 1812. He married Janet, daughter of Archibald Fraser, in 1812. He came to Pictou in October 1818. Peter G. was his eldest son. He married Elizabeth Kennedy, a sister of Donald Kennedy, Sunny Brae. His son, Donald K., is a minister in Illinois. One of his sons is a physician in Illinois.

Donald, son of Charles McIntosh, settled on the lot above Donald McDonald, Roy. He lived there for a few years and then sold to William Ciuin McDonald and removed to Fox Brook. William Ciuin was a teacher but gave it up for other pursuits. In the course of time he started a store in New Glasgow. He put up a frame house on his lot, boarded it, but never shingled it. Donald McDonald, Roy, bought a piece of land near New Glasgow from Dr. Skinner. He exchanged it with William Ciuin for the lot in the Upper Settlement and gave it to his son, John McDonald, Roy. John finished the frame house which William Ciuin had begun and lived in it. It is a question who had the honor of living in the first frame house above Springville. It may have been an honor, but what of it? Were not the men who were born in log houses as strong, as wise and good as the men born in frame houses?

David McIntosh, son of Charles McIntosh, settled a short distance above his brother, Donald McIntosh. David was born in Inverness, Scotland, and married Christie Chisholm. James McIntosh, his son, Island, East River, married Catherine Grant. Two of their sons David C. and Finlay G., entered the ministry. Hugh, another son of David McIntosh, married Isabel Polson and gave that man of weight and wisdom, Rev. Charles D. McIntosh to the ministry. Two other sons entered the medical profession.

Alexander McDonald, Roy, was a native of Glen Urquhart, came to Pictou in 1803, and settled at Sunny Brae. He married Christy Fraser and had four sons and four daughters. Squire McDonald of Springville was his second son. Alexander, his third son, was well known in Sunny Brae for many years. The Rev. Finlay R. McDonald, a minister in Scotland, was the youngest son of Squire McDonald.

John Thompson and his son Alexander settled at Sunny Brae in 1801. Alexander married Bella McIntosh by whom he had John, Andrew, Alexander, William, James, Finlay, Christy, Janet and Mary. John Thompson had a brother Donald who settled at Nine Mile River. Rev. James Thomson of the West River was his grandson.

THE PIONEERS OF PICTOU

Angus McPhie, in Glen Urquhart married Christy, daughter of John Thompson and had Duncan, Christy, John, Ewen, Alexander, Mary and James. He came to Pictou in the ship Aurora in 1803. Duncan, his eldest son, settled at Springville and was an elder in Rev. Angus McGillivray's day. His son, John McPhie, was one of the old Pictou magistrates. He died in May 1912 in the ninety-sixth year of his age.

The first settlers in Sunny Brae were: Robert McIntosh, Donald Kennedy, James Chisholm, John Grant, Duncan McDonald, John Thompson, John McDonald, Peter Cruikshank and John McGregor. They came to Pictou in 1801 and settled in Sunny Brae in 1802.

Peter Cruikshank was a native of Strathspey, and came to Pictou in 1789. In 1792 he had two hundred acres of land and a cow. He was married and had Elizabeth, William, John, Alexander, Marjorie and Peter.

Robert McIntosh married Jessie, daughter of John Thompson, and had John, William, Jessie and others. Finlay, his son settled on Blanchard Road. He married Catherine Fraser. John Robert McIntosh, his son, married Margaret, daughter of Donald McDonald, blacksmith. Their son Finlay H., is pastor in Sydney, C. B.

John McGregor was a man of great strength. When they were making the Big Miller's dam, he stood before a log that was rolling down the bank to stop it, but the log went over him and killed him. The Big Miller's dam was built about the year 1807.

Donald McDonald, Breac, came from Kerrowgare, Scotland, in 1802. He was an intelligent man, and was an elder under Dr. McGregor. In 1811 he had four hundred acres of land, two cows and eight sheep. He had eight children. Finlay settled in Caledonia; Donald, his eldest son, settled in Sherbrooke, and was a tailor.

His son, James McDonald, was born in Scotland in 1801. He was a tailor but gave up the tailoring business for farming. He married Catherine, daughter of Alexander Fraser, Downie. He was ordained to the Eldership by the Rev. D. B. Blair and fully adorned his office. He was succeeded on his farm by his son, the late John A. McDonald, Kerrowgare. James A., his son, is a minister in the United States.

Donald Ross, was born in Eddrachillis, in Sutherlandshire. He came to Nova Scotia in 1816. He lived for one year on Irish Mountain, but removed to Iron Ore, and settled back of Alexander McDonald's place. He lived there twenty-two years. He then purchased the farm of James McIntosh and occupied it. He had eight children. Jessie was married to Kenneth McKenzie, elder, Churchville.

Jane, who was born at Irish Mountain was married to James Cumming, elder, of Sunny Brae. William, his eldest son married Mary, daughter of William Cumming, and had by her, Donald, William, Peter, Hugh and John who settled in Ontario. Donald, his eldest son, has lived in New Glasgow for many years where he is greatly beloved. He has been an honored elder in St. Andrew's Church for nearly half a century.

Hugh Ross was an elder in the United Church, New Glasgow, and died some years ago. William Ross was an elder in Sunny Brae Church. He was married to Christy, daughter of Robert Grant, Finlay's brother. He had a large family, who were all actively identified with the church. Two of his sons, William and Robert D., entered the ministry.

John Grant was born in Glen Urquhart, and came to Pictou in 1801 and settled at Sunny Brae. He married Margaret McIntosh, and had by her Peter, William, Robert, Catherine, and Finlay. Robert was three years old when he came to Pictou. He married Mary McDonald, and had five sons, John, Alexander, Peter, William and Duncan.

A son of Duncan Grant, William M., is a minister in

Ontario. William, who settled in Providence, R. I., married Jessie McDougall, a sister of Roderick McDougall of Westville. One of his sons became a physician, another a lawyer, and two daughters are teachers in the Grammar schools, Providence. Marjorie, daughter, of Robert Grant, married Joseph McKay; two of their sons William R. and Robert G., are clergymen. Catherine, a sister of Finlay Grant, married Duncan McPhie, Springville. They had John, Christy, Alexander, Jessie, Margaret, Mary, Angus and Peter. Their youngest son, Peter McPhie, married Isabella Cruikshank. Their two sons, John P. and Duncan A., entered the ministry.

Finlay Grant was born in 1800 and was one year old when he came to Pictou. He married in 1827, Ann, daughter of Alexander Fraser, Downie, and had Alexander, a merchant in New Glasgow and elder in the United Church. John, an elder in Sunny Brae church who gave two sons Robert J. and William P., to the ministry; William, who entered the ministry, gave two of his sons to the church, Melville and Clarence. The latter died while a catechist. Finlay Grant was ordained to the eldership by the Rev. John Macrae in 1834. He was a clear-headed, well-read and useful man.

The descendants of John Grant who came to Sunny Brae in 1801 were numerous and took a leading part in the activities of the Church. Fifteen of them entered the Christian ministry and fourteen were regularly ordained elders in the church. This is perhaps as many or more than was given by any other family in the county.

CHAPTER II

THE RELIGIOUS HISTORY OF THE COUNTY

PICTOU County is probably the strongest Presbyterian community in Canada. Presbyterianism was first on the ground, and has continued in possession. So far as known, all who came in the "Hope" and "Hector" were Presbyterians, with the exception of one man on the "Hope" and one family on the "Hector" who were Roman Catholics. The South of Scotland settlers were, without exception, Presbyterians.

The first settled minister, Rev. James McGregor, D.D., was an ardent Presbyterian, as was also his coadjutor, Rev. D. Ross. These two, with Dr. McCulloch who came later, for over forty years upheld the blue banner of Presbyterianism, and planted the seed out of which grew many of the leading churches, not only in the County but in the Maritime Provinces.

The early settlers in Pictou were almost exclusively Scottish. They and their descendants have proved themselves worthy of their nationality. They believed profoundly in the Word of God and in the blessings of education. They were ardent lovers of the Sabbath and the Sanctuary. The great truths and principles of Presbyterianism they brought with them to their new home, where they had much to do with the making and moulding of Pictou's religious life and history. No group of Scotsmen could long be content without the ordinances of religion; and hardly had the first ground been cleared and the first seeds planted in Pictou before its pioneers began to ask for the ministrations of their Church.

One hundred and fifty years ago, there was not so far as known, a single Presbyterian minister in Nova Scotia.

PICTONIANS AT HOME AND ABROAD

One hundred years ago there were but eight or nine, and none at all in any of the other Maritime Provinces. Indeed, there were then only three other Presbyterian ministers in all Canada; Revs. George Henry and Alexander Spark of Quebec, and Rev. John Bethune of Montreal, the latter of whom held the first Presbyterian service in that city, on March 12, 1786. West of Montreal there were at that time no Presbyterian ministers. Ontario was an almost uninhabited wilderness, and the Great North West was unknown.

The first minister who labored in Nova Scotia was Rev. James Lyon who was an Ulster Scotsman. He arrived here in 1764 or 1765 and remained about seven years. He was a graduate of Princeton, N. J., and was ordained to the ministry in 1764. He was a member of the Philadelphia Land Company which sent the pioneer settlers to Pictou in the "Hope"; and in all probability it was arranged that he should be the minister for the new settlement. But it is found that for several years he ministered to the people of Halifax, Onslow and Truro. In 1769, he removed to Pictou with his family, remaining only about two years, after which he went to Maine. The only memorial of his visit to Pictou is that he gave his name to Lyon's Brook.

A few years after Mr. Lyon's departure, James Davidson, a schoolmaster, established a Sabbath School at Lyon's Brook for the religious instruction of the young. Mr. Davidson came from Scotland to Truro with Rev. Mr. Cock in 1772. Soon afterwards he removed to Pictou with his family; secured a lot at Lyon's Brook, and made his home there. On week days he taught the children reading, writing and arithmetic; on the Sabbath he gathered them together in his house to teach them the Shorter Catechism and the Word of God.

It is said that his was the first Sabbath School in the County, and probably in the Province. If this is true,

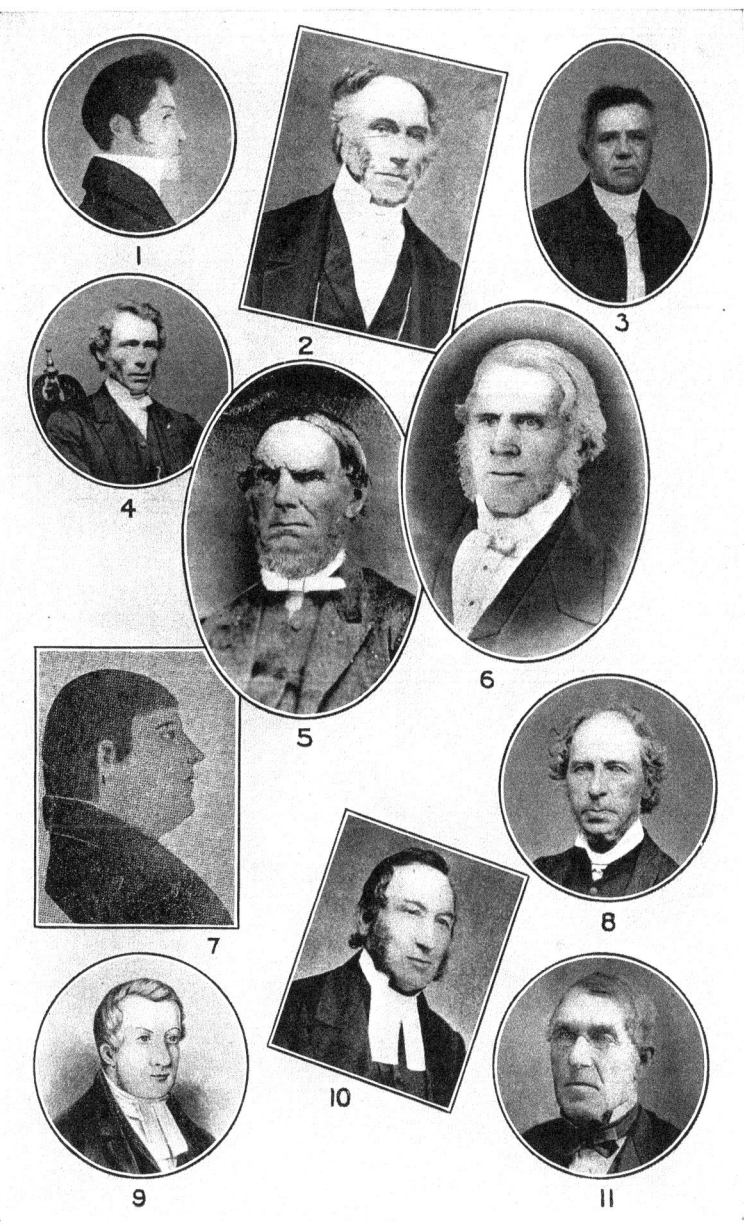

PIONEER MINISTERS OF PICTOU

1 John Maclean
2 David Roy, D.D.
3 Alexander McGillivray, D.D.
4 Alexander Sutherland
5 Robert S. Patterson
6 Angus McGillivray
7 Duncan Ross
8 George Walker
9 Donald A. Fraser
10 John L. Murdoch
11 John Stewart, D.D.

THE RELIGIOUS HISTORY OF THE COUNTY

then to an old-time school master belongs the honor of originating the Sabbath School idea, and Mr. Davidson was the first in line of a noble band of teachers, to whom, the county of Pictou owes much of its fame. This was many years before Robert Raikes began his world-wide Sabbath School movement. Mr. Davidson returned in 1776, to Truro, where he ended his days.

In April, 1818, a Sabbath School was organized in Prince St. Church, Pictou. Its promoters were Robert Dawson and John Geddie. Rev. Thomas McCulloch was pastor when the school started. It began with about eighty scholars. Ten years later the school had increased to 260. The first superintendents were Robert and James Dawson. The first teachers were John Geddie, F. Ross, David Fraser and R. S. Patterson.

In 1823 a Sabbath School Society was formed for the purpose of organizing schools in the outlying districts. In four years the number had increased to 75, chiefly through the agency of this society. The first Sabbath School in New Glasgow was organized about 1838, in St. Andrew's Church, by Rev. John Stewart who was then pastor. He taught the Bible Class, which was held in the church during the summer months, and in the winter months in the manse. Among the first teachers were John McKay, Alexander McKay, Dr. Forrest and the wife of Rev. John Stewart.

From the time of the arrival of the "Hope" and "Hector" the colony increased in numbers and influence. A steady stream of immigrants continued to pour into the county till, in 1786, the total population was about five hundred. These were settled principally along the three rivers, East, Middle and West with a few families scattered around the shore, from Pictou to Merigomish. Rev. Mr. Cock of Truro frequently visited the people and preached to them. Indeed, many considered him their minister, and traveled thirty miles on foot to Truro to observe the Lord's Supper — sometimes carrying their children there for baptism. But the time had come for them to have a minister of their own.

Accordingly, a committee was appointed, consisting of Robert and John Patterson of Pictou, William Smith of the West River, Robert Marshall, Middle River, and Donald McKay of East River, to secure a minister. They agreed to pay eighty pounds for the first and second years. The call was sent to Scotland. It came before the General Associate Synod of Scotland at its meeting on May 3, 1786, when it was accepted by Rev. James McGregor who accordingly sailed for Halifax, from Greenock, in the brig Lily, on the fourth day of June, 1786.

Dr. McGregor was born in Perthshire, Scotland in 1759. He arrived in Nova Scotia in July 11, 1786, when he was 27 years of age. He had had some experience in ministerial work in Scotland. He was a good scholar and a sound theologian. His knowledge of Gaelic was accurate and his mastery of the language complete, as may be seen from his "Gaelic Poems and Hymns," which are still in demand among Highlanders.

He landed in Halifax, after a voyage of 37 days, and at once proceeded to Pictou, where he arrived on Saturday, the twenty-first day of July, 1786. His welcome was cordial. His first sermon was preached in Squire Patterson's barn about a mile west of the present town. He preached in English in the forenoon from the text, "This is a faithful saying, and worthy of all acceptation, that Christ Jesus came into the world to save sinners", and in Gaelic in the afternoon on "The Son of Man is come to seek and to save that which was lost."

The second Sabbath after his arrival, July 30th, he preached at the East River, a little below what was afterwards Albion Mines. The third Sabbath's preaching took place at the lower end of the Middle River, at what was then Alexander Fraser's homestead. It was at this

THE RELIGIOUS HISTORY OF THE COUNTY

time he first met Robert Marshall, who was afterwards his life-long friend and helper. Early in October he visited the upper settlement of the East River. His first sermon in that section was preached at James McDonald's intervale, (now Cameron's) under the shade of a large elm tree, which forms the frontispiece of this book. The tree is still standing and flourishing vigorously. Occasionally, he preached at Mr. Charles McIntosh's, about six miles farther up the River in a grove of trees, and at West Branch at Mr. Donald Chisholm's or at James Cameron's. Late in the Autumn, he paid his first visit to Merigomish, where for thirty years he continued at intervals to give supply. During the summer he preached in the open air, then during the winter, in private dwellings.

For nine years, Dr. McGregor was the sole minister in Pictou County, preaching, visiting, traveling on snowshoes in winter, and in summer literally paddling his own canoe. His congregation was widely scattered, and his mission field extensive.

Among the settlers who came to Pictou in 1783, were three Frasers, who all settled on the East River. Their names were; Thomas, Simon and Alexander Fraser. They are noteworthy because they were the first elders chosen to that office. Having been previously ordained as elders before leaving Scotland, they were elected by the people, and these three men, with Dr. McGregor, as Moderator, formed the first session in Pictou, Sept. 17, 1786, thus completing the organization of the congregation which at that time comprised the whole county.

The next year the session was increased by the addition of Donald McKay and Peter Grant of the East River. Robert Marshall and Kenneth Fraser of the Middle River, John McLean and Hugh Fraser of the West River and John Patterson of the Harbor. They were ordained on May 6, 1787.

During the summer, the people built two log churches, the first in the county. The one was situated near the site of the old Duff Cemetery, a short distance above New Glasgow; the other on the Loch Broom side of the West River, beside a brook, on land, owned at that time, by William MacKenzie, who gave the site. Dr. McGregor describes the building of these churches. During the month of July 1787, the men were chiefly engaged in building the two meeting houses. Instead of having contractors, to build them, they agreed to divide the work among themselves. One party cut the logs and hauled them to the site; another hewed and laid them; another provided the shingles; those who had knowledge of carpentering made the doors and the windows; the glass and nails were bought. Moss was stuffed between the logs to keep out the wind and rain. The churches at first had no pulpits, and, when they were provided at a later date, they were not of mahogany, but of the white pine of Pictou. The buildings were some thirty-five or forty feet long, by twenty-five to thirty feet wide. The only seats in them were logs of wood with the upper side hewed. It is unnecessary to state that they were without cushions. There was a gallery, or rather, an upper story, with a floor seated with logs and slabs to which the young went up by ladders.

Such were the first two churches of Pictou. They had no modern improvements. Even the luxury of a fire in winter was unknown. There were no carriages and no roads at that date Our dear mothers in Israel walked to church, or went by boat or horseback, in bonnet and shawl and gingham dress. The music was far from pretentious. The preacher and his sermon would now be considered antiquated. But the writer of this volume is old fashioned enough to think that no sweeter praise and prayers ever ascended to God than these devout pioneers offered in glen and glade and primitive building.

THE RELIGIOUS HISTORY OF THE COUNTY

With all our knowledge and progress, we have not got beyond them in essentials.

In 1803, the old log church near New Glasgow was replaced by a frame-building at Irishtown, (now called Plymouth). Here Dr. McGregor built a house made of brick, the first of its kind in the Eastern part of the Province. He employed a man from the old country to make the brick. Here he lived till near the close of his life. The fact that Dr. McGregor received no salary until he had been over a year at work did not prevent him from doing his whole duty as a minister. His salary was to be eighty pounds for the first two years, ninety for the third and fourth and one hundred pounds currency per year thereafter, which was a very generous allowance for that time, more particularly in a new and struggling settlement. The salary at first was raised by an assessment on lands and cattle. With certain changes this was continued till 1815, when the method of obtaining the salary was changed to voluntary subscription.

On the 27th day of July, 1788, the first Sacrament was held at Middle River, in the open air. It was dispensed on a beautiful green plot, on the left bank of the river, sheltered by a lofty wood. Here one hundred and thirty sat down in Nature's great cathedral, for the first time in this new land, to own a Saviour's dying love. There the sacred Supper was dispensed annually till 1795. At the first communion thirty-eight new communicants joined. Each year there were a few additions till, in 1793, the number had reached two hundred and forty. At the same time five hundred persons were under training with a view to becoming communicants.

In 1793 a census of the County was taken. In 1769, there had been 18 families and a total population of 120. In 1786, there were 90 families and about 500 people. In 1793, there were 178 families, a gain of one hundred per cent in seven years.

For nine years Dr. McGregor labored alone At the end of that time two young ministers arrived from Scotland, Revs. Duncan Ross and John Brown. They reached Pictou in the summer of 1795, and remained there for a little time to rest. Meantime the sacrament of the Supper was dispensed at Middle River. Messrs. Ross and Brown assisted in preaching and serving the tables.

The next step was for those three to organize a Presbytery. Accordingly, at the close of the sacrament, on Monday, July 7, 1795, Messrs. McGregor, Ross and Brown held a meeting in Robert Marshall's barn, and formed themselves into "The Associate Presbytery of Nova Scotia." On this occasion Dr. McGregor preached on Neh. 2:20, "The God of heaven, he will prosper us; therefore we his servants will arise and build." The meetings of Presbytery, were occasions of rich enjoyment. Business was apparently a secondary matter, at all events, for five years, they kept no minutes of their proceedings. But their meetings were scenes of hearty Christian fellowship and conference about the trials or successes of their work; intelligence from friends in the dear homeland, the new movement in Missions, the meaning of some particular text, or sometimes an hour of harmless mirth and merriment, these engaged their attention and made their meetings times of fraternal enjoyment.

Dr. McGregor and Mr. Ross were associate ministers for the county till July 14, 1801, when a division was made. Thereafter West and Middle Rivers formed one congregation, with Mr. Ross as minister. East River, another, with Dr. McGregor in charge; and the Harbor a third, to be supplied by these two till another minister could be secured.

In Nov. 1803, Rev. Dr. Thos. McCulloch, with his wife and three children, arrived at Pictou from Scotland. His coming was a great event in the ecclesiastical and

HON. JAMES D. McGREGOR
LIEUTENANT GOVERNOR OF THE PROVINCE

THE RELIGIOUS HISTORY OF THE COUNTY

educational history of the County, as well as in that of the Province. He had been assigned to Prince Edward Island, but owing to the lateness of the season, he was unable to secure passage. He was engaged to supply the Harbor congregation till spring. Before winter was over, the people gave him a call, and he was inducted as their minister, June 6, 1804. The town of Pictou, at this time, consisted of something over a dozen houses, a few barns, a blacksmith shop and the Court House. There was no church, and the people met in private dwellings and other places. Until that time the people of the Harbor had worshipped in the log church at Loch Broom, but they now set about the erection of a church of their own, and a frame building was built on the lot at present occupied by Prince St. Church. That building served the congregation till 1848, when the existing church was erected. Dr. McCulloch resigned in 1824 to give his whole time to educational work. He was succeeded by Rev. John McKinlay who continued in charge till his death, 1850. He in turn was succeeded by Rev. James Bayne, D.D. Mr. McKinlay was a native of Scotland, and came to this country in 1817. For several years he was a teacher in Pictou Academy before he became pastor of the Harbor church.

River John was organized into a congregation in 1808, with Rev. John Mitchell as its first settled minister. There were about fifty families at this time in the community. Mr. Mitchell, who came from England, was in early life a rope-maker, but being anxious to preach the Gospel, he prepared himself for the work when about thirty years of age.

He made several missionary tours in Canada before settling in River John. Though originally a Congregationalist, he united with the Presbytery of Pictou. His labors extended over a district now served by five or six ministers. Here he labored with great diligence and faithfulness, giving special attention to the training of the young and the superintendence of prayer meetings. He died in 1841, in the seventy-sixth year of his age. He is described as a man of great cheerfulness.

Rev. William Patrick was the first minister at Merigomish, and the fifth in the county. He came to Merigomish in 1815 and was inducted pastor. In early life he was brought up in the Reformed Presbyterian Church, but connected himself with the Anti-Burgher Church. Mr. Patrick labored with great fidelity, preaching on week days as well as Sabbaths, and faithfully attending to family visitation, prayer services and catechising. On May 7, 1844, the Rev. A. P. Miller was ordained as his colleague. On the 25th of Nov., 1844, he died, greatly beloved by his people, aged 73 years.

An event of much importance to the Presbyterian Church took place on the third of May, 1817, when a union between the Burgher and Anti-Burgher Churches was consummated. The united body assumed the name of The Presbyterian Church of Nova Scotia, and a Synod was formed and divided into three Presbyteries. Rev. James McGregor was chosen as first Moderator. Of the nineteen ministers of the Synod of Nova Scotia, fourteen had been connected with the Anti-Burgher Church, three with the Church of Scotland and two were Congregationalists. This union was productive of much good. The hearts of ministers and people were greatly encouraged. Now they were one body, ready to establish and build up the Kingdom.

Hitherto the Church had been dependent upon Scotland for its ministers; but it had long been evident that they must look elsewhere for their supply. Accordingly, in 1820, the Synod established a Theological Hall in Pictou for the training and education of a native ministry.

Pictou claims the honor of being the birthplace of the first Presbyterian Theological School in Canada. The

THE RELIGIOUS HISTORY OF THE COUNTY

moving spirit in the enterprise was the Rev. Thomas McCulloch, D. D., an enthusiastic educationist and a man of wonderful foresight. As early as 1805, two years after his arrival from Scotland, we find him planning a school for the education of young men which resulted in 1816 in the establishment of Pictou Academy, where several young men who had the ministry in view were prepared for entering upon a theological course.

In the autumn of 1820 the Divinity Hall was opened with Dr. McCulloch as the first Professor of Theology. The classes were taught in one of the rooms at Pictou Academy. Twelve students entered upon the study of theology the first term. The young men supported themselves by teaching and met the professor at intervals of a fortnight to receive instruction in their theological studies. In 1824, the first fruits of the church's educational efforts were realized in the licensing, ordaining and settlement of six of the students. These were Messrs. R. S. Patterson, John L. Murdoch, John McLean, Angus McGillivray, Hugh Ross and Hugh Dunbar. The first four were licensed on June 8, 1824 by the Presbytery of Pictou. Three of these, Messrs. Patterson, Murdoch and McLean before accepting calls, proceeded to Scotland, where after passing a creditable examination they received the degree of Master of Arts from the University of Glasgow.

One of the first of the graduates to be settled was Angus McGillivray. He became the worthy successor of Dr. McGregor in the Upper Settlement of the East River. He was inducted Sept. 1, 1824. For the long period of 40 years he continued to labor, amidst great discouragements, but with great fidelity. In 1864 he tendered his resignation and on the 20th of July, 1869 he died in the 77th year of his age and the 45th of his ministry. His congregation included both the East and West Branch, a district now supporting five Presbyterian ministers. The first meeting house on the East River was at Grant's Lake, on the farm now occupied by Joseph H. Grant. It was a log house, built in 1790, and served the East and West Branches.

Having visited London and Edinburgh, Messrs. McLean, Murdoch and Patterson returned to Nova Scotia reaching Pictou after a passage of forty five days. They were soon settled in pastoral charges. Mr. McLean was ordained in 1825 and in 1826 accepted a call to Richibucto, N. B. In a short time he was compelled to resign his charge on account of ill health. For two years he conducted a private academy in Halifax with success. He died in 1837, in the 37th year of age. During his brief ministry he was distinguished as an able preacher, and a zealous missionary; he took a deep interest in Sunday school work and was one of the first advocates of the cause of temperance.

Mr. Murdoch was settled at Windsor and died there in 1873, in the 74th year of his age. His congregation extended all over western Hants and for nearly fifty years he preached there with ability and success. He was greatly beloved by his people and was the spiritual father of many children. He was a valuable member of the courts of the church. One of the ecclesiastical measures which he brought before the Synod in 1840 was, that this Synod do form itself into a society to be called "The Society for the Propagation of the Gospel in the Lower Provinces." Dr. Keir and Mr. Murdoch drafted the rules which were adopted. The successor of that domestic Missionary Society is the Board of Home Missions of the church of today of which Mr. Murdoch was a member as long as he lived.

Bedeque, in Prince Edward Island was the scene of Mr. Patterson's ministry. At the time of his settlement in 1825 it is said there was not a wagon in the parish or a mile of road in which to run one. The country was almost an unbroken forest. The congregation at first was

THE RELIGIOUS HISTORY OF THE COUNTY

small and during the greater part of his ministry he did not receive more than $300 per year and only half in money. He labored without interruption till a few years before his death in 1882, having been 56 years and a half in the ministry. Mr. Patterson was a distinguished student and a true friend of popular education. His zeal for missions is well known and second only in fervor to Dr. Geddie's.

In 1827 Mr. Ross accepted a call to Tatamagouche and New Annan. Here he continued until 1840 when he accepted a charge in Prince Edward Island, where he died suddenly in 1858.

Mr. Dunbar was an English and Gaelic preacher. He settled at Cavendish, Prince Edward Island in 1827. Resigning in 1840 he engaged in teaching but also preached regularly where he resided. He died in 1857. These six men have this prominence and honor in common that they were the pioneer native ministers of British North America, at all events of the Presbyterian Church.

From this time forward the Church made rapid growth and progress. Congregations were formed, and suitable pastors settled over them. Home missions were established to aid the weaker churches. It was a time of strengthening and enlargement.

On April 16, 1813, over a hundred years ago, a Bible Society was organized at Durham, N. S., the first in the County and the second in the Province, that in Truro being first. The first contribution received for the Bible Society, London, from any place outside of England, came from Pictou County. Money was a rare commodity in those days, but, in 1807, two hundred and fifty-six dollars, and, in 1808, three hundred and twenty dollars were collected in the county and sent to the London Society. In 1825, the Society was reorganized, with headquarters in Pictou. In 1840 the New Glasgow district was organized into a branch of its own.

For forty-four years Dr. McGregor labored in the County. He died on the third day of March, 1830. He had lived to see the congregation of which he was originally the sole Pastor grow and develop into six congregations with settled pastors, a Presbytery and a Synod organized to conduct the business of the church, an Academy and Seminary founded to educate and train ministers, and the cause of Presbyterianism firmly established in the Maritime Provinces.

Dr. McGregor was twice married, first to Ann, daughter of Roderick McKay, by whom he had James, Christina (Mrs. Abram Patterson, Pictou), Roderick, Jessie (Mrs. Charles Fraser, Green Hill), Sarah (Mrs. George McKenzie, New Glasgow), and Robert.

In 1812 he married Mrs. Gordon, widow of Rev. Peter Gordon, by whom he had Mary (Mrs. (Rev.) John Cameron, Nine Mile River), Annabel (Mrs. (Rev.) John Campbell), Sherbrooke, and Peter Gordon.

His successor in the New Glasgow congregation was Rev. David Roy, who was inducted, April 13, 1831.

Four years after Dr. McGregor's death, Mr. Ross died, in the sixty-fifth year of his age. For thirty nine years he wrought with great faithfulness and diligence. Besides pulpit and pastoral duties, he gave considerable time to public affairs. He took a deep interest in education, being a trustee of Pictou Academy from its beginning, till his death. He was a pioneer in the organization of temperance work. The idea of a total abstinence Society originated at the West River, and the honor of forming the first Society on this basis in Nova Scotia, and the second in Canada, belongs to its founders. It was organized in January 1828, and Rev. Duncan Ross, George McDonald and Donald McLeod were the prime movers.

Mr. Ross' last public act was assisting at a Communion service in Pictou, town, and taking a leading part in the ordination of Alexander McKenzie, a young student

THE RELIGIOUS HISTORY OF THE COUNTY

from the Seminary. He married Miss Elizabeth Creelman of Stewiacke, and had a family of fifteen children. Two of the sons were Rev. James Ross, D.D., afterwards Principal of Dalhousie College, who succeeded him, and Rev. E. Ross of Truro. A daughter who was married to Mr. Miller, Rogers Hill, gave three sons to the ministry, and another married to Mr. Crockett, gave two sons.

We now come to the story of the Kirk in the County of Pictou. For many years, a large number of the immigrants, chiefly from the Highlands of Scotland, who had settled in Pictou, belonged to the Church of Scotland or the Kirk. They naturally had great affection for the church of their fathers, but continued to attend the Anti-Burgher Church, which was the only Presbyterian Church within their reach. From time to time, many of them were appointed elders and office bearers in Dr. McGregor's and Mr. Ross' congregations. A spirit of harmony and cooperation prevailed. But, alas! a root of bitterness sprung up. Upon this unfortunate story it would be vain to dwell.

At that time Rev. Donald Allan Fraser came from Scotland and landed at Pictou in 1817. Sometime afterwards a large number of the Kirk people withdrew from the connection altogether, and formed themselves into the Church of Scotland in Nova Scotia with Rev. Mr. Fraser as their leader. Mr. Fraser was a man eminently qualified to gain the hearts and affections of the Highlanders — young and handsome, an accomplished scholar and a powerful Gaelic preacher. The first congregation organized was at McLennan's Brook. There were about forty families settled there at that time, all Highlanders. They extended to him a call which he accepted.

They erected a frame church capable of seating about five hundred persons. This was the first church in the County erected in connection with the Church of Scotland. Beside it, they built a log house for himself and his wife.

Next year a church was built at Fraser's mountain, about six miles from McLennan's Brook and two miles from New Glasgow. There were some twenty-five families connected with it, and it became in course of time, the nucleus from which St. Andrew's Church, New Glasgow was formed. Here Mr. Fraser continued to labor with great acceptance and success until 1837, when, to the regret of his congregation, he removed to Lunenburg. Thence he went to St. Johns, Newfoundland, and founded St. Andrew's Church. He died, Feb. 7, 1845, greatly honored as a preacher and as a man. He was the first Presbyterian minister settled in Newfoundland. His son, late Hon. J. O. Fraser, St. Johns, Nfd., spent his early manhood at McLennan's Brook.

The next Kirk congregation organized was St. Andrew's Church in the town of Pictou. It first met for worship, in the old Court House, in 1822. In 1823, a wooden building was erected. Their first minister was Rev. K. J. McKenzie, a native of Stornoway, Scotland, who came to Pictou in 1824. He was a man of fine ability and a good preacher in Gaelic and English. His labors were chiefly confined to the Town where he took a prominent part in the educational and political questions of the day. He died in 1838, in the 39th year of his age. He was succeeded by Rev. Mr. Williamson. In 1849, Rev. Andrew Herdman became pastor and ministered for thirty years. In 1866, a brick and stone building was erected. It was burnt in 1893, but rebuilt shortly afterwards.

The next organization after Pictou town was West Branch and East River formed into one congregation. The two districts were nearly equally divided in the number of families, between the Kirk and the Anti-Burghers. For many years Dr. McGregor supplied the one section, and Mr. Fraser the other.

Rev. Angus McGillivray succeeded Dr. McGregor in 1824. The Kirk people were without a settled minister

THE RELIGIOUS HISTORY OF THE COUNTY

until 1832 when Rev. John Macrae came from Inverness, Scotland to be their pastor. Both parties now had regular services, but there was only one church in each district occupied by Kirk and Anti-Burghers on alternate Sabbaths. In 1815 framed buildings were erected at St. Paul's, East River, on the hill above the present church, and at the West Branch, on a hill near Cameron's Brook, not far from St. Columba's Church. Mr. Macrae entered upon his work with great zeal and continued to labor most acceptably to the people for 16 years, when he returned to Scotland.

In the Western part of the County, a congregation was organized at Gairloch and Saltsprings. These two districts contained about four hundred families, nearly all from the Highlands of Scotland. There first minister was Rev. Hugh McLeod who settled there in 1822. He was succeeded by Rev. Donald McIntosh who remained until the disruption.

Rogers Hill, now Scotsburn, was formed into a congregation about the same time as Gairloch and Saltsprings. The community was settled by Highlanders from Sutherlandshire, who nearly all belonged to the Kirk. The first church (St John's) was built in 1823, and is the oldest church building in the County. Rev. Roderick Macaulay was the first minister. In a few years he went to Prince Edward Island, where he entered into politics and became speaker of House of Assembly. The next minister was the Rev. Donald McConnichie. He was a powerful Gaelic preacher, and the Highlanders considered him very eloquent in the first and best of all tongues. He left for Scotland in 1844.

In 1827 Barney's River was organized into a congregation, with Rev. Donald McKichan as its first minister. He was a man of some ability and a faithful pastor. After a few years he removed to Cape Breton. At a later date he returned to his first charge, and remained there till 1844. The people of Barney's River were nearly all Kirk men. For ten years the people were dependent on Home Mission supply part of which was given by Rev. Dr. McGillivray of McLennan's Mountain. The next pastor of the Kirk congregation was Rev. James Mair, in 1857.

The Kirk grew and prospered. The grain of mustard seed had grown into a stately tree. During the period of twenty-six years, the Kirk had become strong and influential. Then, suddenly, her progress was arrested by an unfortunate division.

During all those years, a memorable conflict had been going on in the Kirk, in the Old Land, which resulted in the disruption of 1843 and the formation of the Free Church of Scotland, led by Rev. Dr. Chalmers.

The ecclesiastical disturbance took a year to cross the sea, but it arrived in due time, and the Free Church in Nova Scotia was formed. It was a time of excitement and confusion. Old-time ties were severed; venerable associations were broken up. There were painful misgivings and divisions and hard feelings were engendered. But it is not necessary to dwell on this unhappy story. It is a thing of the past; there let it rest. That year, seven of the Kirk ministers in Pictou returned to Scotland to fill pulpits made vacant by Free Church ministers. A majority of the people remained in the Kirk but they were, for most part, as sheep without a shepherd.

Rev. John Stewart, New Glasgow, was of the first to join the Free Church movement. He became pastor of St. Andrew's Church immediately after Mr. Fraser's resignation, in 1837. In 1819 a frame church was built at Fraser's Mountain. It was originally a part of McLennan's Mountain congregation, but was separated in 1830, when the church was moved down to New Glasgow and placed on a site near the present St. Andrew's Church. This was the first church building in New Glasgow.

THE RELIGIOUS HISTORY OF THE COUNTY

When Mr. Stewart left the Kirk, about one hundred and forty-five families, and all the elders, save one, went with him, and they formed Knox Church, of which he became pastor. Mr. Stewart was born in Scotland, in 1800, and came to Nova Scotia in 1833. He was a man of fine natural gifts, enriched by a superior education. He spent himself most lavishly in the best interests of the Church and education. He rendered valuable service in establishing the Free Church College in Halifax and was highly successful in raising funds for it, and in encouraging young men to enter the ministry. He died, May 4, 1880, having completed his four score years in April.

In 1844, a delegation from the Free Church in the Old Country visited the Maritime Provinces. At that time, about one third of the people of the Kirk at Scotsburn joined the Free Church. They worshipped in St. John's Church until 1862, when Bethel Church was built. Rev. Alexander Sutherland became their pastor. He was a stirring and energetic preacher. In 1859 he became a minister of the Scotsburn and Saltsprings Churches, and in both charges gave full and fruitful proof of his ministry. He died in Nebraska, in 1897, in the 80th year of his age.

Knox Church, Pictou, was organized in Jan. 1846, by a handful of mechanics and farmers whose sympathies were with the Free Church of Scotland. The church building was erected in 1848. The first minister inducted was Rev. Murdoch Sutherland. He was called, because of his burning zeal and piety, "the Robert Murray McCheyne of Nova Scotia." On account of ill health he resigned his charge in 1857, and returned to Scotland where he died. The next pastor was Rev. Alexander Ross who was inducted in 1850, and served the people for nineteen years.

The people of Blue Mountain and Garden of Eden with Barney's River joined the movement in 1848, and had for their leader the Rev. D. B. Blair, a rare and remarkable man who was, in his day, the best Gaelic scholar in America. In 1852, Mr. Blair and his people set about erecting a church which was formally opened for service, before a board had been nailed on its walls, because the congregation had no other place in which to worship. In three years it was completed, without debt. For forty years Mr. Blair served this congregation and other sections adjoining with great ability and devotion.

For ten years the Kirk in Pictou County struggled on without pastors. Rev. Alexander McGillivray, D.D., the only Kirk minister who did not return to Scotland after the disruption, wrought manfully and faithfully to repair the breach and to build up the church on the old foundations.

Dr. McGillivray came to Nova Scotia, from Inverness, Scotland, in 1833. For five years he labored at Barney's River and Merigomish. He succeeded Mr. Fraser, in 1838, and continued there to discharge the duties of a minister with a devotion and earnestness rarely equaled, until his death, in 1862. He spread his labors over hundreds of miles of territory, to strengthen and encourage the pastorless churches. It was said of him, that he often tired out his horses, but the indefatigable Dr. McGillivray never tired.

In 1848, the Synod opened a seminary at the West River of Pictou. Professor Ross who was pastor at the West River, had charge of the literary and classical departments and Professors Keir and Smith the Divinity Hall. The classes met in the Temperance Hall in an ill ventilated room above the little country schoolhouse not more pretentious than the log cabin that gave birth to the renowned Princeton Seminary. Each of the students acted stoker in turn, and not only kindled the fire, but also swept the floor. Sometimes the little upper room

THE RELIGIOUS HISTORY OF THE COUNTY

looked tidy and sometimes it did not. The old Temperance Inn where the students boarded is still standing. In 1853 five men graduated, James McGregor McKay, James Thomson, Henry Crawford, John M. Macleod and James Maclean. They were the first graduates who received all their collegiate education at the West River. They all settled in country congregations, were successful ministers, and all lived to participate in their ministerial Jubilee celebration. Revs. Mr. McKay and Mr. Thomson died at the ripe old age of ninety three years. Mr. Crawford died after he passed four score years, and Mr. Macleod lived hale and hearty until he was eighty seven. Mr. Maclean, died in 1914, in his eighty eighth year and the sixtieth year of his ministry.

The West River Seminary gave a great impetus to the life and work of the Presbyterian church both at home and abroad. In 1858 the Seminary and Theological Hall with its professors and students were transferred to Truro, Nova Scotia. The Synod of the Free Church of Nova Scotia, realizing their need of a native ministry, also opened a college in Halifax in 1848. It continued over a period of nearly thirty years. In 1860 the Theological department of the College at Truro was removed to Halifax, and united with the Free Church College.

In 1878, the Synod purchased the property at Pine Hill and the Theological Hall was transferred there where it has since remained. As in the olden times the Ark of the Covenant moved from place to place till David, in the days of Israel's national unity and prosperity, found a permanent resting place for it on Mount Zion, "beautiful for situation," so the Divinity Hall moved from place to place till the church in her unity and prosperity provided a beautiful and, we trust, a permanent home for it in Pine Hill. The present Principal and Professor of Theology is Rev. Clarence Mackinnon, D. D., a native of Pictou County.

The Presbyterian College, Halifax, is the child of the several branches of the Presbyterian Church of the Maritime Provinces, once separated but now happily united. It had its origin in the humble theological school in Pictou nearly a century ago, and since its beginning, has sent out over four hundred ministers, who have gone to almost every part of the land. The good old fathers of the church who founded and maintained this school of learning have left us a splendid educational heritage, and we owe them the debt of a grateful remembrance.

The other denominations have played an important part in religious history of the County.

Among the early settlers of the Eastern part of the County, who came in the years 1791 and 1802 were a number of Roman Catholics who settled in Merigomish and along the Gulf Shore. The first resident priest was the Rev. James McDonald, who came as early as 1793. He was succeeded, about 1800, by the Rev. Alexander McDonald, who remained with the people till his death, in 1816. He died in Halifax, and his remains were carried by his people through the woods all the way to Arisaig where he had had his home.

The first native priest was Rev. Donald McKinnon. He died when quite a young man. The first Roman Catholic church in the county was built at Merigomish, in 1810. In 1834 the first church at Bailey's Brook was built; and, in 1869, that settlement was formed into a separate parish with the Rev. D. M. McGregor, D.D., as its first priest.

Stella Maris, in Pictou town, was begun in 1823. The first priest located there was Rev. Mr. Boland who was settled in 1828. The present church, which stands on one of the most prominent sites in Pictou, was erected in 1865. Father McDonald, afterwards Bishop of Newfoundland, was then in charge. From 1881 to 1892 Rev. Roderick McDonald was pastor. He was succeeded by Rev. J. J. Chisholm.

GROUP OF DECEASED MINISTERS

1 JAMES MACLEAN, D.D.
2 ISAAC MURRAY, D.D.
3 ALEXANDER FALCONER, D.D.
4 JOHN CAMERON
5 GEORGE PATTERSON, LL.D.
6 E. D. MILLER, D.D.
7 WILLIAM McCULLOCH, D.D.
8 P. G. McGREGOR, D.D.
9 J. McGREGOR McKAY

THE RELIGIOUS HISTORY OF THE COUNTY

The Parishes and Priests of the Roman Catholic Church in the county at present are: Rev. W. B. Macdonald, Lourdes, who has been stationed there for 38 years, Rev. J. D. McLeod, New Glasgow, Rev. J. J.McKinnon, Bailey's Brook, Rev. J. A. Butts, Westville, Rev. J. McLennan, Thorburn and Merigomish, Rev. Ronald Macdonald, Pictou.

The Church of England was first established within the county in the town of Pictou. The leading spirits in the first organization were Dr. Johnsone and Robert Hatton, Sr. Through the influence of the latter, a lot was secured, and he himself put up the frame in the year 1826. Three years later the church was completed, Mr. Hatton's son, Henry, being foremost in the work. The church was consecrated in 1829 by Bishop Inglis. The first rector of the parish was the Rev. Chas. Elliott, B. A., who was settled there, the 3d of April, 1832. He was appointed rector of the parish in 1834.

The whole country was then his parish, and he preached once a month at Albion Mines, River John and other places. He was a man greatly beloved by his own church and had the respect of the whole community. He labored in the County for thirty-three years. He was succeeded by Revs. Messrs. Prior, Wood and Geniver. Rev. D. D. Moore was Rector until 1873, when he resigned, and the Rev. T. C. Desbarres was elected. He was followed in the year 1874, by the Rev. James P. Sheraton, now Principal of Wycliffe College. Rev. Wm. Cruden was the next Rector, and in 1877 the Rev. John Edgecombe was appointed.

The old Church having been enlarged at different times and now getting pretty old, it was decided to erect a new one. The corner-stone was laid on the 22d of May, 1879, and the fine large church in which the congregation now worship, was finally completed and the first service held on the 15th day of June, 1881. Rev. H. A. Harley suc-

PICTONIANS AT HOME AND ABROAD

ceeded Rev. Mr. Edgecombe in 1888. In the year 1852, the southern part of the parish, including Albion Mines, New Glasgow and adjoining Country, was constituted a separate parish. In 1876, the settlement of River John was separated from Pictou, and likewise constituted a parish.

Christ Church, Albion Mines, was built in 1851. The earlier pastors were Revs. St. Blois, Wilkins, Bowman and Moore. The first curate at River John was Rev. M. Kaulbach. He was appointed in 1865. The Rectors and parishes at present are: Rev. A. E. Andrews, St. James Church, Pictou, Rev. F. Robertson, M. A., St. George's Church, New Glasgow, Rev. R. B. Patterson, M. A., Christ Church, Stellarton, Rev. J. F. Tupper, St. Bee's Church, Westville, Rev. A. W. L. Smith, M. A., St. John's Church, River John, and Rev. W. W. Clarkson, Trenton.

The first Baptist Society in the County was organized by James Murray, who came to Pictou in 1811, and afterward removed to River John in June 18, 1815, where he baptized two persons and dispensed the communion. The society was formed on the principles of the Scotch Baptists or Disciples. The first society of the regular Baptists was formed in the year 1838 at Merigomish. A congregation was organized at River John in 1844.

In 1874 a church was built at Barney's River and a small congregation worshipped there. The First Baptist Church, New Glasgow, is now the largest in the County. It was formed in 1875. The present pastor, is Rev. J. Clement Wilson. His predecessor was Rev. W. M. Smallman.

The history of Methodism in Pictou County virtually begins with the opening up of the coal mines, although River John had long previously been a regular appointment of the Wallace Circuit. From 1825 to 1848 irregular visits were paid to Albion Mines (now Stellarton) by the Methodist ministers stationed at Wallace, Truro or

THE RELIGIOUS HISTORY OF THE COUNTY

River John. In 1845, in response to a request from the General Mining Association, among whose employees were a number of married Englishmen, Richard Weddal was sent to Albion Mines. There is no further record of appointments to this place until it was made a circuit in 1861, when Rev. J. Cassidy was stationed there.

The Society in River John was organized by Rev. Mr. Snowball, in 1822. They built their first church in 1824. Since that time, River John has been one of the regular Methodist circuits.

Pictou town did not become a circuit until 1868, although one or two unsuccessful attempts had been previously made to place a minister there. This circuit became a mission in 1905.

New Glasgow was, until 1888, a part of the Stellarton Mission. It is to a young woman from River John that New Glasgow Methodism owes its existence today. Miss Ellen Harbourne from that circuit was married to a Mr. Walker and came to live in New Glasgow. She was a loyal Methodist, and united with the Church at Stellarton. At her request the minister from Stellarton frequently preached in a hall at New Glasgow. Rev. Douglas Chapman (1864-67) was probably the first to conduct these services. No serious attempt was made to establish a Methodist Church in New Glasgow until the time of Rev. Isaac Thurlow (1880-83). During his pastorate, the old Free Church building and lot were purchased. It was remodelled and put into its present condition at a cost of nearly $3,000. From a struggling mission, raising only $410 for its minister as late as 1899, New Glasgow became independent under Rev. E. E. England, in 1901, and is now one of the most desirable circuits of the Conference.

Trenton has been attached to New Glasgow since the time of Rev. W. I. Croft (1893-96). Services were first held in the Orange Hall. Later, the little Methodist Church at Piedmont was donated to the Trenton Methodists. The Methodist Circuits with their present ministers are: Pictou, Rev. Robert Williams, Stellarton, Rev. John Phalen, River John, H. D. Townsend, Trenton, Rev. Thomas Hodgson, New Glasgow, Rev. F. E. Barrett.

The census of 1911 gives the number of Presbyterians in the County 24,000, Roman Catholics 5600, Anglicans 2600, Methodists 2500, Baptists 1100. The population of County is 36,000. Out of this number 26,000 are Scotch, 5200 English, 2400 Irish, 1000 French, 376 Swiss, 240 German, 300 Negro, 172 Indian.

The beginnings of the different branches of the Presbyterian Church in the County of Pictou have now been briefly traced; the Anti-Burgher Church from 1786; the Kirk from 1817, the Free Church, from 1844, and likewise, those of the other denominations. The result of the Presbyterian disruption, of 1844 was a renewed activity in that denomination. There was a spirit of rivalry between the churches. If the different branches of the Church did not provoke one another to love, they certainly did provoke to good works.

The Home Mission Board which was founded in 1840, prosecuted its work as never before. Foreign Missionary enterprise was launched in 1845, and Dr. Geddie the first Missionary of the Church, was sent to the South seas in 1846. That event started a new era of zeal and liberality in the Church, never manifested before. It also brought the Churches into closer touch with one another. In 1848 the Presbyterian Church of Nova Scotia and the Free Church established "schools of the prophets," one at West River, another at Halifax.

From these two schools, came a splendid band of ministers and missionaries who went far and wide, founding and building up churches. The Kirk still kept on looking across the sea for a supply of ministers, and they came. In 1853, two young men came from Scotland — Rev.

THE RELIGIOUS HISTORY OF THE COUNTY

Alex. Maclean, D. D., a native of the County but educated in the old country, and Rev. Allan Pollock, D. D., sent over by the Colonial Committee to Nova Scotia, as a minister of the Church of Scotland. Dr. Pollock received and accepted a call to St. Andrew's Church, New Glasgow; and continued to be its pastor till 1875, when he was appointed Professor of Church history in the Presbyterian College, Halifax, and later Principal. In 1904, he resigned, and now resides in Halifax, rich in the love and esteem of the whole Canadian Church.

Mr. Maclean was settled over the Kirk Congregation at Saltsprings, and held pastorates at Belfast, P. E. I. and Hopewell, N. S. In all these charges he gave full proof of his ministry. In 1911, his Diamond Jubilee was celebrated by the Presbytery of Pictou. He now resides at Eureka, N. S., in his ninety-fourth year, enjoying an honorable old age. Four young men, all natives of the County; William McMillan, Simon McGregor, George M. Grant and John Cameron, were educated in Glasgow and returned to Nova Scotia and were settled in important charges.

Gradually the ecclesiastical sky was clearing after the storm. It was found that men were forgetting their old differences and settling down to a new order of things. There were three branches of the Presbyterian Church in the Province, where two was one too many. October 4, 1860 is a memorable day in the history of the Presbyterian Church. On that day the union of the Presbyterian Church of Nova Scotia, and of the Free Church took place under the title of "The Presbyterian Church of the Lower Provinces."

The Synod of the Presbyterian Church of N. S. was represented by Revs. John L. Murdoch and P. G. McGregor, Professors Smith and Ross. The Synod of the Free Church, by Rev. Mr. Forbes, Professor King and Rev. Dr. Forrester. The Union meeting was held in

Pictou. A tent was erected on Patterson's hill, near the town. Over this tent floated a bright, blue banner with the legend in white lilies, "For Christ's Crown and Covenant." The spot selected was where Dr. McGregor preached his first sermon in the County. Here the two parties were declared one, amid great rejoicings.

There followed years of growth and prosperity in all branches of the Church. Congregations multiplied. The supply of ministers increased. Educational institutions were strengthened. Missionary enterprise was promoted, both at home and abroad. "Then had the churches rest and were edified." This prosperity was shared in very largely by the Kirk brethren as well.

With the coming of young men into the ministry a spirit of Union was manifest, and grew rapidly. Churches were tired of controversy and separation; and united co-operatively in educational and missionary, as well as in devotional services. A Union of co-operation was soon followed by a Union of Organization. In 1875, all branches of the Church were merged in the Presbyterian Church in Canada.

Chapter III

PICTONIANS IN THE PULPIT

The Ministers and Churches in the Town of Pictou

A BRIEF history of the local churches in the County, with a list of the clergymen connected with them, from their organization to the present time, is here presented. It is much to be regretted that it is more or less imperfect, owing to the loss of records and the difficulty in securing definite information.

What has long been known as Prince Street Church, Pictou, was originally a section of the field of Dr. McGregor and Mr. Ross. It was formed into a separate congregation in 1801, as the Harbor District. In 1804, Rev. Thomas McCulloch came to it as its first minister. For twenty years he was the only clergyman in Pictou Town. He resigned in 1824, and was succeeded by Rev. John McKinlay who died in 1850. Rev. James Bayne, D.D., was inducted in 1851, and continued as minister until his death, in 1876. Rev. William Donald followed, from 1878 to 1883. He was succeeded by Rev. Alex. Falconer, D.D., who served for nearly a quarter of a century. Rev. Geo. C. Taylor followed. Rev. A. D. Archibald, M. A., the present minister was inducted in 1913.

The first election of elders took place on May 6, 1787, when John Patterson and John Fraser were chosen to represent the Harbor District. In 1809 the session was increased by the addition of Geo. Ives, John Patterson and David Pottinger.

The first minister of St. Andrew's Church was Rev. K. J. McKenzie, who was followed by Rev. Mr. Williamson. Rev. Andrew Herdman, of Scotland, was inducted into the charge in 1849, and ministered for thirty years. He was followed by Rev. Robt. Burnet, in 1880; Rev. John C. Callan, in 1886; Rev. Robt. Atkinson, in 1889; Rev.

Andrew Armit, 1893, and Rev. W. T. D. Moss, 1897. The present incumbent, Rev. L. H. MacLean, M. A., was inducted March 23, 1904.

The first minister of Knox Church was Rev. Murdoch Sutherland. The next pastor was Rev. Alexander Ross, 1860 to 1879. He was followed by Rev. James Carruthers, 1880 to 1885. Rev. Geo. S. Carson, B. A., was inducted in 1885, and resigned to become Editor of the Presbyterian Witness. Rev. Wm. McNally followed from 1908 to 1910. The present minister, Rev. A. W. Thomson, was inducted in 1911. The first Session consisted of Donald Ferguson, Murdoch McKenzie, Alexander McLeod. Alexander McKenzie, William McKenzie and Alexander Murray. Over a dozen young men from this church have given themselves to the ministry.

Below are the names of the clergymen born in Pictou Town with place of birth and brief reference to those who are dead, and the present addresses of those who are still living. A few of the ministers mentioned in this chapter were not born in the county, but came into it when quite young, and were brought up and educated in it. The ministers belonging to denominations other than Presbyterian are so indicated.

ROBERT S. PATTERSON, M.A., Pictou; Died in 1882.
> He was minister of the congregation at Bedeque, P. E. I., fifty-six years and six months. This is, perhaps, the longest unbroken pastorate in one congregation in the history of the Canadian Church.

JOHN L. MURDOCH, M.A., Pictou; Died in 1873.

JOHN GEDDIE, D.D., Pictou; Died in 1872.
> The founder of the New Hebrides Mission.

WILLIAM MCCULLOCH, D.D., Pictou; Died in 1895.
> He was minister of the oldest regularly organized Presbyterian Church in Canada for over fifty years. He was ordained at Truro, Feb. 14, 1839, and his whole life was spent in this one congregation. He was a man of eminence as a pastor, a presbyter and educator. He was a son of Dr. McCulloch of Pictou Academy.

CHURCHES IN NEW GLASGOW
1 First Presbyterian Church   2 United Church   3 St. Andrew's Church

PICTONIANS IN THE PULPIT

DANIEL M. GORDON, D.D., LL.D., Pictou; Kingston, Ont.

D. M. STEARNS, D.D., Pictou; Germantown, Pa.
: Born in 1844; educated in Pictou Academy; teacher for a number of years in the Maritime Provinces; ordained in Boston, 1880. From 1886 to the present time he has been in the Reformed Episcopal Church. In 1892 he went to his present charge, where he is still pastor. He is a noted Bible Class teacher, and conducts Bible Classes weekly in New York, Philadelphia, Washington, etc. His church and Bible Classes help to support over a dozen missionaries in the foreign field.

ISAAC M. PATTERSON, Pictou; Died in 1892.
: He was Pastor in Annapolis, Maryland, Milford, N. J., and Bloomsburg, Penn.

JAMES PATTERSON, Pictou; Deceased.
: He was a son of Matthew Patterson and a minister in the Canadian Northwest. He was formerly a bookseller in Pictou.

FRANCIS A. ROSS, Pictou; New Glasgow, N. S.
: He spent twenty-two years in pastorates in the West Indies. He also served as Chaplain in the Boer War. Retired.

J. R. DOBSON, B.D., Pictou; Montreal, P. Q.
: Pastor of St. Giles Church, one of the leading churches in Montreal.

JAMES C. HERDMAN, D.D., Pictou; Died in 1910.
: Mr. Herdman was a child of the Kirk Manse, born in 1856. He was ordained at Campbellton, N. B., in 1877. In 1885 he went west and took charge of Knox Church, Calgary, until 1902, when he was appointed Superintendent of Missions for British Columbia and Alberta.

WILLIAM C. HERDMAN, M.A., Pictou; Halifax, N. S.

A. W. K. HERDMAN, B.A., Pictou; Calgary, Alta.
: Sons of Rev. Andrew Herdman, late of St. Andrew's Church, Pictou.

PETER M. MACDONALD, M.A., Pictou; Toronto, Ont.

DANIEL J. MORRISON, Pictou; Deceased.
: Graduated from Theological Seminary, Auburn, N. Y., and settled in New York State where he died.

DONALD FRASER, B.A., Pictou; St. Peters, C. B.

PICTONIANS AT HOME AND ABROAD

JOHN W. LOWDEN, Pictou; Newark, Del.

DONALD A. MACKENZIE, Pictou; Tillamook, Ore.

FENWICK W. FRASER, Pictou; Masillon, Ohio.

CHARLES TUPPER BAILLIE, Ph.D., Pictou; Trinidad, B.W.I.
Pastor Susamacher Church, San Fernando, and assistant Professor in the Theological Hall.

A. H. FOSTER, B.D., Pictou Landing; Durham, West River.

D. R. MACLEAN, B.A., Pictou Island; Hazelton, B. C.

CHARLES ELLIOT MACKENZIE, Pictou; Galliopolis, Ohio.
Mr. Mackenzie is a son of the late George A. Mackenzie, Pictou. He entered the ministry of the Church of England from Kings College, about thirty years ago, and after successful work in the Maritime Provinces, went to Ohio where he was appointed Archdeacon of the Diocese of Southern Ohio, U. S. A. He is a brother of President Mackenzie of Dalhousie University.

LEWIS M. WILKINS, Pictou; Deceased.
Son of Hon. Martin I. Wilkins, and pastor of the Episcopal churches in Stellarton and Pictou.

FRANK BEATTIE, Pictou; Deceased.
Mr. Beattie was born in 1834, and died at Wolfville, N. S., 1912, aged seventy-seven years. His first public work was as a temperance lecturer and organizer. In 1870 he was ordained, and gave nearly forty years to the work of the Baptist ministry.

ROBERT MCEWEN, Pictou; Antigonish, N. S.
Roman Catholic Church.

RICHARD POWER, Pictou; Ontario, Can.
Roman Catholic Church.

WILLIAM E. PURCELL, Pictou.
Father Purcell was born in Pictou in 1874. He attended the public schools of Pictou and Pictou Academy. In 1889, he entered St. F. X. college and in 1893, he began his philosophical course at the Grand Seminary at Montreal, where he also took a course in theology. He taught for a time at St. Anne's college, Digby County, as professor of English. He was ordained a priest in 1898 and was curate at Chatham and Bathurst, N. B., and parish priest at Jacquet River before going west. He died in Montana, Aug. 23, 1912.

PICTONIANS IN THE PULPIT

THE MINISTERS AND CHURCHES IN NEW GLASGOW

The History of the churches in New Glasgow is largely the history of the Town, for they have played a foremost part in its life and growth.

In 1787 a log church was built on the West side of the river. This was used until 1803 when a frame church was erected at Irishtown. In 1834 the congregation was incorporated under the name of James Church and in 1852 a large wooden building was erected in the town of New Glasgow.

The first minister was the Rev. James McGregor, D.D. He came in 1786, and died in 1830. He was succeeded by Rev. David Roy, D. D., who came to Nova Scotia in 1830, and the following year was inducted minister of the congregation. He labored faithfully until laid aside by failing health in 1871. He died in 1873, aged 82 years, having preached the gospel for forty years with great energy and power. Rev. E. A. McCurdy, D.D., was minister from 1871-1891. He was succeeded by Rev. James Carruthers, 1892-1904. Rev. G. Ernest Forbes, was inducted in 1904, and continues in charge.

On May 30, 1888, the new St. Andrew's congregation was organized. The ministers have been: Rev. Alexander Robertson, 1888-1896, and Rev. W. McC. Thomson, 1897-1906. On Nov. 5, 1907, James Church and New St. Andrew's united under the ministry of Rev. G. E. Forbes, with the name First Presbyterian Church. On Nov. 5, 1912, the cornerstone of the First Presbyterian Church was laid on the site of old James Church. It was opened and dedicated to public worship, April 12, 1914. The congregation worshipped in New St. Andrew's Church from June 1908 until the opening of their new church home.

St. Andrew's Congregation was formed from the Church at Fraser's Mountain, and Rev. Donald A. Fraser, was minister until 1837. Rev. John Stewart was the second pastor, 1838-1845. For eight years they were without a pastor after the disruption. Rev. Allan Pollock was settled there in 1853 and continued until 1875. The other ministers of this church have been: Rev. George Murray, Rev. George Coull, Rev. Archibald Bowman, Rev. S. J. McArthur, B.D. The present incumbent, Rev. James A. Ramsay, B.A., was inducted in 1898.

Primitive Church was an off-shoot from James Church, and was organized, May 25, 1845. The first meetings were held in the old Temperance Hall. Primitive Church was built in 1849 on the corner of Provost and McLean Streets. In 1848 Rev. George Walker arrived in Pictou from Scotland. He accepted a call to this church and was inducted Sept. 20, 1848. He was its only pastor. In 1873 the church was enlarged. In 1874 it was burnt. In 1845 Knox Church was built by the Free Church adherents. Rev. Mr. Stewart was the minister of Knox Church, 1845-1866. He was succeeeded by Rev. John M. Macleod and Rev. Robert Cumming, D.D.

In the autumn of 1874, the year of the great fire, the two congregations got together and formed the United Church. They continued to worship in Knox Church until January 9, 1876, when the present building was opened and occupied. Rev. Mr. Walker was minister of the United Church until 1878, when he was relieved by the settlement of Rev. E. Scott, the congregation making Mr. Walker, Pastor Emeritus. Mr. Walker was a preacher of great ability and power. He was a most faithful minister, and in every way adorned his calling. He died Feb. 4, 1884, in the seventy-ninth year of his age. Rev. E. Scott, D.D. retired in 1891, and was succeeded by Rev. Anderson Rogers, D. D., who was pastor from July 1893 to March 1908. Rev. John H. MacVicar, D.D. was minister from December 10, 1908 to March 17, 1912. Rev. J. Macartney Wilson, B.D., was inducted in May,

CHURCHES IN PICTOU TOWN

1 KNOX CHURCH
2 ST. ANDREW'S CHURCH
3 HOME OF REV JAS McGREGOR. D.D.
4 PRINCE ST. CHURCH

PICTONIANS IN THE PULPIT

1913. Peter A. McGregor has been treasurer of the United Church since its organization, and, for three years was treasurer of Primitive Church.

The First Presbyterian Church, Trenton, was organized in 1889 and the Church built in 1890. Rev. A. W. Thomson was pastor from 1889 to 1890; Rev. H. R. Grant, April 13, 1891 to April 1904; Rev. D. C. Ross, Nov. 8, 1904 to Sept. 1913. Rev. A. A. Macleod, present pastor, was inducted 1914.

THE FOLLOWING MINISTERS WERE BORN AND BRED IN NEW GLASGOW

PETER G. MCGREGOR, D.D., New Glasgow; Died in 1886.
Dr. McGregor was the son of Rev. James McGregor, D.D. He studied Theology under Dr. McCulloch. In 1843 he was called to Poplar Grove Church, Halifax, where he was minister for twenty-five years. He was an excellent pastor and preacher. In 1868 he was appointed General Agent for the Church in Nova Scotia, the duties of which he discharged with fidelity and success.

JOHN FORREST, D.D., LL.D., New Glasgow; Halifax, N. S.

GEORGE SUTHERLAND, New Glasgow; Died in 1868.
Mr. Sutherland was one of the first graduates of the Free Church Seminary, Halifax, and was settled first in Nova Scotia and afterwards in P. E. I., where he labored for a time. He went to New Zealand in 1886, and was called to Dunedin. In 1870 he was called to Sydney, Australia, where he labored until his death, which was instantaneous, as he was removing his outer clothing on his return from a congregational meeting.

J. A. F. SUTHERLAND, New Glasgow; Winnipeg, Man.

ROBERT J. CAMERON, New Glasgow; Died in 1879.
Mr. Cameron was educated at Glasgow University. He was called to St. Andrew's Church, St. John, N. B., in 1870, and labored there for six years. Resigning that charge, he removed to Scotland, where he obtained an important congregation, the duties of which, however, proved too great for his strength. He died at the Manse, Burnt Island, Scotland, in the thirty-sixth year of his age. Mrs. Cameron was a daughter of the Hon. James Fraser, New Glasgow.

A. H. CAMERON, New Glasgow; Keremeos, B. C.
A brother of the Rev. Robert J. Cameron.

HUGH W. FRASER, D.D., New Glasgow; Vancouver, B. C.
Dr. Fraser studied in Manitoba College; was settled at Fort William, Ontario, and Holland, Manitoba; went to China, and returned from there to San Francisco, where he was a minister for a number of years. In 1904 he came to Vancouver, B. C.

HUGH R. GRANT, B.A., New Glasgow; New Glasgow, N. S.
General Secretary, Nova Scotia Temperance Alliance.

FRANK L. FRASER, New Glasgow; Kennewick, Wash.
Brother of the Rev. Dr. Fraser.

WILLIAM MEIKLE, B.A., New Glasgow; Tuxford, Sask.
Mr. Meikle, with the Rev. J. P. Gerrior, was for many years engaged in Evangelistic work.

WILLIAM L. MACRAE, Abercrombie; Golden, B. C.

DONALD M. GRANT, New Glasgow; Cincinnati, Ohio.

CHARLES J. CAMERON, New Glasgow; Vancouver, B. C.

JOHN R. FRASER, New Glasgow; Avoca, N. Y.

JAMES A. FRASER, B. A., New Glasgow; Pittsburg, Pa.

ALEXANDER W. McLEOD, New Glasgow; Summerland, B. C.
Pastor, Baptist Church.

GEORGE MACDONALD, New Glasgow; Baptist Church, U. S. A.

SAMUEL A. McDOUGALL, New Glasgow; Chester Basin, N. S.
Pastor, Baptist Church.

FRED A. SULLIVAN, New Glasgow; New Hampshire.
Pastor, Methodist Church.

JOHN BURNS, came to New Glasgow when a lad; Died in 1851, aged 27 years.

JAMES BURNS, New Glasgow; Born in 1825; Died in 1907.

WM. HENRY BURNS, D.D., New Glasgow; Evanston, Ill.
Mitchell Burns, who was a potter by trade, came with his wife, Ann Morrow, from the north of Ireland, in 1830 or 1831,

PICTONIANS IN THE PULPIT

and settled on what is now the John Connolly estate at Potter's Brook, to which stream he gave the name. In 1847 the family removed to River John, where Mrs. Burns died in 1858, and Mr. Burns in 1871. They had a large and notable family of seven sons and four daughters. Three of the sons entered the Methodist ministry. John Burns died in early life at Sackville, N. B.

James Burns was educated at Sackville, N. B., served several churches in the Maritime Provinces, and later in Chicago, and Idaho, where he died in 1907. He was a member, at one time, of Dr. Roy's Church. His daughter, Angeline, married Dr. Frederick Holmes, of San Diego, Cal. His eldest son, Jabez B. Burns, practices Dentistry in Poyette, Idaho. Another son, John Burns, is a Dentist in Oakland, Cal.

William H. Burns was born in 1840 in New Glasgow; graduated from the Wesleyan University, Middletown, Conn. He is a member of the Rock River Conference, and spent most of his ministerial life in Chicago and vicinity. He married Miss Ann P. Foster, daughter of Rev. Caleb Foster, Aurora, Ill. He is the author of "The Higher Critic's Bible; or, God's Bible?" "The Crisis in Methodism", and other books. His only son, William Foster Burns, is a graduate of Princeton University and Chicago Law School, and is a barrister in Chicago.

The eldest of the family, Stuart Burns, lived in New Glasgow; was a merchant in River John, but spent his later years as a druggist in Sydney, C. B., where he died. His son, Dr. W. F. Burns, born in River John, is now a practicing Dentist in Sydney, C. B. Anna Burns married William Perrin, farmer and tanner in River John. Their son, Dr. Albert M. Perrin, was born there, and is now practicing medicine in Yarmouth, N. S. Margaret Burns married George Langille, a mill owner in River John. Their son, M. K. Langille, is a Dentist in Truro, N. S.

Robert E. Burns was a real estate dealer in New York and San Francisco, Cal. He died in Portland, Ore. Bion, his son, is a Dentist in San Francisco. Charlotte Burns married Alexander McDonald, a ship builder, River John, who now lives in Victoria, B. C.

Samuel W. Burns, M.D., was born in New Glasgow, in 1836, is now practicing medicine in Shelburne, N. S. His eldest daughter, married Dr. Muir, Dentist, Shelburne. Thomas M. Burns, M.D., born in New Glasgow, 1838, practiced medicine in Shelburne, removed to Oakland, Cal., and died there. His son, Dr. Thomas M. Burns, is a Professor in the Denver Cross Medical College. Another son, Daniel C. Burns, is a lawyer and real estate dealer in Denver, Col.

Carrie N. Burns married C. S. Lane, Dentist of P. E. I. Their eldest son, Franklin K. Lane, was born there July 15, 1854. He lived in Pictou when a child, where his father practiced his profession. The family moved to California, where the son graduated from the University of California, in 1886. In 1889 he practiced law in San Francisco. From 1897 to 1902 he was a member of the Interstate Commerce Commission. In 1913 he was appointed Secretary of the Interior, in President Wilson's Cabinet. Mr. Lane is a Democrat in politics and was his party's candidate for mayor of San Francisco, for governor of the State and for the U. S. Senate. He is a man of fine personality and high character. For a score of years he has been a prominent figure in the public life of the Pacific Coast and is today one of the public men of mark and standing at Washington. George W. Lane, another son, practices law in San Francisco, Cal. Frederick Lane, a third son, is a Dentist in San Francisco. The Rev. F. E. Barret, New Glasgow, N. S., pastor of the Methodist Church is a great grandson of Mitchell Burns.

East River Ministers and Churches

The East River Congregation was formed into a separate charge, in 1824, with the Rev. Angus McGillivray as its first minister. The West Branch Section was connected with it. In 1853 the church at Springville was built. The Church at Sunny Brae was erected in 1854, and was supplied by Rev. Mr. Blair for several years. In 1866, Rev. A. Maclean Sinclair became pastor of the Springville and Sunny Brae Congregations, and served them for a period of twenty-two years. Rev. John Calder was pastor, 1889-1892. In 1892, James Sinclair was settled as minister. In 1894 the Congregation was divided, Springville and Bridgeville forming a separate charge under Rev. Mr. Sinclair. He resigned in 1910; and in 1911 Rev. E. A. Kirker, B. A. became minister. The Bridgeville Church was built in 1894.

PICTONIANS IN THE PULPIT

The first regular minister of the Kirk at St. Paul's was Rev. John Macrae, 1827 to 1847. He was succeeded by his son, Rev. D. Macrae. Rev. Simon McGregor was the minister 1860-1869. He was succeeded by Rev. William McMillian in 1875. He continued pastor until 1888. The present St. Paul's church was built in 1855. The Sunny Brae and St. Paul's congregations were formed into a separate charge in 1894. In 1895 they called Rev. W. P. Archibald who was pastor until 1904. He was followed by the Rev. George A. Sutherland 1904-1911. The present pastor, Rev. D. K. Ross, was inducted Sept. 1912. The first elders of Sunny Brae were Finlay Grant, James McDonald and Duncan McMillian. They had worthy successors in James Cumming, William Ross, John A. McDonald and John Cruikshank. A brother of the latter, D. B. Cruikshank, is now an elder and clerk of the Session.

NAMES OF MINISTERS BORN ON EAST RIVER

WM. MCMILLAN, Churchville; Died 1889.
> He was educated for the ministry in Scotland, and was for a number of years pastor at Earltown, whence he removed to Saltsprings. He was pastor for 13 years at St. Paul's Church, East River. He was a diligent minister, and a warm-hearted friend.

SIMON MCGREGOR, Churchville; Deceased.
> He was minister of the West Branch and East River Kirk Churches for eight years. He spent thirteen years in pioneer work in British Columbia. He went to Scotland in 1881, and was elected minister of Appin, in the North of Scotland, where he labored until he retired. He died in Edinburgh, deeply regretted.

ANGUS MCGILLIVRAY, Springville; Died 1869.

JAMES MACLEAN, D.D., Springville; Died 1914.
> Nearly the whole of Dr. Maclean's ministry was spent in Colchester County at Shubenacadie and Great Village. He was a graduate of the West River Seminary, and finished his studies in 1853. He was an excellent preacher and minister and a most devoted friend.

PICTONIANS AT HOME AND ABROAD

EBENEZER MCLEAN, Springville; Deceased.
   He was a nephew of the Rev. Dr. Maclean, and was a student for the ministry, but died in early life.
JOHN D. MCGILLIVRAY, Springville, Truro, N. S.
   Retired from the Ministry.
JAMES T. MCGILLIVRAY, Springville.
   A student in theology, died Oct., 1856, aged 24 years. Sons of Rev. Angus McGillivray.
ROBERT GRANT, Springville; Died 1898.
   Studied in Pictou Academy and Edinburgh University.
DAVID C. MACKINTOSH, D.D., Springville; Shenandoah, Iowa.
FINLAY G. MCINTOSH, B.D., Springville; Dorchester, N. B.
WM. R. MCKAY, B.D., Springville; Kong Moon, So. China.
ROBT. G. MCKAY, B.A., Springville; So. Vancouver, B. C.
WM. MACDONALD, B.A., Springville; Barney's River, N.S.
ALVER MCKAY, Springville; Hollyburn, B. C.
JOHN A. MACDONALD, B.D., Bridgeville; Died 1890.
   Son of Duncan Macdonald and Mary McPhie; born Nov. 6, 1849. While working at the carpenter's trade in Boston, he decided to devote himself to the ministry, and began his preparation in the New Glasgow High School. His studies being interrupted by a long illness, he was sent as a missionary to Trinidad, 1874 to 1877. He took a special course in Dal. Coll., 1877-79, continuing his study at the Pine Hill Divinity School. He attended Andover Theological Seminary, 1882-84, but seeking a more favorable climate, served as home missionary in Arizona, and afterward at different places in California. He continued his studies at the Pacific Theological Seminary in the class of 1885, and was ordained pastor at Lincoln, Cal., May 21, 1885. The last few years of his life was a continual fight with sickness but he supplied congregations as he was able. His ministry, though brief and only kept up by an indomitable will, bore abundant fruit. He was a man of sincere piety, an earnest preacher and a most devoted friend. His whole life was blameless and beautiful. He died at Elgin, N. S., Jan. 29, 1890, at the age of forty years.

PICTONIANS IN THE PULPIT

A. H. FRASER, Bridgeville; Broken Bow, Neb.

A. J. H. FRASER, Bridgeville; Port Morien, C. B.

JAMES W. FRASER, St. Pauls; Died 1913.
    For forty years pastor of St. John's Church, Scotsburn, N. S.

DONALD K. CAMPBELL, St. Pauls; Ottawa, Ill.

JOHN W. CAMPBELL, St. Pauls.
    Student for the ministry. Died, Delaware, Md., Feb. 18, 1874.

SIMON W. Thompson, B. A., St. Pauls; Kindersley, Sask.

WM. ROSS, B. A., Sunny Brae; Vancouver, B. C.
    Thirty-three years pastor Prince William, N. B.

ROBT. D. ROSS, Sunny Brae; Died 1895.
    As a minister and preacher he won the affectionate confidence of the people. He had a most winsome disposition and a keen sense of humor, which made him a most agreeable companion. He was settled in Wolfville, N. S., in 1882, where he labored for about 10 years, until failing health compelled him to resign.

ROBT. J. GRANT, B.D., Sunny Brae.
    Mr. Grant was cut off in the prime of life June 10, 1898, at Montreal, Can. While attending the General Assembly he and four young friends had gone on bicycles to visit the Lachine Rapids, when returning to the city he was run over by an electric car. His death was instantaneous He was a young man of high intellectual attainments, and devoted piety, and had a distinguished course in college. For two years he was settled at St. George's Church, River John, and his brief ministry was rich in promise. He died in the thirty-first year of his age.

WM. GRANT, Sunny Brae.
    He was educated in the Presbyterian College, Halifax, and an additional year at Princeton Seminary, N. J. His pastorates were at Earltown and West Branch, seven years; at West River Clyde and Brookfield, P. E. I., nine years; at Port Morien, C. B., thirteen years; and at Grand River, eight years; in all some thirty-seven years. In every pastorate his work was a success. His careful preparation for the pulpit was continued to the last, when for a few weeks before the end he was unable to go to the church, he sent the prepared sermon in manuscript to be read. The last of his sermons thus sent

was read in the Grand River Church on Sunday, Dec. 16, 1906. He died on the following Tuesday. Mr. Grant was greatly afflicted in his family circle. Melville, his eldest son was ordained to the ministry, but ill health laid its hand upon him and he died in early manhood. Clarence, a younger brother, was suddenly called away when engaged as a theological student in a mission field, and Mary Sibella, a sister, died soon after her graduation from the university.

FINLAY R. McDONALD, Sunny Brae.
He was educated at the Academy. He pursued his theological studies in Scotland, and after graduation was called to the pastorate of Cooper Angus, an important charge in Scotland, where he labored with fidelity for 21 years. He died in 1900.

WM. P. GRANT, B.D., Sunny Brae; Truro, N. S.
Pastor of the First Presbyterian Church.

WM. M. GRANT, M. A., Sunny Brae; Ayr, Ont.

FINLAY H. McINTOSH, M.A., Sunny Brae; Sydney, C. B.
Pastor, Falmouth Church.

CHAS. D. McINTOSH, M.A., Sunny Brae; River John, N. S.

JAMES A. McDONALD, B.A., Sunny Brae; Youngstown, Ohio.

WM. C. ROSS, B. A., Sunny Brae; Halifax, N. S.

A. W. ROBERTSON, B. A., Centredale; Kennetcook, N. S.

DUNCAN A. MACPHIE, M.A., Centredale; Boston, Mass.
Secretary of the Evangelical Alliance. Office, 507 Tremont Temple.

J. P. MACPHIE, M.A., Sunny Brae; New Glasgow, N. S.

THE MINISTERS AND CHURCHES IN HOPEWELL

Hopewell is a village of about 450 people, with a beautiful country surrounding it. The first church was built in 1820, one and a half miles above the village. Rev. John Macrae was the first minister, 1827-1844. His son, Rev. Donald Macrae, succeeded him, 1857-1859. He returned a second time, in 1870, and remained four years.

PROFESSIONAL MEN OF PICTOU
1 W. E. MACLELLAN 3 JOHN P. MACPHIE 5 ROBERT D. ROSS
2 JOHN A. MACDONALD 4 W. B. MACDONALD

PICTONIANS IN THE PULPIT

It was during his first ministry that St. Columba's Church was built in 1859. From 1860 to 1869 Rev. Simon McGregor was minister. He was succeeded by the Rev. Peter Galbraith 1875; the Rev. Peter Melville 1881, the Rev. Homer Putman 1893, Rev. John Macintosh 1898, and the present Pastor, Rev. C. Munro 1908.

Union Church, Hopewell was organized in 1854. The present church was completed and opened in 1857. The first minister was Rev. John Mackinnon. He was inducted in 1858, and served the Church for eighteen years. He was a preacher of great vigor, and a most faithful pastor. The Rev. A. Maclean, D.D., was his worthy successor, 1877-1891. The first elders were Peter Ross, Robt. Munro, John McLean, Robt. Dunbar, Thomas Grant, Daniel Shaw, Enon McDonald and Angus McPhie. Rev. Simon Fraser was pastor in 1892; Rev. Wm. McNichol, in 1895; Rev. Hugh Miller, 1908, and the present minister, Rev. Geo. A. Logan, 1912. The Ferrona Church was an off-shoot from the Hopewell congregation. It was organized March 3, 1896. Revs. W. H. Smith, A. M. Thompson and J. F. Polley have served it as pastors.

MINISTERS BORN AND BROUGHT UP IN THIS DISTRICT

REV. A. MACLEAN, D.D., Hopewell; Eureka, N. S.
    Retired from the Ministry.

DONALD MACRAE, D.D., Hopewell; Died 1909.

HUGH DUNBAR, Hopewell; Died 1857.

HUGH ROSS, Hopewell; Died 1858.

CLARENCE MACKINNON, D.D., Hopewell; Halifax, N. S.
    Principal, Presbyterian College.

ALBERT G. MACKINNON, M.A., Hopewell; Greenock, Scotland.
    Author of a series of books for young men: "Spiritually Fit"; "Tangible Tests"; "Truths for Today"; "God's Right of Way Through a Young Man's Life".
    Rev. Clarence and Albert G. Mackinnon are sons of the late Rev. John Mackinnon.

JOHN B. MACLEAN, B. D., Hopewell, Huntington, Que.
Author of "The Secret of the Stream", thoughtful religious essays on Life and Literature.

A. D. MCINTOSH, M.A., Hopewell; Souris, P. E. I.

JAS. R. MACDONALD, Hopewell.
He was for many years a teacher in the public schools in the Province. Graduated from Princeton Seminary 1895, held pastorates in Fairville, N. B., Barney's River, Caledonia and Sheet Harbor, N. S. He died at Elmsdale, 1912.

JOHN W. BRITTON, Hopewell; Pugwash, N. S.

ASA J. CROCKETT, B. A., Hopewell; Hopewell, N. S.
Graduated from the Rochester Baptist Seminary.

DONALD ROSS, D. D., Lorne; Died 1907.
At the age of 27 he entered the ministry and for four years was pastor in Seattle, Wash. Twenty-five years were spent in eastern Canada, when he removed to the West. He was a man widely known for his learning and for his faithful work.

JOHN R. FRASER, M.A., Lorne; Uxbridge, Ont.

ALBERT M. MACLEOD, B.A., Lorne; Hyde Park, Mass.

WM. A. ROSS, M.A., Lorne; Moncton, N. B.
General Secretary Sunday School, N. B. and P. E. I.

D. K. ROSS, B. A., Lorne; Sunny Brae, N. S.

JOHN CAMERON, D.D., Glengarry;
Minister of Dundee, Canada for some time and for many years Parish minister of Dunoon, Scotland, where he died.

JOSEPH HALLIDAY, Glengarry; Orange City, Fla.
Pastor Congregational Church.

THE MINISTERS AND CHURCHES OF STELLARTON.

St. John's Church was organized in connection with the Kirk body. It was an offshoot from St. Andrew's Church, New Glasgow. Rev. Wm. M. Phillips was the first minister, inducted in 1863. In 1871, Rev. Chas. A. Dunn was settled over the congregation. He was followed by Rev. E. H. Burgess and Rev. D. M. Matheson. Rev. W. L. Cunningham, the present minister was inducted in 1908.

PICTONIANS IN THE PULPIT

Sharon Church is a child of old St. James' Church, New Glasgow. The original Sharon Church was built on the banks of the River, near Dr. Donnelly's house. On the 5th of June, 1856, Rev. A. J. Mowatt, D.D., was settled as the first pastor of the church. Wm. McPherson was the father of the session of Sharon Church. He opened the first Presbyterian Sunday School when there were only eight scholars; and afterwards became the first Superintendent of the Sunday School. Dr. Mowatt was followed by Rev. Thos. Cumming, D.D. who served the church for ten years, 1875-1885. The Church was fortunate in having such able and eloquent ministers at its beginning. Rev. J. H. Turnbull was pastor another ten years, 1885-1895. Rev. Wm. M. Tufts, B.D., became the fourth pastor in 1896, remaining twelve years. Rev. M. S. Fulton was ordained 1909, and resigned in 1913. The present pastor is the Rev. C. C. McIntosh, B.A., inducted 1913.

Ministers Born in Stellarton and Riverton.

GEORGE M. GRANT, D.D., LL.D., Stellarton; Died 1902.

CHAS. M. GRANT, D.D., Stellarton; Dundee, Scotland.
Retired from the Ministry.

JOHN MORTON, D.D., Stellarton; Died 1913.

THOS. CUMMING, D.D. Stellarton; Stellarton, N. S.
Retired from the Ministry.

ROBERT CUMMING, D.D., Stellarton; Trinidad, B. W. I.

JAMES FALCONER, Stellarton; Santa Clara, Calif.

PETER A. DUNN, B.D., Stellarton; Arbuthnott, Scotland.
Minister of the Parish Church, Arbuthnott, Scotland.

WM. H. MCDONALD, Stellarton; Denver, Col.

JOSEPH S. MCKAY, Stellarton; Port Hill, P. E. I.
Mr. McKay, well known evangelist, was ordained by presbytery of P. E. I., in 1913.

CHAS. J. CONNOLLY, Ph.D., Stellarton; Antigonish, N. S.
St. Francis Xavier College.

RICHARD GILMORE, D.D., Stellarton.
He was born in Scotland but came to N. S. with his parents when four years old. They settled at Plymouth, opposite Stellarton, where they lived for several years. Afterwards they moved to Ohio, U. S. A. His parents were Presbyterians but he entered the Roman Catholic Church and rose to be Bishop of Cleveland, where he died some years ago. He was the author of several religious works.

ALEXANDER MCKENZIE, Riverton; Died 1860.
He was the son of Thos. McKenzie and an uncle of Thos. Grant, Riverton. He went to Upper Canada where he spent most of his ministry. He founded the church at Goderich, Ont. For several years he was an instructor in the grammar schools at Goderich.

JOHN CAMERON, Riverton; Died 1907.
His grandparents were among the earliest settlers in Pictou County. He had the distinction of being Dr. McCulloch's last student, and of ministering to him during his last illness. In 1844 he was inducted at Nine Mile River, Gore and Kennetcook, Elmsdale, where he labored with great energy and faithfulness for 32 years. Later he labored for some years at Bridgewater, N. S. He then retired to Bridgetown, N. S., where he died in the 90th year of his age, and the 63d of his ministry. Mr. Cameron was an ardent friend of education, a fearless champion of temperance.

ALEXANDER FALCONER, D.D., Riverton; Died 1913.
He became pastor successively in Zion Church, Charlottetown; St. James' Church, Dartmouth; Greyfriar's Church, Trinidad; and Prince St. Church, Pictou. In 1906 he was chosen Moderator of the General Assembly. With rare qualifications of head and heart he efficiently discharged the responsible duties pertaining to all the important positions which he occupied during his long and busy life. He was a ripe scholar, and a faithful workman in the service of Christ.

ALEXANDER CAMERON, Riverton; Died 1913.
He held pastorates at Middle Stewiacke and Bass River, N. S., and at New London, P. E. I. He gave 31 years of devoted service to the church. He was a brother of Rev. John Cameron.

RETIRED MINISTERS

1 JOHN McMILLAN, D. D.
2 A. MACLEAN, D. D.
3 ROBERT CUMMING, D. D.
4 THOMAS CUMMING, D. D.
5 A. MACLEAN SINCLAIR, LL.D.
6 JOHN MURRAY
7 SAMUEL C. GUNN, D. D.

PICTONIANS IN THE PULPIT

JAMES D. CAMERON, Riverton; Lonsdale, R. I.

DAVID K. GRANT, M.A., Riverton; Olds, Alberta.

SAMUEL MACNAUGHTON, M.A., Riverton; Preston, England.

> Graduate of Dalhousie University, and completed his course in Edinburgh. He settled in the Presbyterian Church at Preston, England, in 1877, where he has since remained. He is a devoted temperance worker and the author of several books, among them, "Doctrine and Doubt", "Our Children for Christ", "The Wines of Scripture".

THE MINISTERS AND CHURCHES OF MIDDLE RIVER INCLUDING WESTVILLE AND GAIRLOCH

St. Phillip's Church was built and completed Jan. 8, 1871, with Rev. Wm. M. Phillips in charge. He was succeeded by Rev. Chas. Dunn who resigned in 1887; Rev. T. D. Stewart, 1888-1899; Rev. G. B. McLeod, 1900-1902; Rev. D. M. Gillies, 1902-1903. Rev. W.W. McNairn, present pastor, was inducted, 1904.

The first Carmel Church was erected in 1870, but while the dedication services were in progress, it was burned to ashes. A new church was soon erected, and Rev. John Lees was called to be pastor, 1873 to 1879. Rev. Robt. Cumming, D.D., was called in 1881 and resigned in 1912, closing a most happy and successful pastorate of 31 years. Rev. D. A. Frame is present pastor, 1913.

The first minister in Gairloch was Rev. Hugh McLeod, 1822. The second pastor, was Rev. Donald McIntosh, 1833-1844. The church was vacant for nine years. The next minister was Rev. A. Maclean, 1853-1857. He was also pastor at Saltsprings. Rev. Alex. McKay, 1859-1867. Rev. Neil Brodie was pastor for 13 years. He was followed by Rev. Thos. Irving and Rev. J. C. McLeod. In 1907, the Gairloch and Middle River sections were united with Rev. A. O. Morash, as pastor. Rev. Geo. Christie is the present pastor, inducted in 1911. The present church was built in 1858.

PICTONIANS AT HOME AND ABROAD

Ministers Born in this District.

John D. Murray, Middle River; Died 1906.
He was settled at Port Hill, P. E. I., in 1865. He held pastorates at Moncton, Buctouche and Red Bank, N. B. He died, aged 72 years, of which he had been 41 years in the ministry.

Alexander McBean, Middle River; Deceased.
Secretary for the British American and Tract Society, Halifax, for many years.

Duncan R. Crockett, Middle River; Deceased.
For some years he rendered good service to the church in N. B. In 1882 he went to the U. S. locating at Greenwood, Mo. In 1891 he was called as Home Missionary in the Indian Territory, where he labored for many years among the Indians.

John Thos. Crockett, Middle River; Deceased.
Pastor of the Adventist Church, Nashville, Tenn. and other places. Both sons of the late John Crockett, Middle River. Their mother was a daughter of Rev. Duncan Ross, West River.

Wm. Douglas, Middle River; Died 1904.
He was born in 1856, studied at the Moody Institute, Chicago; for seven years engaged in Evangelistic work; for seven years pastor in Minnesota. In 1904, he went to the Pacific Coast. He died at Portland, Ore.

A. Murray Porter, B.A., Alma.
Graduated Union Theological Seminary, N. Y., 1914.

John R. Douglas, B. A., Concord; Lake Megantic, P. Q.

Alex. Robinson, Concord; Died 1904.
Educated at the Springfield School of Workers. Settled in Nebraska, 1888, and afterwards in Wyoming. Died in Boulder, Col.

Duncan McDonald, Gairloch; Strathcona, Alta.; Retired.

Robert McDonald. Gairloch.
Brother of Duncan McDonald, a student for the ministry, Free Church College, Halifax. Died of smallpox, Jan. 12, 1850.

PICTONIANS IN THE PULPIT

WALTER ROSS, Millbrook; Died 1882.
    He was settled at Carleton Place, Ont., in 1862, where he did faithful work. This was his only pastorate. He died in the 48th year of his age.

A. H. DENOON, B.D., Westville; Antigonish, N.S.

THOS. JOHNSTONE, Westville; Maxville, Ont.

CHAS. CUMMING, Ph. D., Westville,
    Professor in the Theological Hall, San Fernando, Trinidad. Son of Rev. Robert Cumming, D.D.

JOHN KINGON, Westville; Park River, Minn.

J. H. HAMILTON, B.A., Westville; New Waterford, C. B.

JOHN P. GERRIOR, Granton; Oakland, Calif.

MINISTERS AND CHURCHES IN MCLENNAN'S MOUNTAIN, BLUE MOUNTAIN, EAST RIVER ST. MARY'S AND BARNEY'S RIVER

Hugh Fraser, who came to Pictou on the *Hector* settled on McLennan's Brook. One son, Donald, known as Donald Miller came with him. Another son, John, long known as John Squire arrived a few years later. John McLennan another *Hector* passenger settled at the mouth of McLennan's Brook and gave his name to that stream.

Rev. Donald A. Fraser was the first settled minister in McLennan's Mountain, 1817 to 1837. The second pastor was Rev. Alex. McGillivray, 1838 to 1862. Rev. Wm. Stewart succeeded him in 1863, and was pastor for 44 years. In 1908 McLennan's Mountain congregation and McLennan's Brook united and Rev. E. A. Kirker had charge for two years. The present pastor Rev. Wm. Dawson, B.D., was settled in 1910.

The first settlers at Blue Mountain came from Glen Urquhart, Scotland in 1818. The first church was built about 1834. The walls were built of logs, as boards had to be sawed by hand. The second church was erected in 1856, and the present church, in 1906. From 1834 to 1850 they had no regular pastor, but occasional supplies. The first settled minister was Rev. D. B. Blair, from 1850 to 1890 when he resigned, and Blue Mountain and Garden of Eden became a separate charge. Other pastors were Rev. D. M. Henderson, Rev. E. J. Rattee, and Rev. F. L. Jobb. Present pastor, Rev. W. H. Sweet, came in June 1909.

The first settlers of Barney's River were from the Highlands of Scotland. William McKenzie settled at Barney's River in 1807. He had six sons who were all land surveyors and roadmakers. John, the eldest son had a high name as a civil engineer. He acted as assistant to James Crearer, Pictou, in locating and building the Albion Mines Railroad. He was a number of years in the Crown Land office, Halifax.

Adam, second son, was for many years supervisor of roads from Colchester County to the strait of Canso. James was deputy surveyor for the County of Inverness. Francis spent much time in Cape Breton making roads. Hugh, the youngest son, was for many years a surveyor in South Africa.

Donald Bruce came to Pictou in the ship *Harmony* in 1822 and settled at Upper Barney's River. Angus McKay, Donald McKay, Donald Douglass, John McLeod and Alexander Grant came on the same ship. Margaret, daughter of Donald Bruce married Edward Jackson, Pine Tree. George, his second son married Christy, daughter of Hector Murray, by whom he had Hector and other children. He was an elder under Dr. Blair.

Donald Robertson came from Perthshire, in 1801 and settled above Avondale in 1819. He died in 1834 aged seventy three years, leaving a large family. His wife died in 1870, aged one hundred years, one month and one day. They had forty-eight grandchildren, of whom Rev. Hugh A. Robertson, D.D., Erromanga, is one.

Angus Murray, a native of Sutherlandshire, married Elizabeth McKay, by whom he had William, Andrew, and three daughters. He came to Pictou with his family in

PICTONIANS IN THE PULPIT

1812. He taught school in New Glasgow for some time. His eldest son, William married in 1821 and had Angus, Andrew, Helen, Jane, Eliza and Mary. Eliza was married to William Murray, at Grand Narrows, C. B. and was the mother of the present premier of Nova Scotia. Premier Murray narrowly escaped being born a Pictonian.

In 1830 a church was erected at Kenzieville. It stood near the Cemetery. At the same time a church was built at Lower Barney's River, near John Copeland's place. Rev. D. McKichan, Kirk minister, was pastor of the two churches for many years.

In 1846, Rev. D. B. Blair, Free Church, came to Barney's River and for 40 years was minister of the Free Church congregation. Other ministers of the Kirk were: Revs. James Mair, James McDonald, A. J. McKichan, J. R. McDonald, J. A. Cairns, E. Gillies, and D. K. Ross. The present pastor, Rev. Wm. MacDonald, came Feb. 25, 1913.

The present church at East River St. Mary's was completed in 1873, when the Kirk and the Free Church united. The following ministers served the congregation: Revs. Hugh McKenzie, Alex. Campbell, C. B. Pitblado, Robt. Cumming, John Ferry, Andrew Boyd, J. D. McFarlane, A. D. Sterling, and Wm. MacDonald. Rev. J. H. Kirk is the present pastor.

Ministers Born in This Section

WM. FRASER, D.D., McLennan's Brook; Died 1892.

Dr. Fraser was born at McLennan's Brook, May 19, 1808. He received his academic and theological education at Pictou Academy of which Dr. McCulloch was then the head. At the age of twenty-six he was sent as a missionary to Upper Canada, and a year later, was settled at Bond Head, Ontario, his first and only pastorate. Here he labored most faithfully for forty-six years until his retirement in 1881 when he removed to Barrie.

He was active in educational work; an earnest advocate of temperance and always a close attendant on church courts. In 1851 he was appointed clerk of the U. P. Synod; at the union of 1861 to the Joint Clerkship of the Canada Presbyterian Synod; and in 1875, to the Joint Clerkship of the General Assembly of the Presbyterian Church in Canada. He continued in this office until 1892, in his 85th year.

Dr. Fraser was a man of calm, judicial spirit, excellent business qualities, unvarying industry and punctuality and always in perfect health till his latest years. He died on Christmas day, 1892. He was thrice married. In 1834 to Jane Geddie, sister of the Rev. John Geddie, by whom he had three children. Second, to Nancy McCurdy of Onslow, N. S., in 1844. Three sons of this marriage were Rev. J. B. Fraser, M. D., Annan, Ont., Rev. R. Douglas Fraser, D.D., Editor and Business Manager, Presbyterian Publications, Toronto; and W. H. Fraser, M.A., Professor of Spanish and Italian, University of Toronto. Miss Jane Wells Fraser, daughter of the Rev. R. D. Fraser, D.D., is assistant editor of the Presbyterian Publications.

Third, he married Maria James Nicholas of Cuyahoga Falls, Ohio, and the children of this marriage were: George A. H. Fraser, M.A., Barrister, Denver, Colorado; and Miss Emma M. N. Fraser, M.A., Ph.D., Wheaton College, Norton, Mass.

SIMON FRASER, McLennan's Brook; Died 1912.

He was a son of Alexander Fraser and Margaret Campbell, daughter of Alexander Campbell, Elder, McLennan's Brook. He was a graduate of Free Church College, Halifax. He settled in New Brunswick for some time, but went to Texas where he spent the remainder of his ministry. He died in the seventy-eighth year of his age.

ALEXANDER CAMPBELL, McLennan's Brook; Died 1908.

He was born in 1855. His first pastorate was at Noel, 1887; the second, Merigomish, 1892. He died in the 53d year of his age. His death came most unexpectedly. Having gone to Noel to attend the funeral of a loyal supporter of the Presbyterian Church, he was stricken while in the pulpit, and in a short time passed away in the same pulpit in which he began his ministry.

> "How beautiful it is for man to die,
> Upon the walls of Zion! To be called
> Like a watch-worn and weary sentinel
> To put his armour off—and rest—in heaven."

WM. McHARDY, McLennan's Brook.

Died while preparing for the ministry.

REV. WILLIAM FRASER, D. D.

PICTONIANS IN THE PULPIT

JOHN F. FORBES, Blue Mountain; Died 1905.

He was born in 1834; received his education in Halifax and in Princeton Seminary. He was ordained 1867, as pastor of Union Centre and Lochaber, where he labored for 19 years. In 1886 he accepted a call to Durham, and from there, 8 years later, to St. Andrew's Church, Sydney, C. B. In all these charges he served with fidelity and success. He died in the 71st year of his age.

ADAM G. FORBES, Blue Mountain.

He came to Pictou when an infant; educated at the Free Church College, Halifax; his first charge was at Buctouche, N. B. From there he went to Ontario and some years later with a colony of his people, he went to No. Dakota, where he died in 1894.

GEO. M. ROSS, B.A., Blue Mountain, North Honan, China.

DAVID C. ROSS, B.A., Blue Mountain; Lower Stewiacke, N. S.

ALEX. L. FRASER, B.D., Blue Mountain, Great Village, N. S.

Published three volumes of poems. "Sonnets and other Verses", "At Life's Windows", "Fugitives".

HUGH MILLER, M.A., Garden of Eden; Glace Bay, C. B.

SAMUEL MCINTOSH, Garden of Eden; Deceased.

Student for the ministry.

REV. A. MACLEAN SINCLAIR, LL.D., Glenbard; Hopewell, N. S.

Rev. A. Maclean Sinclair is the highest authority in Canada on the Gaelic language and literature, and owns one of the best Gaelic libraries on the continent. He is also recognized in the Old Country as an eminent Gaelic scholar and student. He is the author of "Clarsach Na Coille", a collection of Gaelic hymns and songs, "Gaelic Bards", from 1411 to 1825, "The Mac Bards", two vols; "The Clan Gillean, or the History of the Macleans". This is a large and handsome octavo volume, and is the standard work on the history of the Clan. He is a regular contributor to the Celtic Magazine, Edinburgh, and other periodicals. He is a grandson of John Maclean, the well known Gaelic poet. In 1907, he was appointed lecturer in the Gaelic Language and Literature in Dalhousie University.

PICTONIANS AT HOME AND ABROAD

JAMES MCGREGOR MACKAY, East River St. Mary's; Died 1911.
 His father was Alex. MacKay, one of the first settlers at East River St. Mary's. He prosecuted his studies at West River Seminary, being one of Dr. Ross' first students. In 1855 he was inducted into the charge of Parrsboro, which at that time had ten preaching stations, and was forty miles in length. In 1860 he was called to Economy and Five Islands where he remained for 18 years. His next charge was at Woodstock, N. B. In 1884 he accepted a call to Shediac. After 37 years of service he retired, in 1892, to New Glasgow, where he died in the 93d year of his age. His physical powers were remarkable. As a preacher he was evangelical; as a presbyter he was loyal to the Church; as a friend his hospitality was unfailing. It is noteworthy that he never missed a meeting of Synod; never had a month's holiday, and, during his public ministry, there were only two Sabbaths on which he was unable to preach.

SAMUEL C. GUNN, D.D., East River St. Mary's; Boston, Mass.
 For nearly twenty years minister of Scotch Church, Boston. Retired from the Ministry.

WM. GUNN, East River St. Mary's; Died 1900.
 Mr. Gunn was educated at Colgate University, N. Y., and was a pastor of the Baptist denomination. His first charge was at Springfield, N. Y. In 1878 he was appointed Chaplain of the Prison, Fort Madison, Iowa. For 20 years he served in this capacity, and accomplished a great work in the reformation of the inmates of the prison.

ADAM GUNN, East River St. Mary's; Died 1903.
 Mr. Gunn was pastor for 16 years at Gore and Kennetcook, N. S., and at Cardigan, P. E. I., 10 years. In 1902 he went to the Northwest, but in the following year he died.

A. D. GUNN, East River St. Mary's; Died 1898.
 In 1883 he was called to Upper Stewiacke, where he labored for four and a half years, until failing health compelled him to resign. He was a brother of Rev. S. C. Gunn of Boston.

DUNCAN CAMERON, East River St. Mary's; Pittsburg, Pa.
 Rev. A. G. Cameron, B. Sc., Sylvania, Pa. and Rev. A. H. Cameron, M.A., Detroit, Mich., are cousins of Rev. Duncan Cameron.

PICTONIANS IN THE PULPIT

WM. A. MASON, B.A., East River St. Mary's; Wetaskiwin, Alta.

JOHN S. CLARK, East River St. Mary's; Minneapolis, Minn.
: Prof. of Latin, University of Minneapolis.

HUGH A. ROBERTSON, D.D., Barney's River; Erromanga, New Hebrides.
: Author, "Erromanga, the Martyr Isle".

A. J. MCKICHAN, Barney's River; Winnipeg, Man.
: Retired from the Ministry.

A. D. SUTHERLAND, Barney's River; Fort Sill, Okla.
: Chaplain Field Artillery, United States Army.

L. A. MACLEAN, B.A., Barney's River; Danville, Quebec.

WM. CRAIGIE, Barney's River; Died 1890.
: Pastor, Baptist Church.

ALEX. J. MCLEOD, Barney's River; Denmark, N. S.
: Pastor, Baptist Church.

WM. GORDON, Barney's River.
: Pastor of the Methodist Church. He labored in California, where he died in 1904.

MINISTERS AND CHURCHES IN MERIGOMISH, SUTHERLAND'S RIVER, THORBURN, LITTLE HARBOR AND BAILEY'S BROOK

The present church at Merigomish was built in 1869. The French River Church, in 1861 or 1862. The two churches maintained a separate existence from 1860 to about 1895, when they were united into one charge. The ministers in order of induction were: Revs. Wm. Patrick, A. P. Miller, K. J. Grant, H. McD. Scott, Daniel McGregor, C. S. Lord, Wm. R. Muir, Alex. Campbell, and A. S. Weir. The present pastor is A. F. Fisher, B. D., April 13, 1911.

Rev. Mr. Cock of Truro preached the first sermon in Merigomish at Morrison's house, about 1784. The first elders were Walter Murray, John Small, and George Roy.

The first settlers at Sutherland's River were from the Highlands of Scotland. The River was named after Sutherland, whose son, John, was the first child baptized belonging to Sutherland's River. Feb. 3, 1854 a site was bought for a church and the people proceeded to build. The congregation was made up of members from the three branches of the Presbyterian Church: the Kirk, the Free Church and the Presbyterian Church of N. S., united. This was the first union Presbyterian Church in the Province.

The Congregation of Thorburn was organized in 1875, and the two made one charge. Rev. W. T. Bruce, M.D. was called in 1876, and resigned in Jan. 1881. Rev. Isaac Murray, D.D. was inducted pastor in 1882; Rev. A. W. McLeod 1885; Rev. James A. Mackenzie 1899. His successor was Rev. John Harris, 1912. James W. McLean has been clerk of the Session for 28 years, and choir leader for over 40 years.

The Little Harbor Congregation was organized in 1864, and Rev. J. A. F. Sutherland was the first pastor. He was followed by Rev. Wm. Maxwell in 1868, who also had charge of Fisher's Grant. During his ministry the church was built. He resigned in 1880, and the pastors who succeeded him were: Revs. Robert Laird, McLeod Harvey, John B. Maclean, John W. Penman, R. J. Douglass, A. D. McIntosh and A. J. McDonald (1910) the present pastor.

Ministers Born and Bred in this District

JOHN CAMPBELL, Merigomish; Deceased.
    For some years he was pastor of St. Andrew's Church, Halifax, and for 18 years minister of Buccleuch parish Church, Edinburgh, Scotland, where he died.

ISAAC S. SIMPSON, Merigomish; Chicago, Ill.

WM. H. SMITH, B.D., Ph.D., Merigomish; Fredericton, N. B.
    Pastor, St. Paul's Church.

PICTONIANS IN THE PULPIT

Edwin Smith, M.A., Merigomish; McLeod, Alta.

A. A. Smith, B. A., Merigomish; Verschoyle, Ont.

F. W. Thompson, B.A., Merigomish; St. John, N. B.
   Pastor, Calvin Church.

Lawrence B. Campbell, Merigomish.
   Theol. Student. Son of late Rev. Alexander Campbell.

W. B. MacDonald, Merigomish; Lourdes, N. S.
   Pastor of the Roman Catholic Church.

John Chisholm, B.A., Sutherland's River; Montreal, Can.
   Pastor, Victoria Church.

Alex. W. McKay, Sutherland's River; Deceased.
   Pastor for some time at Streetsville, Ont.

James M. Sutherland, Sutherland's River; E. Pepperell, Mass.
   Pastor, Methodist Church.

John Lamont, Sutherland's River; Deceased.
   Graduated but never had a charge. For many years he was a successful colporteur for the National Bible Society, in the Maritime Provinces.

John A. MacGlashen, B.D., French River; Bridgeport, C. B.

A. W. Pollock, B.A., French River; Deceased.
   Student in Theology. Drowned at French River.

James A. McLean, B.A., Thorburn; Mahone Bay, N. S.

John J. MacDonald, Thorburn; Brooklyn, N. Y.
   Pastor, South Presbyterian Church.

Wm. MacPherson, Thorburn; Waterville, N. S.

A. S. Weir, Thorburn; Swan River, Manitoba.

J. F. McKay, Thorburn; Clyde River, N. S.

William Forbes, B.A., Little Harbor; Tatamagouche, N. S.

G. Ernest Forbes, B.A., Little Harbor; New Glasgow, N. S.
   Pastor, First Presbyterian Church.

John G. Golquhoon, B.A., Little Harbor; Millerton, N. B.

PICTONIANS AT HOME AND ABROAD

EDWIN H. BURGESS, Little Harbor; Sydney, C. B.
Editor, "Canadian Commonwealth". Author "At the Place which is called Calvary", a volume of sermons, and "For Canada and the Old Flag".

THOMAS F. MCGREGOR, Chance Harbor; Hawarden, Sask.

THE FOLLOWING ARE CLERGYMEN OF THE ROMAN CATHOLIC CHURCH

DONALD MACKINNON, Ardness; Died at Grand Narrows, C. B.

DUGAL MACKINNON, Ardness; Died at Dundas, Ont.

J. J. MACKINNON, Ardness; Bailey's Brook, N. S.

C. F. MACKINNON, Bailey's Brook; Sydney Mines, C. B.

M. W. MACKINNON, D.C.L., Lismore; Vancouver, B. C.

DONALD M. MACGREGOR, D.D., Lismore; Judique, C. B.

RONALD MACDONALD, Lismore; Pictou, N. S.

MINISTERS AND CHURCHES IN WEST RIVER AND GREEN HILL

The West River is one of the oldest congregations in the County. Rev. Duncan Ross took the pastoral oversight of the congregation in 1795 and continued to be pastor for 39 years. He was succeeded by his son, Rev. James Ross, D. D., who was inducted in 1835, and resigned in 1852.

James Watson followed him and remained for 5 years. In 1858 the congregation was divided into two separate charges. The one known as Central Church called Rev. James Thomson and the other congregation, Rev. George Roddick. At the close of 20 years' service, both resigned, when a reunion was effected, in 1879, and Rev. A. W. McLeod settled as pastor. In 1886 Rev. J. F. Forbes was inducted and Green Hill was united with West River. Rev. J. R. Coffin was called in 1895 and Rev. C. J. Crowdis in 1907. The present pastor is Rev. A. H. Foster, inducted

GROUP OF CHURCHES

1 Presbyterian Church, Springville
2 Presbyterian Church, Durham
3 St. John's Church, Scotsburn
4 Sharon Church, Stellarton
5 Hopewell Village and Church
6 Salem Church, River John
7 St. James Church, Pictou
8 Village of Sunny Brae
9 Carmel Church, Westville

PICTONIANS IN THE PULPIT

in 1913. The West River congregation has always been a centre of educational and missionary endeavor.

The church at Green Hill was built in 1848. Rev. George Patterson, D.D., was the first minister, inducted 1849, resigned 1876. Rev. William Stuart was pastor 1877 to 1884. The other pastors were: Revs. Forbes, Coffin, Crowdis and Foster.

Names of Ministers Born in this District, with Place of Birth and Addresses of Those Still Living

JAMES ROSS, D.D., West River; Died 1886.

EBENEZER ROSS, West River; Died 1891.
> Mr. Ross was inducted at Folly Village, 1849, and remained in this, his only charge until 1877, a ministry of 28 years. He then resigned on account of ill health, and removed to Truro, where he resided until his death. He was possessed of rare vigor and much learning.

DUNCAN MCDONALD, West River; Deceased.
> He was a member of the first class of theological students under Dr. McCulloch.

JOHN MCDONALD, West River; Deceased.
> Student for the ministry.

JOHN J. RICHARDS, West River; Died 1889.
> Mr. Richard's whole ministry was spent in Brockville Presbytery, Ontario, where he was held in high esteem as a faithful pastor and preacher.

JAMES D. MURRAY, West River; Died 1914.

ANGUS MCKENZIE, West River; Died 1911.
> He went to Kansas in 1872, and to the Pacific Coast in 1874 where nearly all his ministry was spent. He married Anna McPherson, Nova Scotia, in 1888. He was a faithful minister and did good work in the organization of new churches.

JOHN D. MCLEAN, West River; Deceased.
> Missionary to Japan.

D. STILES FRASER, B.A., Durham; Elderbank, N. S.
His son, E. J. O. Fraser, B.A., was appointed Missionary to Korea in 1914.

JOHN M. MACLEOD, West River; Deceased.
Mr. Macleod was one of the first who received his education at the West River Seminary. In 1853 he began his ministry at Richmond Bay, P. E. I., where he spent 6 years. His next pastorage was at Newport, N. S. From there he went to Knox Church, New Glasgow, N. S. In 1871 he was called to Zion Church, Charlottetown, where for 18 years he labored with zeal and success. He left the island in 1889 and went to Vancouver, to minister to a new congregation. Mr. Macleod was a vigorous preacher and a faithful pastor, and his memory is cherished in all his congregations. He was the author of "The History of Presbyterianism in Prince Edward Island".

WILLIAM McC. THOMSON, M.A., Durham; Port of Spain, Trinidad.
Pastor, Greyfriars Church.

A. W. THOMSON, M.A., Durham; Pictou, N. S.
Sons of the late Rev. James Thomson.

D. McDONALD CLARK, B.A., Durham; Middle Stewiacke, N. S.

DAVID CLARK, Durham; Died 1882.
He was a son of the late David Clark, elder, and had the ministry in view.

HENRY MACDONALD, Durham; Deceased.
He died at Paterson, N. J., in 1899, just after being ordained.

D. G. COCK, M.A., West River; Mhow, Central India.

FOREST L. FRASER, Durham; Penn Yan, N. Y.
Pastor, Baptist Church.

JOHN MCLEAN, M.A., Green Hill; Died 1837.

ALEX. BLAIKIE, D.D., Green Hill; Died 1885.
Born 1804, educated at Pictou Academy and Halifax, a Missionary in the Western States, 1831-1835. In 1836 he became pastor at York, N. Y. and continued for nine years. In 1846 he came to Boston and established a congregation in connection with the United Presbyterian Church, and continued pastor of it until he retired in 1880. His work in

Boston was marked by great labor and patience. He was the author of "Philosophy of Sectarianism", and "History of Presbyterianism in New England", and other works. William Blaikie, author, lawyer, athlete, was his son.

JOHN W. MCKENZIE, D.D., Green Hill; Australia.
Retired from Missionary Work.

JAMES A. MACKENZIE, B.A., Green Hill; Elmsdale, N. S.

EDWARD GRANT, Green Hill; Died 1894.
In 1869 he was inducted at Kempt and Walton, and in 1872 was called to Upper Stewiacke to succeed the late Rev. Prof. Smith, D.D., and from that, in 1891, to Middle Musquodoboit, to succeed the late Rev. Dr. Sedgwick. Mr. Grant was 52 years of age, and for nearly 25 years he was a most faithful minister in the Church.

D. W. CAMERON, Green Hill; Died 1903.
For many years Mr. Cameron was the pastor of Presbyterian Churches in Canada and the United States, but in later years entered the Church of England at Yonkers, N. Y., where he died.

JOHN G. CAMERON, Green Hill; Died 1897.
He was educated at Princeton Seminary, and ordained at the early age of twenty-one. The whole of his ministry was spent in Prince Edward Island, where he was greatly beloved as a man and a minister. His charges were in Bonshaw, Souris and Murray Harbor.

GEORGE GORDON MAHY, D.D., Green Hill; Philadelphia, Pa.
Secretary of the General Assembly's Committee on Evangelism, Presbyterian Church in U. S. A.

THOMAS MCLEAN, Green Hill; Deceased.
Was preparing himself for missionary work when he died.

NORMAN G. REID, Green Hill; Halifax, N. S.
Theological Student.

PICTONIANS AT HOME AND ABROAD

Ministers and Churches of Scotsburn, Including Rogers Hill and Plainfield

St. John's Church (Kirk) was built in 1838. It was the first church in the place and is still standing. Rev. R. Macaulay and Rev. D. McConnachie were the first ministers. Rev. John Sinclair was pastor for five years. In 1860 Rev. John Goodwill was inducted and resigned in 1871 to go as missionary to New Hebrides. The last minister of the Kirk church was the Rev. J. W. Fraser who spent his whole ministry at Scotsburn.

The Free Church was formed, after the disruption, in 1844, and in 1862 Bethel Church was built. Rev. Alex. Sutherland was the first minister. The other pastors in order of induction were: Revs. Alex. Stirling, 1871; J. A. Cairns, 1887; Thos. Cumming, D.D., 1898; W. A. Ross, 1908. Upon Mr. Fraser's retirement in 1907, St. John's Church and Bethel were united. Rev. A. D. Stirling is the present pastor, inducted 1910.

Ministers Born in this District

JOHN MURRAY, Scotsburn, Stanley Bridge, P. E. I.
    Retired from the Ministry.

JAMES MURRAY, B.D., D.D., Scotsburn; Toronto, Ont.
    Pastor, Erskine Church.

ROBERT C. MURRAY, Scotsburn; Died in India, 1888.

GEORGE MURRAY, Scotsburn; Nicola, B. C.
    Retired from the Ministry.

JOHN GORDON, Scotsburn; Nelson, B. C.

AENEAS GORDON, Scotsburn, Kings Kettle, Fifeshire, Scotland.

HUGH MCLEOD, Scotsburn.
    Born 1826, graduated, Amherst College 1851, studied, Bangor Theological Seminary. Settled in Springfield, Ohio, as pastor of the Congregational Church. In 1857 went to New Hampshire, where he spent the most of his ministerial life. During the Civil War he served honorably as Chaplain in the Army. He died at Cambridge, Mass., Feb. 19, 1900.

MINISTERS OF TODAY

1 James A. MacKenzie
2 D. Stiles Fraser
3 H. W. Fraser, D. D.
4 James Murray, D. D.
7 Wm. H. Burns, D. D.
5 Duncan Cameron
6 Hugh R. Grant

PICTONIANS IN THE PULPIT

DANIEL W. MCLEOD, Scotsburn; Hollywood, Calif.
Relinquished his studies for the ministry on account of ill health. Prominent elder on the Pacific Coast for many years.

ISAAC MURRAY, D.D., Scotsburn; Died 1906.
He received his theological training in West River Seminary, and Princeton Seminary, N. J. In 1849 he was inducted pastor of the congregation of Cavendish and New London, P. E. I., successor to Dr. Geddie. Here he labored for 27 years, wielding a large influence not only as a minister, but as an educationist and writer. In 1877 he was called to Thorburn and Sutherland's River. Here he remained for seven years, when he was settled in North Sydney, where he remained until his retirement in 1896. Dr. Murray was a man of fine attainments, and one of the most faithful in his attendance upon Church courts.

J. ALLISTER MURRAY, Scotsburn; Died 1894.
In 1857 he was settled at Annapolis, N. S. Three years later he accepted a call to Bathurst, N. B. He afterwards removed to Ontario where he labored during the remainder of his life. His chief work was at London, Ont., where he ministered for about twenty years. Mr. Murray was a very effective and forcible preacher. He was a brother of the Rev. Isaac Murray.

A. D. STIRLING, B.A., Scotsburn; Scotsburn, N. S.

JOHN STIRLING, B.A., Scotsburn; Cavendish, P. E. I.
Sons of the late Rev. Alexander Stirling.

JOHN STEWART, Scotsburn; Deceased.
Student for the ministry. He entered Dal. Univ., 1874 and won a scholarship. During his second year in college he died, aged twenty-three. He was a young man of fine ability.

HUGH MCINTOSH, Scotsburn; Deceased.

ALEX. MCKENZIE, Scotsburn; Deceased.
Mr. McIntosh and Mr. McKenzie were both students for the ministry and promising young men.

E. D. MILLER, D.D., Rogers Hill. Died 1909.
Rev. Mr. Miller was a grandson of Rev. Duncan Ross. After a successful course of study he was ordained, on Oct. 28, 1872, in Shelburne. After he left Shelburne he labored with great zeal and energy in Lunenburg and Yarmouth, and was eminently successful in both places. After 16 years of work in Yarmouth he was called to Chalmer's Church, Halifax.

He settled there in 1907. He was an instructive preacher, a sympathetic pastor, and deeply interested in all the enterprises of the Church. His ministry spanned thirty-six very busy years.

DUNCAN MILLER, Rogers Hill; Deceased.

JAMES MILLER, Rogers Hill; Deceased.
Brothers of the Rev. E. D. Miller, and died while preparing for the ministry.

JOHN W. MATHESON, Rogers Hill; Died in New Hebrides, 1862.

ANDERSON ROGERS, D.D., Rogers Hill.; Halifax, N. S.
Dr. Rogers enjoys the honor of having formed the first Christian Endeavor Society in N. S., at Yarmouth, in 1885.

JAMES FITZPATRICK, B.A., Rogers Hill; New Annan, N.S.

JOHN R. FITZPATRICK, Rogers Hill; Died 1893.
Educated at Dalhousie and Presbyterian College, Halifax. Settled at Carleton, N. B., but resigned on account of ill health. He was brother of the Rev. James Fitzpatrick.

RODERICK MCKAY, B.D., Rogers Hill; Kingston, Ont.

JOHN A. FRASER, Rogers Hill; Oakland, Calif.

ROBERT MURRAY, Rogers Hill; O'Leary, P. E. I.

WILLIAM B. MACCALLUM, Rogers Hill; New Richmond, Quebec.

RODERICK C. Jackson, Rogers Hill; Farmington, New Mexico.

ALEXANDER SUTHERLAND, Plainfield; Died 1897.
He was born in Lairg, Scotland, 1816. While a child his parents came to Nova Scotia. He was sent to Edinburgh to complete his education, and at the age of 28, he entered upon the ministry. His first charge in Pictou Presbytery, was 40 miles in extent. In seven years four congregations were organized and five new churches. In 1852 he removed to Prince Edward Island, where he labored for seven years and organized four congregations with two new churches. A call was sent to him three times from his former field, the third time urging him to return on the ground that four congregations that hesitated would enter the union of 1860 if he should return, which he did, and these congregations entered

MINISTERS OF TODAY

1 J. R. DOBSON
2 WILLIAM P. GRANT
3 WILLIAM. H. SMITH
4 ANDERSON ROGERS, D. D.
5 F. H. MACINTOSH
6 G. ERNEST FORBES
7 J. A. MACGLASHEN

PICTONIANS IN THE PULPIT

without a dissenting voice. During the next few years he occupied Earltown, West Branch, Scotsburn and Saltsprings, gathering the fruits of seed sown during previous years. In 1874 he went to Canada where he labored until Aug., 1897. His ministerial jubilee was celebrated at Ripley, Ontario, 1896. Seventeen ministers were present and over one thousand people. He was always punctual in fulfilling appointments. Many times did he break the road before his horse through deep snows, while his coat was frozen about him. A large number of the ministers of our church received their first impulses and ideal under his ministry.

WILLIAM SUTHERLAND, Plainfield; Deceased.
His whole ministry was spent in Ontario, where he died.

ALFRED FITZPATRICK, B.A., Plainfield; Toronto, Ont.
Director and Superintendent of Educational Work among the lumber camps of Canada.

LUTHER L. YOUNG, B.A., Millsville; Ham Heung, Korea.

MINISTERS AND CHURCHES IN THE SALTSPRINGS DISTRICT

The first minister of St. Luke's Church, Saltsprings, was the Rev. Donald McIntosh. He was followed by the Rev. Hugh McLeod, from 1833 to 1844. For seven years the church was vacant. The other ministers in order of induction were: Revs. A. Maclean, D.D., 1851-1857; Alexander McKay, 1859-1867; William McMillan 1868-1876; James Fitzpatrick 1879-1891; Alexander Roulston 1892-1898; A. H. Denoon 1899-1908; Wm. F. Burns 1909-1913.

In 1845, twenty families went out from St. Luke's Church and were organized into a Free Church of Scotland. The following year they began the erection of Ebenezer Church. In 1859 Rev. Alex. Sutherland became minister of the united congregations of Bethel Church, Scotsburn and Ebenezer Church. He was followed by the Rev. Alex. Stirling, 1871, Rev. J. A. Cairns 1887, Rev.

PICTONIANS AT HOME AND ABROAD

Thos. Cumming, 1889. In 1908 St. Luke's and Ebenezer churches were formerly united. The present pastor is Rev. A. T. Macdonald.

From 1845 to 1896 West Branch River John was part of the Earltown congregation. In 1896 it was united to St. George's Church, River John. It became a separate charge in 1910 under the Rev. Thomas Johnstone who remained two years. The Rev. C. J. MacInnes, B.A., present pastor was inducted March 3, 1913.

MINISTERS BORN AND BROUGHT UP IN THIS DISTRICT

HUGH J. FRASER, B.D., Saltsprings; Summerside, P. E. I.

NORMAN T. MCKAY, Saltsprings; Ready, Ont.

J. FRANK MCLEOD, Saltsprings; Harbor Creek, Pa.

ALEX. RETTIE, M.A., Saltsprings; Millerton, N. B.

DANIEL MCGILLIVRAY, Brookland; Deceased.
 He received his early education in Pictou Academy, and took his theological course in Queen's University, Kingston. His first charge was Brockville, Ont., where he ministered for 14 years, after which he settled at London, Ont., where he remained 8 years. He was then called to Lunenburg, N. S., and remained 13 years in this charge, when his health broke down, and he went to British Columbia. He was forty years in the ministry. Mr. McGillivray was a man of genial disposition and his memory is cherished in all the congregations where he ministered.

ANDREW GRAY, Brookland; Murray Harbor West, P. E. I.

ARCHIBALD GUNN, Six Mile Brook.
 Studied at Dalhousie University and graduated from the Presbyterian College, Halifax, in 1878. His first charge was at Little Bay, Nfd. From there he was called to Windsor, N. S. He was for seven years minister at St. Andrew's, N. B. and another seven years at Bloomfield, P. E. I. Failing health compelled him to retire from the ministry. He removed to Westville where he made his home for eight years. He died on the evening of Easter, 1912.

PICTONIANS IN THE PULPIT

GEORGE GORDON MATHESON, Six Mile Brook.; Died 1897.
> He attended Pictou Academy in 1887 and studied at Springfield School for Christian Workers. He was ordained to the ministry at Fergus Falls, Minn., 1893. For several years he was Sunday School Missionary in the Red River Presbytery Minn., holding evangelistic services, founding and aiding churches and Sunday Schools. He was an earnest Christian worker.

ARTHUR ROSS, M. A., Black River; Dawson, Y. T.

JOHN S. ROSS, Black River; Vancouver, B. C.

JOHN LIVINGSTON, West River Station; Deceased.
> He was pastor of Dundee, Ont., for nine months, when he died. The congregation erected a monument to his memory with the inscription,—"In memory of John Livingston, born at West River Station, Apr. 6, 1821, died in Dundee, Aug. 15, 1860, aged 29 years. He was ordained to the pastoral charge in Dundee Nov. 30, 1859. He was a burning and a shining light."

W. A. MACKAY, B.D., West Branch River John; Blackwater, Ont.

Earltown, adjoining Pictou County on the Colchester side has produced a splendid lot of men in almost every profession and line of calling. Among the clergymen are: Neil McKay, Adam McKay, Robt. Murray, editor of Presbyterian Witness, William Murray, Alexander Ross, Donald Sutherland, A. L. McKay, Angus McDonald, John D. McKay, missionary to South America, James Ross, Geo. A. Sutherland, J. H. Stewart, D. W. McDonald, R. J. Douglass and Melville Grant.

MINISTERS IN THE SCOTCH HILL, HARDWOOD HILL AND CARIBOO DISTRICT

Some of the families belonging to Scotch Hill and Hardwood Hill, attended the Scotsburn Church. Others worshipped in Pictou. Cape John was formerly connected with St. George's Church, River John. In 1908, Cape John and Cariboo was organized into a separate charge. Rev. G. R. McKean was the only settled minister.

PICTONIANS AT HOME AND ABROAD

Ministers Born in this District

JOHN MCMILLAN, D.D., Scotch Hill; Halifax, N. S.
Stated Clerk, Halifax Presbytery.

GEORGE MCMILLAN, Scotch Hill; Died 1913.
For 16 years he was the faithful minister at Kentville, N. S. Previous to this he ministered to congregations at Malpeque, P. E. I., and Harbor Grace, Nfd. He was a brother of the Rev. John McMillan, Halifax, and a scholarly and impressive preacher.

A. N. MCQUARRIE, B.A., Scotch Hill,; Died 1909.
Mr. McQuarrie graduated from Queen's University in 1865, and went to Quebec, when for a number of years he was a successful professor in Morrin College. From there he went to Washington, D. C., where he taught for several years. For fifteen years he was a minister in Manitoba. He died at Winnipeg Dec. 1, 1909, aged 70 years. He was a diligent student, an acceptable preacher, and was held in high esteem by those to whom he ministered.

JOHN CAMPBELL, Scotch Hill; Died 1873.
Born at Scotch Hill, December, 1809. Studied at Pictou Academy, and Theology under Dr. McCulloch, licensed by the Presbytery of Pictou, April, 1837. Ordained at St. Mary's, 1st November, 1837. Died September 4, 1873. Endowed by nature with strong mental gifts, great powers of physical endurance, animated with the spirit of his Master, he gave himself to his work with energy and zeal, undergoing the most arduous labors, in discharging his duties as a minister over a widely scattered field.

KENNETH J. GRANT, D.D., Scotch Hill; Vancouver, B. C.

WM. L. CAMPBELL, Scotch Hill; Yarmouth, N. S.
Collector of Customs.

ALEXANDER HAMILTON, Scotch Hill; Old Orchard, Me.
Pastor, Methodist Church.

KENNETH MCKAY, Hardwood Hill; Died March 28, 1914.
In 1872 he was ordained at Richmond, N. B., where he remained 16 years. In 1888, he became pastor of a mission Church at Houlton, Me., thus organizing the first Presbyterian Church in the state. He resigned in 1910. Mr. McKay was an able and earnest preacher and one of the most genial and lovable

PICTONIANS IN THE PULPIT

of men. He married Miss Margaret Grant, a sister of Rev. Dr. K. J. Grant. He is survived by his widow and seven children.

ALEXANDER MCKAY, Hardwood Hill; Deceased.

Mr. McKay was the first Nova Scotian who studied for the Church of Scotland, and returned to labor among his countrymen. In 1852 he commenced his ministry in his native parish, Rogers Hill, and at the end of 2 years went to Belfast, P. E. I. From 1859 to 1867, he labored with great success at Gairloch and Saltsprings, N. S. In 1868 he removed to Ontario. He died in the 63d year of his age, and the 35th of his ministry. He was a devoted minister of the Gospel.

D. O. MACKAY, B.A., Hardwood Hill; Kingsville, Ohio.

HECTOR MCQUARRIE, Hardwood Hill; Deceased.

Settled at Wingham, Ont.

HECTOR B. MCKAY, Cariboo; Died 1912.

Mr. McKay was for some time a teacher in the Free Church Academy, Halifax. In 1855, he was ordained at Chipman, where he spent the first 7 years of his ministry. In 1861 he was called to Salem Church, River John, where he labored with great success. This pastorate lasted 24 years. In 1885 he went to Wallace where followed 11 years of great usefulness. He retired from the ministry in 1897, and lived thereafter in Halifax, where he died, at the venerable age of 87 years.

KENNETH MCKENZIE, Cariboo; Died 1904.

For a year he was in charge of Baddeck, C. B., before his call and ordination there in 1857. This was his first and only charge. For 35 years he labored here, until his resignation and retirement, in 1891. For 5 years during his ministry he inspected all the schools of Victoria County.

GEORGE RODDICK, Cariboo; Died 1910.

In 1858 Mr. Roddick was inducted into the congregation of West River, Pictou, where he was a faithful pastor for 21 years. Then catching the first strain of the call to the west he removed with his family, and a portion of his congregation, to Brandon Hills, Manitoba. There he engaged in farming and preached as opportunity offered. After an absence of 25 years he returned to his native County and settled in the town of Pictou.

DANIEL MCKAY, Cariboo; Addison, N. Y.

MURDOCH, S. MacKAY, B. A., Cariboo; Waweig, N. B.
ALEXANDER MACAULAY, Cariboo; Vancouver, B. C.
ARCHIBALD SUTHERLAND, Cariboo; Trenton, N. S.
Graduate Presbyterian College, Halifax, 1914.

MINISTERS AND CHURCHES OF RIVER JOHN

The early settlers of River John were of Swiss origin. Having undergone untold persecution in their native land, some of them left their native country and came to Halifax, N. S. From thence they proceeded to Lunenburg, where they endured the hardships of the first settlers. In 1772 twelve or thirteen families came to Tatamagouche and formed the first settlers of that place. In 1785 four families: George Patriquin, James Gratto, John Patriquin and George Langill, removed to River John, where they could obtain crown land. They became the first settlers there and had a noble ancestry. The first preaching received by River John's early settlers was by Dr. McGregor. Between Pictou and River John, at this time, there was an unbroken forest. Not a single dweller was to be found along the shore between these two places. The first settled minister was Rev. John Mitchell, who began his labors in 1808, and gave 35 years of service to this congregation. The Rev. James Waddell, was settled over the people in 1844. He resigned in 1858. Mr. Waddell was succeeded by the Rev. H. B. McKay in 1861, who ministered to this people for 24 years. In 1887 the Rev. G. L. Gordon was inducted, and was minister for 21 years. The present pastor is Rev. C. D. McIntosh, settled there Dec. 9, 1909.

Two congregations existed for many years in River John, Salem and St. George's congregations. The latter belonged to the Kirk body and was organized by the Rev. Geo. M. Grant. Its first pastor was the Rev. Robt. McCunn, who was settled in 1863, and spent a long and faithful ministry there. Then followed the Rev. J. A. Crawford from 1898 to 1906. In 1896 the Rev. R. J. Grant was ordained. His ministry was a short one, and terminated in his tragic death at Montreal, in 1898. On the 4th of January 1911, the two charges in River John were happily united.

MINISTERS BORN AND BROUGHT UP IN THIS DISTRICT

DAVID W. JOHNSON, D.D., River John; Truro, N. S.
    Editor of the Wesleyan, organ of the Methodist denomination.
JOHN G. BIGNEY, River John; Hantsport, N. S.
    Retired Methodist minister.
WM. H. LANGILLE, River John; Glace Bay, C. B.
    Pastor, Methodist Church.
ROBERT F. ALLEN, B.A., River John; Annapolis Royal, N. S.
    Pastor, Baptist Church.
CHARLES W. ALLEN, River John; Hamilton, N. Y.
    Student Colgate University. Baptist.
JAMES A. FORBES, River John; Earltown, N. S.
PAUL F. LANGILLE, B.A., River John; Fingal, Ont.
GILBERT W. LANGILLE, B.A., River John; Edgerton, Alta.
GEORGE P. TATTRIE, B.D., River John; Tabusintac, N.B.
JOHNSON A. HENDERSON, B.A., Toney River; Chicago, Ill.
CHARLES ROSS, Toney River; Deceased.
    Pastor, Congregational Church.
MALCOLM McKAY, River John; Oxford, Me.
    Pastor, Congregational Church.
A. A. McKAY, B.A., River John.
    Theological student, Presbyterian College, Halifax.
LINTON DWYER, River John; Pawtucket, R. I.
    Pastor, Episcopal Church.

PICTONIANS AT HOME AND ABROAD

PETER MELVILLE, B.D., Cape John; Died 1912.

Mr. Melville was pastor in New Brunswick and at Hopewell, N. S., for many years, where he left a record of efficient work. His scholastic attainments were of a high order. For eight years he studied in the University of Glasgow, and won valuable prizes in sharp competition with many others. He spent the closing years of his ministerial life in a parish in the North of Scotland. He died in Edinburgh in 1912.

Chapter IV

PICTONIANS IN THE MEDICAL PROFESSION

ROBERT Louis Stevenson said there are men and classes of men that stand above the common herd—the soldier, the sailor and the shepherd not infrequently, the artist rarely, the clergyman rarelier still, the physician almost as a rule.

On the score of priority in the field the physicians from Pictou may justly enter a claim for precedence over the other professions. For foremost among the little band of settlers, who, on June 10, 1757, arrived aboard the Brig Hope and laid the foundations of the town of Pictou, came Dr. John Harris, an agent of the Philadelphia company.

It is to be taken for granted that Dr. Harris did not depend for a living upon his practice, for the Hope brought only 35 or 40 passengers, all told. Incidentally, it may be remarked that the first white child born in the county came into the world the very night of the arrival of the brig, when the doctor's own family received the addition of a son. He afterward became known as Clerk "Tommy" Harris, having the position of Clerk of Peace for many years. He died in 1809, and was buried in the Pictou cemetery, where a monument stood to his memory, long since fallen, on which was the inscription, "The first descendant of an Englishman born in Pictou." We may add that Dr. Harris' daughter, afterward Mrs. Robert Cook, born in 1769, was the first female child born in Pictou of English parentage.

Since that day, a century and a half ago, generation after generation of his successors carried on their appointed labors, and of many even the names have passed from the memory of men. Naturally, the earliest of these were not natives of the county. Among pioneer physicians of

PICTONIANS AT HOME AND ABROAD

Pictou town and vicinity were Dr. Skinner, Dr. Johnstone, Dr. Kirkwood and Dr. Anderson. The physicians who first settled in New Glasgow were Dr. Wade, Dr. James Skinner, Dr. John Fox, Dr. Alexander Forrest, from 1832-1875. Dr. James Donnelly practiced at Albion Mines, now Stellarton, for many years. He was a native of the North of Ireland. He died in 1866 in the fifty-sixth year of his age.

But with the gradual increase of population, of worldly goods and of educational advantages, her young men began to take advantage of their opportunity to qualify themselves for more ambitious careers. The practice of the healing art evidently appealed with force to a considerable proportion as the partial list appearing upon subsequent pages will indicate. It is practically impossible to give a complete list of all the native sons and daughters of Pictou who, since the first settlement, have given themselves to the medical profession. But of this list, it may be said with truth, of all her sons, of none may the county more reasonably feel proud than of those whose names appear herein. Far and wide are they scattered, living or dead, but in whatever place their lot was cast they brought credit to their native land. Not a few arose to eminence in the profession. The county in which they were born today is recognized as a section where the best standards of medical knowledge and professional ethics are maintained.

The list below, with the name, place of birth, alma mater and present address, if living, shows 190 physicians of whom knowledge is available:

ANDERSON, ALEXANDER, M.D., Pictou; Harvard Univ., 1864; Petaluma, Cal.

ANDERSON, SMITH, M.D., Pictou; Univ. N. Y., 1892; Pictou, N. S.

ANDERSON, WALTER, M.D., Pictou; died in Vallejo, Cal.

PHYSICIANS AND SURGEONS

ARBUCKLE, JAMES, M.D., Merigomish; deceased.

BAILEY, CAMERON, V., M.D., New Glasgow; McGill Univ. 1909; Montreal, Can.

BAILEY, WILLIAM J., M.D., New Glasgow; Univ. Penn., 1895; Connellsville, Pa.

BELL, JOHN, M.D., C.M., New Glasgow; McGill Univ., 1898; New Glasgow, N. S.

BENVIE, ROBERT MCLEAN, M.D., C.M., Saltsprings; McGill Univ., 1907; Stellarton, N. S.

BRUCE, JAMES GARFIELD, M.D., C.M., Barney's River; Dal. Univ., 1908; Westville, N. S.

BURNS, SAMUEL WESLEY, M.D., New Glasgow; Bell Med. Col., 1864; Shelburne, N. S.

BURNS, THOMAS M., M.D., New Glasgow; deceased.

CALDER, ALLISTER, M.D., C.M., Springville; Dal. Univ., 1909; Glace Bay, C. B.

CALDER, JAMES SQUAIR, M.D., Springville; Harvard Univ. 1886; Los Angeles, Cal.

CAMERON, ALEXANDER, M.D., Glengarry; Glasgow Univ.; deceased.
> Dr. Cameron settled at Huntington, Quebec, where he was a distinguished and successful practitioner. Brother of Rev. John Cameron, D.D., Scotland.

CAMERON, CLARENCE B., M.D., C.M., New Glasgow; Dal. Univ., 1911; Halifax, N. S.

CAMERON, HAROLD, M.D., C.M., River John; Dal. Univ., 1901; River John, N. S.

CAMERON, JOHN THOMAS, M.D., Hopewell.
> Died at River John, N. S.

CAMERON, MURDOCH, M.D., Saltsprings; Mexico.

CAMERON, OWEN HALIBURTON, M.D., River John; Balt. Med. Col., 1892; Maccan Station, N. S.

CAMERON, WILLIAM, M.D., Saltsprings; deceased.

CAMPBELL, ALBERT E., M.D., St. Paul's; Univ. of Buffalo 1886; Chicago, Ill.
    Health Officer for the Illinois Central Railway system, Chicago, Ill.

CAMPBELL, ALEX. R., B.A., M.D., Merigomish; Dal. Univ., 1913; Yarmouth, N. S.

CAMPBELL, DUNCAN, M.D., West Br. River John; Tulane Univ., 1891; West Br. River John, N. S.

CAMPBELL, ROBERT, M.D., West Branch River John; deceased.
    He practiced in River John for a few years, then removed to Dartmouth, N. S., where he died.

CHISHOLM, HUGH D., M.D., C.M., Springville; Dal. Univ., 1907; Springville, N. S.

CHISHOLM, JAMES, M.D., New Glasgow; McGill Univ., 1900; Everett, Wash.

COLLIE, JAMES ROSS, M.D., Middle River; Harvard Univ., 1869; River John, N. S.

COLLIE, JOHN R. M., M.D., C.M., River John; Dal. Univ., 1911.
    Post Graduate course, London, England.

COPELAND, GEORGE, M.D., Merigomish; deceased.

CULTON, ALBERT, M.D., Stellarton; Balt. Med. Col., 1897; Port Greville, N. S.

CUMMING, ALLISON, M.D., Stellarton; McGill Univ., 1905; Vancouver, B. C.

DELANEY-BARBOUR, ISABEL, M.D., Churchville; Women's Med. Col., N. Y; New York City.

DICKSON, CHARLES H., M.D., C.M., Pictou; Dal. Univ., 1901; Springfield, N. S.

DICKSON, MINAR S., M.D., Pictou; Univ., N.Y., 1890; Dartmouth, N. S.

DOULL, JAMES A., B.A., M.D., New Glasgow.
    Graduate, Dal. Medical Univ., 1914.

PHYSICIANS AND SURGEONS

DUFF, DUNCAN, M.D., Churchville.
: Died in Detroit, Mich.

DUNBAR, WILLAIM R., M.D., C.M., Abercrombie; McGill Univ., 1897; Truro, N. S.

DUNN, GEORGE A., Lyon's Brook; Dal. Col., 1906; Pictou, N. S.

DUNN, JAMES B., M.D., Merigomish; Pittsburgh, Pa.

ELLIOTT, ALFRED, M.D., River John; Balt. Col. Phys. & Surg.; Bridgewater, Conn.
: Medical director of the State Farm Hospital.

FALCONER, A. F., M.D., Hopewell.
: Died in Sherbrooke, N. S.

FERGUSON, JOHN A., M. D., Cariboo; L. I. Col. Hosp; N. Y.; Brooklyn, N.Y.

FERGUSON, WILLIAM, M.D., Pictou; McGill Univ., 1894; New York City, N.Y.

FORBES, ALBERT E., M.D., C.M., Durham; Dal. Univ., 1900; Upper Stewiacke, N. S.

FORBES, ARTHUR E. G., M.D., C.M., Little Harbor; McGill Univ., 1906; Lunenburg, N. S.

FRASER, ALEXANDER, M.D., C.M., West River; Dal. Univ., 1897; New York City.

FRASER, HUGH D., M.D., Bridgeville; Jefferson Med. Col.; Philadelphia, Pa.

FRASER, JAMES, M.D., New Glasgow; Edinburgh Univ.; deceased.

FRASER, JOHN B., M.D., New Glasgow; deceased.

FRASER, JOHN F., M.D., West River; Harvard Univ., 1892; New York City.
: Brother of Dr. Alexander Fraser.

FRASER, J. W., M.D., Pictou; deceased.
: Practiced in Prince Edward Island, brother of Rev. F. W. Fraser.

FRASER, WILLIAM F., M.D., Westville; L. I. Med. Col., 1897; Lynn, Mass.

PICTONIANS AT HOME AND ABROAD

FRASER, WILLIAM, M.D., F.R.C.S., New Glasgow; deceased.
Was born at Island, East River, studied in Glasgow University, practiced in New Glasgow twenty-seven years, where he died June 20, 1900. Son James Fraser, Downie; was married to Mary M., daughter of late Basil Bell, New Glasgow.

FULLERTON, THOMAS, M.D., Lyon's Brook; Harvard Univ.; deceased.

GRAHAM, JOHN, M.D., New Glasgow; deceased.

GRAHAM, JUDSON V., New Glasgow; Dal. Univ., 1914; medical student.

GRANT, DANIEL, M.D., Caribou; McGill Univ., 1896; Portland, Ore.

GRANT, JOHN, M.D., Little Harbor; deceased.

GRANT, JOHN P., M.D., C.M., Linacy; McGill Univ., 1895; New York City.

GRANT, NORMAN McKAY, M.D., C.M., Stellarton; Queen's Univ., 1889; New Zealand.
Brother of Rev. Hugh R. Grant and the Grant Bros. Druggists, New Glasgow.

GRANT, WILLIAM R., M.D., Springville; deceased.
Was born in 1811 and died in Philadelphia in 1852, in the forty-first year of his age. Early destined for the church by his parents, he entered Pictou Academy where he received his early education. While there, he relinquished the study of Theology and in 1834 entered the office of Dr. Alexander McDonald, Antigonish, as a medical student.

Two years later he went to Philadelphia, which was to be his home and the scene of his labors and distinctions. Graduating from Jefferson Medical College in 1839, he was immediately appointed demonstrator of Anatomy in his Alma Mater. In 1843, he was appointed Professor of Anatomy in the Pennsylvania Medical College—a position which he held to the close of his life and which he filled in an eminent degree.

Dr. Grant was a distinguished physician and surgeon, as well as an excellent instructor. His many qualities of mind and heart endeared him to all, and few men were better fitted by nature and education for his work.

Prof. WILLIAM R. GRANT, M. D.

PHYSICIANS AND SURGEONS

In 1840, he was ordained a ruling elder in one of the leading churches in Philadelphia, and in the same year, he married into the well-known family of John McAllister of the same city. He left a wife and three children. It was in discharge of a professional duty that his last illness was contracted. He died like a faithful sentinel of humanity, at his post with his arms on his back.

GRANT, WILLIAM R., B.A., Springville; Dal. Col.; deceased.
> Nephew and namesake of Prof. W. R. Grant. Died in 1881, in the first year of his Medical course.

GREEN, FRED W., M.D., C.M., Pictou; McGill Univ., 1903; Glace Bay, C. B.

GORDON, DAVID, Pictou; Edinburgh Univ.; deceased.

HATTIE, WILLIAM H., M.D., C.M., Pictou; McGill Univ., 1891.
> Provincial Health Officer for Province, Halifax, N. S.

HENDERSON, JOHN, M.D., Mt. Thom; Harvard Univ.; deceased.

HERDMAN, WILLIAM H., M.D., C.M., L.M., Stellarton; Dal. Univ., 1911; Bass River, N. S.

JOHNSTONE, GEORGE M., M.D., Pictou; London Univ.; deceased.

KEAY, ARNOLD, M.D., C.M., New Glasgow; Royal Victoria Hosp.; Montreal, Que.

KEAY, THOMAS, M.D., C.M., New Glasgow; McGill Univ., 1907; New Glasgow, N. S.

KEITH, SILVANUS, M.D., C.M., Stellarton; Queen's Col., 1886; New Glasgow, N. S.

KENNEDY, EVAN, M.D., Bridgeville; Boston Univ., 1876; New Glasgow, N. S.

KIRKWOOD, HENRY, M.D., Pictou; Jefferson Med. Col.
> Died in 1859, son of late Dr. Kirkwood, Pictou. At his father's death took his practice.

LINDSAY, ANDREW W. H., B.A., M.D., C.M., Pictou; Dal. Univ., 1875, and Univ. of Edinburgh, 1877; Halifax, N. S.

In 1866 he won the first professors' scholarship offered by Dalhousie College. He is secretary and registrar Provincial Medical Board of Nova Scotia. Dr. Murdoch A. Lindsay, Professor of Pathology Dal. Univ., and Dr. W. S. Lindsay, Halifax, are his nephews. Their father, Murdoch Mackenzie Lindsay, was a native of Pictou.

LIPPINCOTT, HENRY, M.D., New Glasgow; Jefferson Med. Col., 1863; died in 1908.

Dr. Lippincott was born in 1839, served as assistant surgeon in civil war, saw distinguished service throughout the country, notably in the Indian campaigns with General Custer. Directed the medical department of the Philippine expedition during the Spanish-American war under General Merritt, later with General Otis. Returned to America broken in health, but in 1901 was appointed chief surgeon, Department of the East, at Governor's Island, N. Y., the most important medical appointment in the United States army after the post of surgeon-general. Was retired when 64. Married Mary Agnes McClenthen, who survives him with two sons, Dr. Walter M. Lippincott and Capt. Aubrey Lippincott, U. S. A. He was a brother of Dr. J. Aubrey Lippincott. Dr. Henry Lippincott was a man of unusually strong character, highest principles and his whole life aptly illustrated by his family motto, *secundis dubiiaque fortis.*

LIPPINCOTT, J. AUBREY, B.A., M.D., New Glasgow; Dal. Col., 1867; Pittsburgh, Pa.

Dr. J. Aubrey Lippincott was born in 1847. After Dalhousie College, he graduated from the Jefferson Medical College, Philadelphia, in 1873. Settled in Pittsburgh in 1877, becoming an ear and eye specialist. Has written extensively for medical journals, was one of the authors of The American Text Book of Diseases of the Ear and Eye, and was renowned for his researches on physiological optics and improvement in the operation for cataract.

LOVE, ANDREW, M.D., C.M., New Glasgow; McGill Univ. 1891; Sydney Mines, C. B.

PHYSICIANS AND SURGEONS

MAXWELL-FULTON, ANNIE, M.D., C.M., Mount Thom; deceased.
   Dr. Fulton-Maxwell was the wife of Elder Samuel Fulton, Stewiacke. She died in Lake City, Minn., in 1881, 34 years old. Dr. Archibald Maxwell was a brother.

MAXWELL, ARCHIBALD, M.D., Mt. Thom.
   Died at Bear River, N. S., in May 23, 1882, of Apoplexy.

MILLER, CHARLES J., M.D., Merigomish; Harvard Univ., 1876; New Glasgow, N. S.

MILLER, CLARENCE, M.D., C.M., Stellarton; McGill Univ., 1905; Stellarton, N. S.

MITCHELL, FREDERICK W., M.D., C.M., Merigomish; Balt. Med. Col., 1898; Houlton, Me.

MITCHELL, WILLIAM, M.D., Merigomish; deceased.
   Graduated Jefferson Medical College 1859, practiced Medicine in New Glasgow from 1860 until his death in Dec. 1896.

MORTON, JOSEPH S., B.A., M.D., Fraser's Mountain; deceased.
   He died in Shelburne, N. S., in the fifty-eighth year of his age. To his church he was ever loyal, and, with great interest filled the office of treasurer for 27 years. He was an ardent educationalist. His first work for Shelburne was as Principal of the Academy for several years, in which position he was very successful; and during the 30 years of medical practice, he never lost his interest in education. He was the moving spirit in securing the erection of the fine Academy Building which is a splendid monument to Dr. Morton's memory. He was a brother of late Rev. Dr. Morton, Trinidad. Died February 25, 1911 from illness contracted while attending to his professional duties, a signal instance of self-sacrifice for the good of others.

MUNRO, CHARLES H., M.D., West River.
   Dr. Munro died in 1909, after practicing his profession at West River 40 years.

MUNRO, CRANSWICK B., M.D. C.M., River John; Dal. Univ., 1895; Boston, Mass.

MUNRO, HENRY W., M.D., River John; Balt. Col. Phys. & Surg.; Quincy, Mass.

MUNRO, HUGH R., M.D., West River.
  Dr. Munro died in 1910, in the Aberdeen Hospital, New Glasgow, after an active practice of more than 20 years in Stellarton, N. S.

MUNRO, JAMES G., M.D., C.M., River John; Dal. Univ., 1899; Winnipeg, Man.

MUNRO, KENNEDY, M.D., West River; deceased.
  Dr. Kennedy Munro died in 1898, after practicing medicine in Kansas, U. S. A., and Millsville, N. S. He and two brothers Charles H., and Hugh R., were sons of William Munro, West River.

MURRAY, ALEXANDER, M.D., West Br. River John; Chicago Med. Col., 1892; Deer Island, N. B.

MURRAY, ANGUS J., M.D.
  Was born in Logansville, October 23, 1855 and was the eldest son of John Murray. He received his education in Pictou Academy and the Provincial Normal School and taught school several years in various parts of Nova Scotia. He graduated from Halifax Medical College, 1884. He was in poor health for years, suffering from pulmonary tuberculosis. He died at Fredericton Junction, where he practiced for many years, April, 1913.

MURRAY, DANIEL, M.D., Plainfield; McGill Univ., 1886; Campbellton, N. B.

MURRAY, DANIEL, M.D., C.M., Meadowville; Dal. Univ., 1903; Tatamagouche, N. S.

MURRAY, DUNCAN A., M.D., C.M., Meadowville; McGill Univ., 1889; River John, N.S.

MURRAY, DUNCAN, M.D., C.M., Meadowville; Dal. Univ., 1896; Pictou, N. S.

MURRAY, GEORGE, M.D., Barney's River; Penn. Med. Col. 1850; deceased.
  Dr. George Murray was born in 1825. His grandfather, Walter Murray, came out from Sutherlandshire to Pictou in the ship, Hector, in 1773. He was educated at Pictou Academy, graduated from Penn. Medical College 1850. Practiced for four years in his native place, and in 1854 settled in New Glasgow. While a general practitioner he was noted for his skill

PHYSICIANS AND SURGEONS

in surgery, having performed successfully a large number of operations for cataracts, etc. In 1854 he married Mary, daughter of Robert P. Patterson. Died February 12, 1888. His son Howard Murray is Professor of Classics in Dalhousie University.

MURRAY, HARVEY V., M.D., Scotsburn; New York Univ.; Honolulu, Hawaii.

MURRAY, JAMES A., M.D., C.M., Pictou; Dal. Univ., 1905; Sydney, C. B.

MURRAY, JOSEPH HOWE, M.D., Barney's River; deceased.
He was educated at Dalhousie College and graduated at University of New York. Died in Boston, 1893, aged 43 years.

MACDONALD, JOHN J., B.A., M.D., Pine Tree; Dal. Univ., 1910; New Glasgow, N. S.

MACDONALD, MICHAEL R., M.D., Lismore; Georget. Univ., 1895; Lourdes, N. S.

MACDONALD, WILLIAM FORBES, M.D., C.M., Westville; McGill Univ., 1900; Vancouver, B. C.

MACDONALD, ROBERT J., B.A., M.D., Hopewell; Univ. N. Y., 1894; Wilkie, Sask.

MACDONALD, RONALD ST. JOHN, M.D., C.M., Bailey's Brook; McGill Univ., 1903; Montreal.
Lecturer on hygiene at McGill University, Montreal.

MACDONALD, PETER, M.D., C.M., L.C.P., Pictou; Hamilton, Ont.
Parents from Inverness, Scot., settled in Pictou Co., 1830, and moved to Huron Co., Ont., 1846; born in Pictou 1835; educated in Trinity Univ., Toronto, graduating 1872; married Miss Margaret Ross in 1865; succssfully practiced his profession at Wigham, Ont. Entered politics 1887; appointed Postmaster London, Ont., 1909. His daughter, Annie C., is National Sec'y for Y. W. C. A., Japan. A man of broad views and high personal character.

MCDONALD, CLIFFORD, M.D., Pictou; Cerra Del Pasco, South America.

McDonald, Daniel R., M.D., C.M., Saltsprings; Dal. Univ., 1905; Athabasca Landing, Alta.

McDonald, Henry K., M.D., C.M., Lyon's Brook; McGill Univ., 1896; Halifax, N. S.

McDonald, John C., M.D., C.M., Pictou; Dal. Univ., 1895; Edmonton, Alta.

McDougall, John G., M.D., C.M., Blue Mountain; McGill Univ., 1897; Amherst, N. S.

McGillivray, Alexander D., M.C., Springville; deceased.
> Graduating in medicine he took up his residence in Sydney, C. B., where for 40 years, he was one of its best known and most progressive citizens. He was one of the first elders elected by the Falmouth Street congregation. He died in 1907 in the 66th year of his age.

McGillivray, Donald, M.D., McLennan's Brook; deceased.
> Son of Rev. Dr. McGillivray, born 1842, educated Edinburgh Univ., Began practice in New Glasgow in 1864. Died at Thorburn, May 1, 1890.

McGregor, Andrew, M.D., McLennan's Brook; deceased.
> Dr. McGregor died in 1889, aged 31 years. Son Dan McGregor, McLellan's Brook, practiced medicine in Providence, R. I., for a few years.

McIntosh, Cyrus R., B.Sc., M.D., Sunny Brae; Manitoba, Med. Col., 1908; Lauder, Man.

McIntosh, Daniel, M.D., Springville; Harvard Univ., 1871, L.R.C.P., Edinburgh, 1873; Pugwash, N. S.

McIntosh, Daniel, M.D., Hopewell; Harvard Univ.; Died in Seattle in 1888.

McIntosh, John, M.D., Springville; Jefferson Med. Col. Phila., 1866.
> He died at Whycocomagh, C. B., November, 1882, in the 66th year of his age, where he practiced for many years. For 10 years he was an elder in the Presbyterian church. He carried much of the spirit of his Master into his visits among the sick and the poor.

PHYSICIANS AND SURGEONS

McIntosh, James W., M.D., C.M., Sunny Brae; Jefferson Med., Col., Phila.; died in 1907.
Dr. McIntosh was a demonstrator in surgery at the college when he died. He was in his thirty-seventh year.

MacKay, Hector H., M.D., C.M., Plainfield; McGill Univ., 1890; New Glasgow.

MacKay, J. Melville, M.D., River John; McGill Univ., 1886; died in Spring Hill, N. S.
Dr. MacKay was the son of Rev. H. B. MacKay, River John, and achieved success as a medical practitioner. He died in 1897 at the early age of 36 years.

MacKay-McKenzie Katherine Joanna, Plainfield; Dal. Univ., 1895; Coquitlam, B. C.

MacKay, William A., M.D., New Glasgow; Bellevue Hosp. Med. Col., 1905; Thorburn, N. S.

McKay, Alexander, M.D., West River; deceased.

McKay, Alexander P., M.D., Barney's River; Jefferson Med. Col., Phila., 1881; Catalina, Nfd.

McKay, Daniel A., M.D., C.M., Welsford; Dal. Univ., 1908; Hamiota, Man.

McKay, Daniel McG., M.D., Lorne; Jefferson Med. Col., 1896; Vancouver. B.C.

McKay, George F., Pictou; N. Y. Med. Univ., 1894; North Sydney, C. B.

McKay-Buchanan, Mary B., B.A., M.D., Riverton; Ladies' Med. Col., Toronto; Amkhut, Central India.

McKay, William, M.D., C.M., Scotsburn; Dal. Univ., 1903; Vonda, Sask.

MacKenzie, David H., Scotsburn; Univ., N.Y., 1889; Millbrook, N. Y.

MacKenzie, Luther B., M. D., West River; Bellevue Med. Hosp. Col., 1904; New York City.

MacKenzie, Kenneth A., M.D., C.M., Cariboo; Dal. Univ., 1903; Halifax, N. S.

MacKenzie, Thomas H., M.D., Churchville; Harvard Univ., 1871; Trenton, N. J.

MacKenzie, William P., M.D., Churchville; Univ., Mich., 1870; Chester, Ill.

MacKenzie, John J., M.D., C.M., Pictou; Dal. Univ., 1902; Pictou.

MacKenzie, Jemima, M.D., C.M., Cariboo; Dal. Univ., 1904; Cawnpore, India.

MacKenzie-Smith, Mary, M.D., C.M., Cariboo; Dal. Univ., 1905; Verschoyle, Ont.

McKenzie, George I., M.D., Durham.
> Graduated from Jefferson Medical College 1866, practiced in Maitland, N. S., from 1866-1871, removed to Pictou in 1871 where he remained until his death in 1905. He was prominent in church and state, as well as skillful in his profession. His son J. J. McKenzie takes his practice. A daughter is teacher in Trinidad mission schools.

McKenzie, J. W., M.D., River John; Med. Col., Ind., 1900; Indianapolis, Ind.

MacKinnon, Albert H., M.D., C.M., Pictou Landing; Dal., Univ., 1913; Upper Musquodoboit, N. S.

McKinnon, John, M.D., Bailey's Brook; deceased.

Maclean, Duncan, M.D., Springville; Harvard University, 1860.
> He practiced medicine in Shubenacadie, N. S., for nearly forty years. He was a devoted and self-sacrificing physician and well-known as a public spirited citizen. He married Margaret, daughter of Richard McHeffey. The eldest son, Dr. Edwin D. Maclean is located at Truro, N. S. Brother of Rev. James Maclean, D.D.

McLean, David, M.D., Green Hill; deceased.

Maclean, Emmeline, M.D., Green Hill; New York City.

McLean, John, M.D., Scotsburn; Spokane, Wash.

McLean, John J., M.D., Saltsprings; Halifax Med Col., 1860; Jersey City, N. J.

PHYSICIANS AND SURGEONS

MACLELLAN, EDWARD K., M.D., C.M., Pictou; Dal. Univ., 1909; Halifax.
: Proprietor, Halifax Hospital for Women. Son W. E. Maclellan, Post Office Inspector, Halifax.

MACLELLAN, ROBERT G., M.D., C.M., Pictou; Dal. Univ., 1909; Lunenburg, N. S.
: Son Principal Maclellan, Pictou.

McLEOD, DAVID, M.D., Scotsburn.
: Practiced medicine in Chicago and died there.

McLEOD, WILLIAM A., M.D., C.M., Lansdowne; Dal. Univ., 1907; Hopewell, N. S.

McMILLAN, FINLAY, M.D., C.M., Churchville; Dal. Univ. 1872; Sheet Harbor, N. S.

McMILLAN, PETER H., M.D., Churchville; deceased.
: Practiced at Ava, Ill.

NICHOL, ANGUS, M.D., Pictou; Hamburg, Ont.

NORRIE, WILLIAM, M.D., Lime Rock.
: Died at River John, aged 60. The deceased was well and favourably known. Skill in his profession, his sympathy and benevolence endeared him to many.

OLDING-HEBB, CLARA MARY, M.D., C.M., Pine Tree; Dal. Univ., 1896; St. John, N. B.

OLIVER, C. W., Westville.
: Student McGill Univ.; died in 1904.

PARK, JOHN E., M.D., Thorburn; McGill Univ., 1910; New Glasgow, N. S.

PATTON, JOHN W. T., M.D., C.M., Barney's River; McGill Univ., 1900; Truro, N. S.

PATERSON, EDWARD MORTIMER, M.D., Barney's River; Harvard Univ., 1871; Oakland, Cal.
: Dr. Paterson was a professor of physiology in the Medical College at San Francisco. His son, Dr. Frank H., is practicing in San Francisco.

PERRIN, ALBERT M., M.D., River John; Univ. N. Y., 1873; Yarmouth, N. S.

PRIMROSE, ALEXANDER, M.D., M.B., C.M., Pictou; Univ. Edinburgh, Scotland; 1886; Toronto.
Son of late Howard Primrose, Pictou, and Oliva, daughter of late Hon. Alexander Campbell, Tatamagouche, N. S., studied for his profession in Edinburgh University and Middlesex Hospital, London. Appointed professor of Anatomy, Toronto Medical College, 1895, resigned in 1907, now devotes himself exclusively to surgery. Author, "The Anatomy of the Orang-Outang", "The American Practice of Surgery".

PRIMROSE, ALEXANDER J., M.D., Pictou; Col. Phys. & Surg., N. Y., 1885; New York City.

PROUDFOOT, JAMES A., M.D., C.M., Saltsprings; Dal. Univ., 1905; Inverness, C. B.

ROBERTSON, THOMAS, M.D., Churchville; Wash. Univ., St. Louis, 1887; Churchville, Ill.

ROSS, ALBERT, M.D., Blue Mountain.
Graduated McGill Univ., 1914.

ROSS, HUGH, M.D., C.M., Telford; McGill Univ., 1894; Hazel Hill, N. S.

ROSS, JAMES D., M.D., Pictou; Harvard Univ., 1861; Edinburgh Univ., 1865.
Only son of late Principal Ross, was in active medical practice forty-seven years. Died March 31, 1911, aged 71 years.

ROY, JOHN J., M.D., C.M., Westville; McGill Univ., 1897; Sydney, C. B.

RUDOLPH, ROBERT DAWSON, M.D., F.R.G.S., Pictou; Edinburgh and London Univ.; Toronto.
Son William N., and Catherine (Dawson) Rudolf, born in Pictou, 1865, practiced 5 years in Bengal, India, associate professor of Medicine, Toronto, Univ. Author numerous scientific articles.

SCOTT, WILLIAM J., M.D., New Glasgow; McGill Univ.; Montreal.
Dr. Scott for five years was a medical missionary to China. Son of Rev. E. Scott D.D., Montreal.

PHYSICIANS AND SURGEONS

SMITH, JOHN P., M.D., Merigomish; Harvard Univ., 1869; deceased.
> Dr. Smith was born in 1838, practiced for twenty years at Lower Barney's River and for seven years in New Glasgow. He then removed to Green's Pond, Nfd., where he remained another seven years. He died at Tilt-Cove Nfd., Sept. 2, 1904, aged 66 years.

SMITH, CECIL V., M.D., Lower Barney's River; Balt. Med. Col., 1906; Twillingate, Nfd.

SMITH, LEONARD H., M.D., Lower Barney's River; Balt. Med. Col.; deceased.
> Dr. Smith died at Hearts Content, Nfd., 1899, where he practiced for three years.

SMITH, V. OWEN, M.D., Lower Barney's River; Balt. Med. Col., 1895; Fogo, Nfd.
> Drs. Leonard H., Cecil V., and Owen V. Smith were sons of late Dr. John P. Smith.

SMITH, HENRY THOMAS, M.D., Merigomish; McGill Univ., 1891; North Sydney, C. B.

SMITH, JAMES J., M.D., Barney's River; Balt. Univ., 1897; Norris Arm, Nfd.

SMITH, SANDY SIMON, M.D., Merigomish; Balt. Med. Col., 1890; Brookville, Nfd.

STRAMBERG, CHARLES W., M.D., C.M., River John; Dal. Univ., 1910; Trenton, N. S.

SUTHERLAND, GEORGE R., M.D., C.M., Hudson; McGill Univ., 1897; Leduc, Alta.

SUTHERLAND, JAMES A., M.D., C.M., River John; McGill Univ., 1896; Vancouver, B. C.

SUTHERLAND, MURDO, M.D., Saltsprings; Harvard Univ., 1871; Westville, N. S.

SUTHERLAND, ROBERT H., M.D., C.M., River John; McGill Univ., 1907; Spring Hill, N. S.

SUTHERLAND, NEIL, M.D., Saltsprings, Harvard Univ., 1868; Strathcona, Alta.

SUTHERLAND, RODERICK, M.D., River John; deceased.

THOMSON, CHARLES A., M.D., Durham; Univ. Berlin and Chicago, 1914; Chicage, Ill.
Son late Rev. Jas. Thomson, Durham.

THOMPSON, GEORGE H., M.D., C.M., New Glasgow; McGill Univ., 1899; North Adams, Mass.

WILLIAMSON, DANIEL W., M.D., C.M., West Br. River John; Dal. Univ., 1896; Yarmouth, N. S.

YOUNG, A. MCGILLIVRAY, M.D., Millsville; McGill Univ., 1906; Winnipeg, Man.

YOUNG, ROBERT M., M.D., C.M., Millsville; Queen's Univ., 1901; Millsville, N. S.

A few natives of the county entered upon practice of Dentistry. A partial list is: Wm. F. Burns, D.D.S., Sydney, C. B; Harry G. Dunbar, D.D.S., New Glasgow, N. S.; John C. Grant, D.D.S., Glace Bay, C. B.; M. K. Langille, D.D.S., Truro, N. S.; David P. Meikle, Henry Matheson, deceased.

Chapter V

THE BENCH AND THE BAR

THE first practicing lawyer in the County, as far as is known, was Nicholas Purdue Olding. For many years he was not only the father but the grandfather of the Bar. Born in England, 1751; educated at Oxford; his friends intended him for the Church, but on completing his course, he turned his attention to law. Having finished his law course, he came to America at the time of the American Revolution and took arms in defence of the mother country. At the close of the war, he came to Halifax with his wife and two children.*

In 1784 he was admitted to the Bar, and entered upon the practice of his profession with great promise. But he had received a wound in the head, which rendered him unfit for the excitement of the Bar and the social habits of the time. About 1797 he received a grant of land at Merigomish from Governor Wentworth. Soon afterwards he moved there and settled on Point Betty Island, where he lived the remainder of his life.

He did not regularly practice as a barrister, but did considerable law business, writing deeds and issuing legal documents. He generally attended the court at Pictou until near the close of his life. Though brought up in the Church of England, he joined the Presbyterian Church, under Dr. McGregor's ministry. His wife died in 1841 in the 87th year of her age, and he in 1845, in his ninety-fifth year. They had lived together for the long period of sixty-four years. Mr. Olding was well educated, had a high sense of honor, and maintained throughout his life a reputation for integrity and justice.

Among the early members of the legal profession in the county were: Robert Hatton, who came from Ireland in

+ Mary Collard of Morrisania N.y.

* Harriet Spry - Heaton Olding Copeland and

1813; Thomas Dickson, who was a Colchester man; Henry Blackadar of Halifax, who represented the district in the legislature for nearly a dozen years; Martin I. Wilkins, born at Windsor, practiced law in Pictou, and afterwards became Prothonotary of Supreme Court in Halifax, which office he held up to time of his death. He was a Barrister of marked ability, but was rather eccentric in his manner. Daniel Dickson, born at Truro, N. S., died December 27, 1878, was father of Wm. A. Dickson of Pictou. A. C. McDonald the second son of George McDonald was born at the West River in 1821. Having been admitted to the Bar, he entered into partnership with Daniel Dickson for the practice of law. In 1853 he married Sarah Brown DeWolfe of Pugwash. He died in 1869, in the forty-eighth year of his age. He was a man of good judgment; and fair dealing characterized his legal career.

John MacKinlay, son of Rev. John MacKinlay at one time pastor of Prince St. Church, practiced law in Pictou town for many years and died there December 1888. James Fogo, was born in Glasgow, came to Pictou when a lad, was educated at Pictou Academy, studied law in the office of Jotham Blanchard, was admitted to the bar in 1837, became Judge of Probate 1850. He died in 1897. Edward Roach was a native of Cumberland County and practiced in New Glasgow. David Matheson was born at West River and died September 1886. For the last twenty-five years of his life he was Prothonotary and Clerk to County Court at Pictou.

One of the best known of the earlier members of the bar, was Jotham Blanchard. He was, by birth, a New Englander, but by education and residence a Pictonian. Inasmuch as his whole public life was spent in Pictou, the County can fairly claim him as one of her sons. Mr. Blanchard was born at Peterboro, N. H., in 1800. He was the eldest son of Jonathan Blanchard. When he was fifteen months old, his parents removed with him to Truro. A few years later the family removed to West River, Pictou, where his father bought George McConnell's farm and built what was known as the Ten Mile House.

Afterwards they removed to Pictou Town, where Jotham studied at Pictou Academy, being one of the first class of students in that institution. He studied law in the office of Thomas Dickson, and was admitted to the Bar in 1821. He soon became one of the most eminent practitioners in Eastern Nova Scotia. His time and energies were largely devoted to fearless advocacy of popular rights and to support of Pictou Academy and higher education.

Mr. Blanchard was an able lawyer, a keen debater, a forceful writer; and he used his powers unstintedly for the best interests of the country. He ended his brilliant career in 1840—in the fortieth year of his age and it is not to the credit of his fellow countrymen, that his grave lies unmarked in the Old Cemetery in Pictou.

Hon. Hiram Blanchard was born in Pictou, in 1820, educated at Pictou Academy, and called to the bar of Nova Scotia in 1843, when only twenty-three years of age. He practiced law for some years in Halifax. He represented the County of Inverness in the Legislature for several years, and was for a short time Premier of the Province. He died in 1874.

Sir Charles Townsend, Chief Justice of Nova Scotia says: "Hiram Blanchard was at one time regarded as one of the best and most successful lawyers in the Province. While he could not be called a well-read and diligent student of the law, yet he possessed in an eminent degree, the faculty of quickly absorbing all the facts, and the law bearing thereon in the case in hand." He was a brother of Jotham Blanchard.

A well-known name of later years, was that of Hon. James McDonald, who was born at Bridgeville, East River,

July 1, 1828. He was familiarly known and honored by his generation in Pictou County as "Jim" McDonald. His family was amongthe first Scottish Highlanders who came to Nova Scotia and settled on the East River. His grandfather, James Macdonald, known as "The Deacon," was one of the founders of the Anti-Burgher Church, and, like all the family was in politics a strong Radical. His father settled in New Glasgow where his son was educated. Some of the older people still remember him as the bright, active lad, who without any advantages, got himself an education and fought his way up to the high position of Chief Justice of the Supreme Court of Nova Scotia. He studied law in the office of the well-known Hon. Martin I. Wilkins and was admitted to the Bar when only twenty-three years of age.

He practiced law first in Pictou for twelve years, and in 1863 removed to Halifax where he was conspicuous among the leaders of the Bar. In 1878 he was made Minister of Justice in the Sir John Macdonald's Government. He was appointed Chief Justice of Nova Scotia in 1881; retiring on a pension in 1904, he was presented with a handsome piece of silver by the bar of Nova Scotia as a testimonial. He declined the honor of Knighthood, and passed the closing days of his life at "Blink Bonnie" on the Northwest Arm, where he died October 3, 1912, in the 85th year of his age. Almost his entire life was spent in his native province.

He was married, in 1856, to Jane Mortimer of Pictou, by whom he had a large family. Two of his sons are in the legal profession; Wallace McDonald at Edmonton, Alta., and James A. McDonald at Halifax. One of his daughters is married to Sir Hibbert Tupper, Victoria, B. C., and another to Mr. Stuart Tupper, Winnipeg, Man., both sons of Sir Charles Tupper, a third is married to the Rev. L. H. Jordan, D.D., Oxford, England. In that great historic debate of giants in what is known as the Pacific Railway Scandal, in 1873, the palm was unanimously awarded to

THE BENCH AND THE BAR

1 Hon. John D. McLeod
2 Hon. George G. Patterson
3 Hon. Simon H. Holmes
4 Hon. James McDonald
7 Jotham Blanchard
5 Hon. James G. Forbes
6 Hon. Angus McGillivray

THE BENCH AND THE BAR

Hon. James McDonald, for his aggressive debating power and skill in defence. At that time Sir John A. Macdonald said of him, "As true as steel; and is, I think, the ablest man in the House of Commons."

On the first day of October, 1845, there was born at East River another lad, who afterwards became one of Pictou's most popular sons—Duncan C. Fraser. He too, was without material advantages; but he was of good Scottish ancestry. By push and perseverance he worked his way up until he attained the Governorship of the Province.

He received his education in the common schools, and later at the Normal School, Truro. After graduating with a B.A. degree from Dalhousie College, he taught school for some time before being called to the bar in 1873. He had a strong instinct for political life, and was a popular debater. Local politics paved the way for his career at Ottawa, where he represented the County of Guysboro for many years. He occupied a seat on the Bench of the Supreme Court of Nova Scotia for a few years, but gave it up to take the Lieutenant Governorship of Nova Scotia. His appointment was received with acclamation, and he was very popular with the people.

Governor Fraser had a notable career in Parliament, at the Bar, and on the Bench. His influence was widely felt throughout the country. He was one of the best stump speakers of his day, a rare story-teller, and a genial companion. Because of his ready wit and powers of oratory he stood out prominently in the public life of his time.

He received the degree of LL.D., from Dalhousie College, and D.C.L., from St. Francis Xavier and King's Colleges. He died in 1910. In 1878 he married Bessie G. Graham of New Glasgow. One of his sons, Alister Fraser, is practicing law at Moose Jaw, Sask.

Hon. James G. Forbes, has for nineteen years been County Court Judge of St. John, N. B., and a pillar of the

Presbyterian Church of that city. For many years he has been connected with the Canadian Bible Society and the Lord's Day Alliance and also with the British and Foreign Society of London, of which he is one of the Vice Presidents.

He is a brother of the Revs. John F. and Adam G. Forbes and a native of the County, born in 1838. He took a course in law at Harvard University, and was admitted to the bar in 1865. He was long a successful practitioner in St. John where he has resided for over half a century.

Hon. Angus McGillivray was admitted to the bar in 1874, practiced in Antigonish, and was retained in many important cases, civil and criminal. He was appointed Judge of the County Court in 1902 and was Speaker of the House of Assembly in 1883. He resides at Antigonish, N. S.

East River has the distinction of having given to Canada, three political leaders, Hon. James McDonald, Hon. D. C. Fraser, and Hon. Simon H. Holmes. Mr. Holmes was born at Springville, in 1831, a son of Hon. John Holmes, Senator. He was admitted to the bar, and practiced successfully in Pictou for many years, devoting part of his time to journalism. For four years he was Premier of the Province. He resides at Halifax where he has been Prothonotary of the Supreme Court for thirty-two years.

John D. McLeod is at present, Judge of Probate for the County of Pictou, a position he has held for a number of years. He was born at West River, being descended from an old Highland family, was educated at Pictou Academy, studied law, and was admitted as a barrister in 1866.

Charles D. Macdonald, B.A., son of A. C. Macdonald, was born in Pictou in 1854. He entered Dalhousie College in 1869 when only 15 years of age. At 21 he was admitted to the bar. He practiced in his native place until 1890, when he removed to Halifax. In 1897 he located in Edmonton, Alta., where he died some years later. He was a brilliant linguist. For several years he was editor of the Pictou News.

Hon. George Geddie Patterson was born at Green Hill, and is a son of the late Rev. George Patterson, D.D. He is a graduate of Dalhousie University and Law School, and practiced in New Glasgow, where he now resides. He was appointed Judge of the County Court in 1907.

Edward Mortimer Macdonald, was born in 1865. Educated at Pictou Academy and Dalhousie University, he was admitted to the bar in 1887. He has successfully practiced his profession at Pictou, where he is head of the firm of Macdonald, Ives and Chipman. He has represented the County of Pictou in Parliament since 1897. Mr. Macdonald has always taken an active part in political matters and is today one of the most influential leaders and supporters of the Liberal Party.

The leader of the Conservative party in the Local House, Halifax, is Charles E. Tanner, also a lawyer and a native of Pictou town, born there in 1857. In 1888 he was appointed Recorder and Stipendiary Magistrate for the Town and still holds that office.

The list below gives 63 names who entered the legal profession from the County. The place of birth and present location is given.

BELL, ISAAC, New Glasgow; Winnipeg, Man.
    Son of late Hon. A. C. Bell.

BLANCHARD, HIRAM, Hon., Pictou; Died 1874.
    Premier for the Province.

BROWN, ROBERT, Saltsprings; California.

BROWNRIGG, WM. H., Pictou; Deceased.

CAMERON, JOHN MCKINLAY, Scotch Hill; Calgary, Alta.

DICKSON, WM. A., K.C., Pictou; Pictou, N. S.

DOUGLAS, JOHN C., B.A., LL.B., Stellarton; Glace Bay, C. B.
    Member of the Legislative Assembly.

DOULL, JOHN, LL.B., New Glasgow; New Glasgow, N. S.

ELLIOTT, GEO. H., Pictou; Deceased.
   Mr. Elliott was the son of the Rev. Charles Elliott, the first Episcopal minister in Pictou. Born in 1842, admitted to the bar in 1868, died in 1904. He practiced law in Pictou.

FITZPATRICK, H. K., B.A., LL.B., Scotsburn; New Glasgow, N. S.
   Brother of Rev. Jas. Fitzpatrick, New Annan, N. S.

FOGO, JAMES, HON., Pictou; Died 1897.
   Judge of Probate.

FORBES, JAMES G., HON., Blue Mountain; St. John, N. B.
   Judge of the County Court.

FRASER, ALISTER, B.A., LL.B., New Glasgow; Moose Jaw, Sask.

FRASER, DUNCAN C., HON. B.A., LL.D., Churchville; Died 1910.
   Lieutenant Governor of the Province.

FRASER, JAMES A., New Glasgow; Deceased.

FRASER, JAMES H., B.A. Harvard Univ., Alma; Toronto, Ont.

FRASER, THOMAS M., LL.B., Hopewell; Saskatoon, Sask.

GRAHAM, ROBERT H., B.A., K.C., New Glasgow; New Glasgow, N. S.

GRAHAM, RODERICK D., New Glasgow; Graduated, 1914.
   Brother of Robt. H. Graham.

GRAY, WM. S., B.A., LL.B., Hopewell; MacLeod, Alberta.

GUNN, ALEX. D., LL.B., East River, St. Mary's; Sydney, C. B.
   Mayor of Sydney.

HOLMES, SIMON H., HON., K.C., Springville; Halifax, N.S.
   Prothonotary of Supreme Court.

HUGGAN, M., IRA, Avondale; Boston, Mass.

IVES, WELSFORD B., LL.B., Pictou; Pictou, N. S.

LANE, CHARLES W., Pictou; Lunenburg, N. S.

LANGILLE, ROBERT M., M.A., LL.B., River John; Sydney, C. B.

MACDONALD, ALVIN F., B.A., LL.B., Hopewell; Halifax, N. S.
Editor, Morning Chronicle.

MACDONALD, CHAS. D., B.A., Pictou; Died in 1908.

MACDONALD, DONALD D., Bailey's Brook.
Grad. of Law School, Halifax, 1914.

MACDONALD, EDWARD M., K.C., M.P., Pictou; Pictou, N. S.

MACDONALD, JOHN W., B.A., Pictou.
Son E. M. Macdonald, M.P.

MACDONALD, WILLIAM C., B.A., Bailey's Brook; Halifax, N. S.
Wm. C., and D. D. Macdonald are sons of late D. D. Macdonald, Bailey's Brook.

McDONALD, A. C., West River; Died in 1869.

McDONALD, A. J., Lismore; Died at Mabou, C. B.

McDONALD, JAMES, HON., Bridgeville; Died in 1912.
Chief Justice of the Supreme Court of Nova Scotia.

McDONALD, WILLIAM, Pictou; Pictou, N. S.

McGILLIVRAY, ANGUS, HON., Bailey's Brook; Antigonish, N. S.
Judge of the County Court.

McGILLIVRAY, JOHN, McLennan's Brook; Died in 1901.
Born April 2, 1847. Educated at Dal. College. Began the practice of law in New Glasgow, 1877.

McINNES, HECTOR, K.C., Lyon's Brook; Halifax, N. S.
Lecturer on the Practice and Procedure of Law, Dalhousie University, Halifax. Firm McInnes, Mellish, Fulton & Kenny.

MACKAY, ADAMS A., K.C., River John, Halifax, N. S.

MACKAY, ALEX. T., B.A., Pictou.
Grad. Halifax Law school, 1913.

MacKay, Ira W., M.A., Ph.D., Scotsburn; Saskatoon, Sask.
: Prof. Political Economy, Univ. of Saskatchewan.

MacKay, Harry B., LL.B., Scotsburn; Westville, N. S.

McKay, Neil F., West River; Kaslo, B. C.

McKay, Roderick G., LL.B., East River, St. Mary's; New Glasgow, N. S.

McKinlay, John, Pictou; Died in 1888.

Mackenzie, Geo. A., Four Mile Brook; Deceased.
: Rev. Chas. E. Mackenzie, Galliopolis, Ohio, and A. Stanley Mackenzie, President of Dal., University, Halifax, are sons of late Geo. A. Mackenzie.

Maclellan, R. W., B.A., LL.B.
: Mr. Maclellan was a son of W. E. Maclellan, Post Office Inspector, Halifax. He was seriously injured in a game of football, from which he died November 10, 1910, at the age of 23. He was a young man of great promise, clever, manly, and to all appearances had a brilliant career before him.

Maclellan, W. E., LL.B., Durham; Halifax, N. S.
: Post Office Inspector for Nova Scotia.

McLeod, John D., K.C., West River; Pictou, N. S.
: Judge of Probate.

Maddin, Jas. W., LL.B., Westville; Sydney, C. B.

Martin, John J., B.A., LL.B., Stellarton; Cranbrook, B. C.

Matheson, David, West River; Died 1886.

Munro, Henry T., B.A., Pictou; Cambridge, Mass.
: Asst. Prof., International Law, Harvard University.

Patterson, Geo. G., Hon., M.A., LL.B., Green Hill; New Glasgow, N. S.
: Judge of the County Court and Lecturer on evidence at Dalhousie University, Halifax, N. S.

Power, John J., M.A., K.C., Pictou; Halifax, N. S.

Ross, John U., K.C., Pictou; Pictou, N. S.

THE BENCH AND THE BAR

SINCLAIR, DONALD C., B.A., LL.B., New Glasgow; New Glasgow, N. S.

STEWART, JAMES MCGREGOR, B.A., Pictou.
: Grad. Halifax Law school, 1914. He is a son of James McGregor Stewart, who took his degree of B.A., from Dalhousie in 1876; afterwards practiced law in Pictou. Dr. John Stewart, Halifax, and Rev. Thos. Stewart D.D., Presbyterian College, are brothers of the last named. Their father was Rev. Murdoch Stewart, Whycocomagh, C. B.

TANNER, CHAS. E., K.C., M.P.P., Pictou; Pictou, N. S.
: Leader of the opposition in the House of Assembly, Halifax, N. S.

TURNER, J. W. M., Merigomish; Died in California.

TWEEDIE, T. M., LL.B., Stellarton; Calgary, Alta.
: Harvard Law School, Member Legislative Assembly.

VAIR, JAMES D., B.A., Pictou.
: Grad. Halifax Law School, 1913.

PICTONIANS AT HOME AND ABROAD

PICTOU'S OLD ACADEMY

Perchance some scoffing passer-by may smile
  In wonder at thy frame, so quaint and crude,
  Considering not, through ignorance, the brood
That found thee wondrous kind and wise, the while
Outstretched, thy wings protected them from guile:
  Upbrought and nurtured them to war with rude
  Strong error, rooted in the multitude
And for the heraldings that reconcile.

Commerce and Culture felt thy fine foresight;
  Altar and Court-room, Science, Arts of Skill,
Drew from thy sons safe leaders, and the State
Enlisted many a stalwart potentate,
  Made fit in thee to sense the people's will
Yet strong to boldly dare and do the right.

Peter M. MacDonald

Chapter VI

THE STORY OF PICTOU ACADEMY

PICTOU Academy will be one hundred years old, March 26, 1916. It is one of the best known and probably, the most famous academy of learning in Canada. Over it was fought the battle of the nineteenth century against unconstitutional government and religious intolerance. It was largely over the rights and wrongs of the Academy, more than any other question, that the fight was waged and won for responsible government in Nova Scotia. It was a great educator in our provincial politics. Under it and through this great conflict our ablest statesmen were educated. The life of the Presbyterian Church hung upon it, for if it was to be perpetuated and extended, it must have a school to educate and train a native ministry. From the walls of the Academy has gone forth a constant stream of strong men and women into all parts of the world, who have graced almost every profession and walk in life. Its founders of rugged Presbyterian stock, esteemed education of next importance to the Bible, and quickly planted a school, on the lines of Edinburgh University, in their eyes, the ideal of what a college should be. It was to attract students from every clime and send them forth to every land.

The history of the Academy divides itself conveniently into five periods:—

The College Period, 1816 to 1831

The Grammar School Period, 1832 to 1844

The Union Academy Period, 1845 to 1864

The Special Academy Period, 1864 to 1884

The County Academy Period, 1885—

PICTONIANS AT HOME AND ABROAD

The College Period

The institution had its origin in the brain of its founder and first President, the Rev. Thomas McCulloch, D. D., —Nova Scotia's greatest pioneer educationist, and the father of higher education in the Atlantic Provinces.

Born in Scotland in 1766, educated at Glasgow University, where he took a course in Medicine, as well as in Arts, studied theology at Whitburn, ordained as minister in Ayrshire, offered his services as Missionary to the Colonies, arrived in Pictou, N. S., 1803, and inducted in charge of Prince St. Church June 6, 1804—these are the main facts in his life. But it is as the champion of liberal and religious education in Nova Scotia that his fame chiefly rests. In the old Academy he laid deep and strong, in a life of great courage and unremitting toil, the foundation of higher education in Nova Scotia. The country is still reaping the fruits of his intellectual activity and zealous labors.

Dr. McCulloch was a man of a rare type. He was possessed of fine natural ability, a strong personality, a mind finely disciplined and of extensive literary attainments as his writings show.

He wielded the pen with ease and felicity, and when needs be, with pungency. He was a born fighter. He lived in a stormy time, and to accomplish his purposes for church and school, he needed to be to some extent a man of war. But amid prejudice and opposition his fearless courage and self-sacrifice shone forth in the higher interests of the people and country. In 1805, two years after his arrival in Pictou, we find him projecting an institution to give promising young men a collegiate education. One day when musing sadly over the ignorance he found among the young, he said to himself, "Why not attempt to train the youth of the Province for better things, and perhaps for the Ministry." It was a difficult task, on account of

REV. THOS McCULLOCH, D. D.

THE STORY OF PICTOU ACADEMY

the condition of the country and small means at hand, and it required the faith and force of a Livingstone or a Lincoln to attempt it. Though unable to carry out the idea for a time, he never relinquished it, and in due time, it resulted in the establishment of Pictou Academy.

His idea was to establish a college for higher education open to all classes and creeds alike. For this purpose a society was formed in Pictou and subscriptions collected amounting to a thousand pounds—Dr. McCulloch Dr. McGregor and Mr. Ross each giving fifty pounds. He opened a school in a log building near his own house, but it was soon destroyed by the hand of an incendiary. Another was soon erected in its place.

In 1811—on the passing of the "Grammar School Act"—Dr. McCulloch received the grant allotted to the Pictou district amounting to a hundred pounds a year. This School attracted students from all over the Province —some coming as far as the West Indies. Dr. Patterson tells us that Messrs. McGregor and Ross tutored boys in Latin and Greek with the idea of matriculating in the contemplated College. Thus the leavening power of Dr. McCulloch's ambitious ideals were producing fruit, and preparing the people throughout the province for the carrying out of his early formed and favorite plans. The time seemed now favorable. Edward Mortimer represented the District of Pictou in the legislature, and Sherbrooke was Governor—a man more liberal-minded than Wentworth, who occupied the position in 1805. An Act of Incorporation was sought and obtained March 26, 1816.

In the autumn of 1817, the first class comprising 23 students met in a private house, with Dr. McCulloch as Principal. Rev. John McKinlay assisted in teaching classics and mathematics, the rest of the Academic work was done by the Principal. It was not until 1818 that the Academy building was ready to be occupied. The Trustees finding that the thousand pounds subscribed was not enough to build the Academy, petitioned Governor Dalhousie for a grant. This was at first refused, but afterwards he granted the sum of five hundred pounds.

Pictou Academy has had a very eventful and chequered career. It had to fight its way to recognition and aid. Early in its history it had to contend with opposition and prejudice; notably, the opposition of the "Council of Twelve," and the unfriendly rivalry of King's College, Windsor, founded in 1790. This college was receiving a grant of nearly $2,000 a year from the provincial treasury and $5,000 a year from the British Government. But its doors were barred to all but Episcopalians. Dissenters, as all other Protestants were called and who formed four-fifths of the population of the Province, were destitute of all means for an advanced education. Naturally, the trustees of the Academy applied to the Council for aid. They were refused, for the "Council of Twelve" appointed by the Imperial Government were composed entirely of adherents of the Church of England, with the Bishop as one of its most influential members. They considered money spent on the education of Dissenters as worse than wasted. They could not tolerate the Pictou idea of a non-sectarian College. The House of Assembly, elected by the people, and representing their wishes, was always in hearty sympathy with the Academy, while the Council were deadly opposed—hence the long and bitter struggle.

In 1819 an application was made to Lord Dalhousie to have Pictou Academy changed into a college, with power to confer degrees, and also asking for the establishment of a professorship of Divinity. These requests were both flatly refused. For the next four years the council granted about $800 a year on application by the trustees. In 1824, application was made for a permanent grant of $2,000 a year, which was passed by the assembly but rejected by the council. Thus year after year the struggle went on. Bill after Bill providing grants for the academy were passed

THE STORY OF PICTOU ACADEMY

by the House of Assembly but negatived by the council. In this matter the council vetoed the voice of the assembly no less than fifteen times.

This continued opposition of the council to the will of the people so roused the energy and righteous indignation of such men as Joseph Howe and Jotham Blanchard, who waged such a vigorous contest, that the agitation finally ended in the demolition of the council and in the establishment of Responsible Government in Nova Scotia. The academy greatly suffered from their rivalries. Unfortunately at this time a section of the Presbyterian Church joined forces with the opponents of the Academy. The trustees became discouraged for lack of funds to carry on the work. In 1830 it was on the brink of ruin.

Finally, in 1831 Jotham Blanchard was sent to England, as the agent of the trustees to lay the whole case before the British Government. His mission to England was successful. Virtually all the claims of the academy were sustained by the Colonial Office.

GRAMMAR SCHOOL PERIOD

In attempting to take advantage of this decision compromise was necessary. Those representing the "Established Church of Scotland" with the Universities and Theological Halls in Scotland were not interested in the higher work of a college which would under local conditions very materially aid the preparation of candidates for the ministry of the dissenting Presbyterians known as antiburghers, while the established Kirk expected to draw their ministers from Scotland or from among Pictonians educated in Scotland. These wanted nothing more than a grammar school; but if there were to be college studies they would have to be conducted in the same building—not in a separate one. The Trustees under the reform Act of 1832 represented the two parties; but the internal friction prevented the successful development of either the college or grammar school grades of the academy.

In 1838 Dr. McCulloch with $800 of grant, was at last transferred to Dalhousie College and made president, which position he continued to hold until his death in 1843. His remains rest in the old Pictou cemetery where his students erected a monument to his memory. From 1832-1842, the academy was reduced to the level of a Grammar school, with Michael McCulloch, Geo. A. Blanchard, Wm. McDonald and Mr. McNaughton as teachers. In 1842 the grant totally failed. The academy lingered on until August 1844 when its doors were closed. The building was in a state of dilapidation. The library was mouldering on the shelves, the scientific collections were sold abroad.

The Union Academy Period

This state of affairs, however, soon aroused the people. Public meetings were called by the two great parties of the county. The Act of 1845 carried in its preamble a record of the desire of the people interested in the Pictou Academy to co-operate—"as to unite the two parties existing in that county in the support thereof." It is at this time the motto "Concordia Salus" was probably adopted. It was certainly the first time an effective local effort was made to carry out the principle. This period is therefore well known as one of union in academic development; and united local support has since carried the academy on through subsequent changes with ever growing success. The old board of trustees resigned and a new union board was elected. The new board of trustees set to work energetically in repairing the building, organizing the departments, and securing teachers.

In 1846 the academy re-opened and next year the three departments were in good working order. Basil Bell was Principal and classical master, with Charles H. Hay and

PRESENT ACADEMY

PICTOU'S OLD ACADEMY

THE STORY OF PICTOU ACADEMY

Alexander McPhail in the other two departments. In December 1847 Mr. McPhail resigned and was succeeded by Wm. Jack, who continued in this department until 1865. At this time John William Dawson delivered a course of lectures on natural history. Mr. Hay suddenly died in 1847 and some time elapsed before his place was filled.

In 1850 William R. Mulholland was appointed mathematical teacher. At the same time W. G. T. Jarvis succeeded Mr. Bell, and three years later, he was succeeded by T. R. Mulholland. In 1855 W. R. Mulholland was transferred to the Normal School, Truro, and T. R. Mulholland resigned. In the same year, John Costley became classical master, and continued in charge until 1865, when a new era was inaugurated throughout the province in educational matters. In that year the Nova Scotia Free School system was enacted, and the academy was organized into a special academy.

The Special Academy Period

The Free School Act of 1865 provided grants of $600 each for county academies, to which students passing the entrance examination from any part of the county would be admitted free. Pictou Academy and about a half a dozen other leading institutions were classed as special academies. It was to function as a county academy; but on account of its superior equipment received a grant of $1000 instead of $600 per annum. Until the Act to encourage Academic education in 1885, the academy and public schools of the town of Pictou was governed by a board of trustees from the Board of the academy and the board of the public schools, thus making the academy the head of the Pictou public school system. This arrangement proved most satisfactory, and under this plan the academy made another forward step. Herbert A. Bayne was appointed first principal and the organizer of the new order of things, which he did most successfully. In the autumn of 1867 Mr. Bayne left to complete his course in Dalhousie College and Aubrey Lippincott, B. A., one of the first graduates of Dalhousie College, was appointed substitute principal for a year. He also, was very successful in winning the respect and affection of his students and carried forward the work most efficiently. He is now a successful eye specialist in Pittsburgh, Pa.

In the following year Mr. Bayne returned accompanied by J. J. MacKenzie. Mr. MacKenzie at first taught the preparatory department, but shortly afterwards the two departments were combined, Principal Bayne teaching classics and science and Mr. MacKenzie English and Mathematics. These gentlemen both resigned in 1873 to take a post graduate course in Germany where each won a Doctor's degree. Returning to Canada, Dr. Bayne took a position in the Military College, Kingston, and Dr. MacKenzie the professorship of Physics in Dalhousie College. Both were cut down by death in early manhood.

In 1873 A. H. MacKay (now Dr. MacKay, Superintendent of Education for Nova Scotia) became principal. With him was associated F. W. George, M. A., Principal MacKay teaching, Mathematics and Science and Mr. George, English and Classics. In October 1876, Mr. George resigned to enter upon Church work. In 1876, Robert Maclellan, the present principal, was appointed to the Classical and English department which position he held until 1883, when he resigned to take the position of Inspector of Schools for Pictou and South Colchester.

Under Principal MacKay's strong administration the Academy made rapid strides. It became celebrated throughout the province and far beyond its limits. Students flocked in from all quarters until there was not room enough to receive. Larger quarters became absolutely necessary, and the citizens of Pictou, with a public spirit worthy of their ancestors, raised about $20,000 for a new building. It was erected in 1880 on the site of the present building. Although it would be entirely inadequate for the present day, it was far in advance of any other high school building in the province. It contained four class rooms, Convocation hall, a small chemical laboratory capable of accommodating five or six students. At the same time a third instructor became necessary and Roderick MacKay, B. A., was appointed teacher of Mathematics. After two years Mr. MacKay resigned to enter the ministry and is now pastor of a congregation in Ontario. Mr. W. R. Fraser, B. A., (now Ph. D., Johns Hopkins) was appointed as his successor. Mr. Fraser taught until 1888 when he resigned to take a post graduate course in Johns Hopkins.

Meanwhile in 1883 Mr. Maclellan resigned as before stated, and was succeeded by Mr. Hector McInnes, now K. C., and head of one of the most influential law firms in Halifax. Mr. McInnes taught Mathematics while the Classical subjects were divided between Principal MacKay and Mr. Fraser.

The County Academy Period

In 1885 the "Act to Encourage Academic Education" consolidated the County Academy system of the Province and provided a scale of grants somewhat proportional to the equipment and educational work of each academy. The Pictou Academy was qualified for the highest scale of grant which was an advance upon the previous special Academic grant. In 1885 Mr. McInnes was succeeded by Mr. Humphrey Mellish, B. A., also at present a prominent member of the Halifax Bar. In the same year a fourth teacher became necessary and Mr. Isaac Gammell, B. A., was appointed as instructor in English and History. Three years later, in 1888, Mr. Mellish was succeeded by R. M. Langille, B. A.; and David Soloan, B. A., was appointed to the position vacated by Mr Gammell, who accepted a position in the Montreal High School which he still holds; and Mr. Fraser was succeeded by J. C. Shaw, B. A.

It may be here mentioned that a great boom was given to the Academy between the years 1880 and 1891 by the Munro Exhibitions and Bursaries offered for competition to students matriculating into the University of Dalhousie. Five Exhibitions of the value of $400 each and ten bursaries of $300 each were presented annually by George Munro, of New York, (an old Pictou Academy student by the way). Pictou Academy was always successful in winning the lion's share of these prizes.

In 1889 Principal MacKay resigned to take the principalship of Halifax Academy, which he held for two years and was then appointed Superintendent of Education for Nova Scotia. At the same time Mr. Langille and Mr. Shaw resigned; the former to enter upon practice of Law and the latter to take a teaching position in Vancouver, where he shortly afterwards died. Robert Maclellan was appointed principal and instructor in Ancient Classics and modern languages; Mr. V. S. Frazee, B. A., took commercial branches and mathematics and Mr. H. M. MacKay, B. A., mathematics and science.

In 1891 Mr. Frazee and Mr. Soloan resigned, the former to take a teaching position in Providence, and the latter to the Principalship of the Presbyterian College in St. John's, Nfd. Mr. Frazee was succeeded by A. O. Macrae, B. A., and Mr. Soloan by A. C. L. Oliver, B. A. H. M. MacKay resigned in 1892 to take a course in engineering in McGill College, in which he won very high standing, distancing all competitors. Mr. C. L. Moore succeeded Mr. MacKay in the mathematical and science department. In 1893 C. B. Robinson, B. A., succeeded Mr. Macrae, who resigned that year to take up the study of theology. He is at present principal of a college in Calgary.

GROUP OF EDUCATIONISTS

1 Robert Maclellan LL.D.
2 Henry M. MacKay, M. Sc.
3 Daniel A. Murray, Ph.D.
4 Chas. B. Robinson, M.A.
5 A. H MacKay, LL.D.
6 George M. Dawson, LL.D.
7 Howard Murray, LL.D.

THE STORY OF PICTOU ACADEMY

On October 26, 1895, the Academy building was set on fire by lightning, and all the walls destroyed. In addition to the destruction of the building, interesting records and the greater part of a valuable museum were lost. This apparent calamity resulted in good. The building had become inadequate to the advancing requirements of the work. The people of Pictou responded heroically to the call thus made on them and the present building, double the size of the former, was erected in the summer of 1896 and was ready for occupancy in the beginning of 1897. In the autumn of 1896, A. C. L. Oliver, one of the best-loved teachers the Academy has ever had, was cut off by typhoid fever in the flower of his age and usefulness. He was succeeded by H. P. Duchemin, B. A. In 1897 Mr. Robinson resigned to follow a post-graduate course in Science in Cambridge, England; and H. M. MacKay, with the degree of B. Sc., from McGill, returned to take his place and remained till Mr. Robinson's return in 1899. In the same year Mr. Moore resigned to take a post-graduate course in Science at Johns Hopkins, and was succeeded by J. T. McLeod, who taught for one year and was followed by H. F. Munro, B. A. In 1901 Mr. Duchemin resigned to engage in the practice of law in Sydney in partnership with Mr. C. L. Moore, who had meanwhile dropped science for law. Mr. Duchemin was succeeded by R. S. Boehner, B. A. In 1906, Dr. Robinson accepted an important position under the U. S. Government in connection with botanical work in the Philippines, and W. P. Fraser, B. A., was appointed to succeed him. In December 21, 1913, he was killed by the natives of the Philippine Islands, while on a botanical expedition.

In 1905 Mr. Fraser and Mr. Boehner both resigned, the former to complete his course in Cornell, the latter to take the position of chemical demonstrator in McGill. Angus McLeod, Esq., who had been for a number of years the efficient principal of Kentville Academy was appointed to the mathematical department and Mr. C. L. Moore, who had soon wearied of the quirks of the law, returned to his old love, the teaching of science. He remained, however, only a few years, tempted by a much higher salary to take the supervisorship of the Sydney Schools. He is now Prof. in Biology, University of Dalhousie, Halifax, and Dean of the Rural Science Faculty in the Provincial Normal College at Truro.

In 1907 Mr. McLeod accepted the principalship of the Canso High School, and was succeeded by R. H. McLeod, Esq., a graduate of Pictou Academy with an excellent record as a successful teacher, and Mr. W. P. Fraser, B. A., returned to fill the science department vacated by Mr. Moore. Mr. Fraser is now on the staff of the Macdonald College, Quebec. On account of ill health Mr. McLeod resigned in 1909, and as no regularly qualified successor could be obtained the department was conducted by three substitutes in succession, J. L. Tanch, Norman Robson and John G. McLean. The present staff of Pictou Academy includes Robert Maclellan, LL. D., foreign languages; John Crerar McDonald, sciences; Howard Hersey Mussells, B. A., Mathematics; Robert Ebenezer Inglis, B. A., English.

Looking back over the history of the academy we can see how great its influence upon the country has been. It has been an important factor in its religious and political development. Though crushed and oftimes defeated, yet out of the struggles have come a great inheritance. It is estimated at least over five or six thousand students have passed through its halls. More than three hundred of these have entered the Gospel ministry, men who have not only done valiant work in the homeland, but have distinguished themselves in Foreign fields. Its lawyers, doctors, politicians, merchants and mechanics, are to be found in every quarter of the globe.

THE STORY OF PICTOU ACADEMY

Confining ourselves to the students of the olden time, we find the academy giving the world among others, Sir T. D. Archibald, baron of the English court of Exchequer; Judge Ritchie, of the Supreme court of Canada; Sir A. G. Archibald, Governor of Nova Scotia; Judge Young of Charlottetown; Jotham Blanchard; Geo. R. Young; Sir J. W. Dawson, President of McGill University; Dr. Ross, Dalhousie; D. M. Gordon, D. D., of Queen's University; President Ross Hill, of the State University of Missouri; Dr. Robinson, Chief Superintendent of Education for British Columbia. These are only a few of the more prominent names of the past. There are hosts of men of later days, whose names stand high in business and professional life.

Not only in men but in measures is the Academy notable. From the crushed Pictou Academy sprang the non-sectarian Dalhousie College, now a large provincial University. The little class in theology first started by Dr. McCulloch was the germ of Pine Hill, the Halifax Presbyterian Theological College. The impetus given and the interest awakened in the cause of Education by the Academy, has made Pictou County ever since the banner spot of Nova Scotia educationally. The present Pictou Academy is still doing a noble work. When its centenary is celebrated, from every part of the country, its children will turn to it with warm hearts and sincere appreciation.

Chapter VII

PICTOU EDUCATIONISTS

PICTOU County might be called the Home of Educators. It has given eight college Presidents to Canada,—many more than any other single county in the Dominion has contributed. Although only a few of its educators have attained great eminence, a large number have made a commanding place for themselves in the educational, literary and scientific world. The county was predestined to become an educational centre, for, from its earliest days, its Scottish settlers, resolved that, whatever the superstructure might be, education and religion should form the corner stone and the foundation of their community.

It was Pictou's good fortune, at the beginning of its history, to have as leaders men of decided scholarship and marked ability, who were firmly convinced that education necessarily went hand in hand with morality and civilization. Others followed them so that there has never been a decade in its history in which a number of men have not stood out as leaders in the cause of education. Dr. McGregor, the first minister in Pictou County, was a man of much natural ability. He had, moreover, enjoyed the benefits of a thorough College training, and was an excellent scholar. From the beginning of his work he made the establishing of schools and the education of the people second only to the preaching of the Gospel. He was ably assisted by his colleague, Rev. Duncan Ross, who was also a university graduate. In 1803, a third minister arrived in the field; and it may safely be said of him that no man ever lived in Nova Scotia who has exercised a more potent influence on education. Thomas McCulloch was a student, a scholar, and a born teacher. From the day of his arrival he became a power in educational matters. He was the founder of Pictou Academy, and the influence of Pictou County on the intellectual life of Canada has been largely concentrated in Pictou Academy ever since.

The pioneers realized that education was a better heritage for their children than gold. Their well-organized public schools were proof of this; but it was particularly reflected in the sacrifices which made Pictou Academy possible. It afterwards became more or less articulated with the common school system, and the question in every household having sons and daughters was: "Which one shall we send to the Academy?" The home was back of it. No wonder that from such soil sprang such a crop of college Presidents, Professors and Teachers.

The first schoolmaster was James Davidson, a native of Edinburgh. He came to Pictou about 1772, and taught school at Lyon's Brook. He returned to Truro, in 1776, and spent the rest of his days there. The first teacher in Pictou town was Peter Grant, who came from Halifax in 1793; he opened a school and taught for six years. S. L. Newcomb took up the work in 1802. He married the daughter of Matthew Harris, and had a family of children, several of whose names became well-known in later years. George Glennie, a graduate of Aberdeen College, succeeded him. He was an excellent teacher and scholar, and left his impress upon the youth of that generation.

First upon the list of Pictou's eminent educators and College presidents, stands the name of Sir J. W. Dawson, LL. D., F. R. S. His life-work extended over a long period of years, and he is the most widely known of all Canadian educationists and scientists. John William Dawson was born at Pictou, on the 13th of October, 1820. While at school in Pictou he developed a love for natural science, inherited from his father, James Dawson; and made a large collection of fossils from the coal measures so well exposed

SIR WILLIAM DAWSON, LL. D.

in the County. When only sixteen years of age, and still attending the Pictou Academy, he read before the local Natural History Society his first paper—"On the Structure and History of the Earth." He graduated from the University of Edinburgh, at the age of twenty-two; and returned to Nova Scotia in company with Sir Charles Lyell who began his geological explorations in the Province in 1842. Mr. Dawson was then appointed to direct a geological survey of the coal fields.

In 1850 he became the first Superintendent of Education for Nova Scotia; and did the pioneer work which resulted in the founding of the Provincial Normal School in Truro, in 1854, and the passing of the Free School Act of 1864. In 1855, he was appointed to the Principalship of the McGill University, Montreal. McGill rapidly developed under his guidance. He gave course of lectures in chemistry, botany, zoology and geology. His "Acadian Geology" was published in 1855. But from 1842 up to that event, no less than thirty-two papers were published by him, including three Annual Education Reports, 1851-3, a geography and a text book on Agriculture. From this time his published works increased in number, until, up to 1901, his bibliography numbered 551 titles of papers, pamphlets and books. His earlier papers on geological subjects had reference chiefly to the coal formation of Nova Scotia; and to his discoveries of the earliest known reptiles of that age. He also had the opportunity of studying along the St. Lawrence, the earliest Geological deposits, and this, with the investigation of Indian remains before the advent of the white man in Canada, gave him a broad outlook on the question of primitive man in relation to geology. So he was enabled to express in his books, sound and well-founded views regarding primitive man and his first surroundings.

Dawson's influence great as it was in field of Education swept yet a broader horizon in the field of letters. As a Bible student and expositor, Sir William stood high. He ploughed deep in the books of Holy Writ; and subjected those writings to the same keen, critical analysis to which he referred various other problems in the scientific world. He brought out many hidden truths from the Word of God, which had been hitherto obscure. "Egypt and the Holy Land, their geology and natural resources." "Eden Lost and Won," "Archaia," "The Mosaic Cosmogony," "Modern Science in Bible Lands," "The Origin of the World, According to Revelation and Science," form part of a series of writings of an apologetic character, which in his day, Sir William Dawson deemed necessary to combat certain views that were thrust upon the more or less observant and thinking world, regarding the origin of man as well as of other species living upon this planet.

As a writer, who sought to present in popular form the results of geological science to a larger audience than greeted him on the college benches, he was eminently successful. Among the most conspicuous of his popular writings, in which the relations existing between science and revelation usually formed a portion of his theme, the following may be mentioned; "The Story of the Earth and Man," "Facts and Fancies in Modern Science," "Fossil Men and their Modern Representatives,""Modern Ideas of Evolution," "The Meeting Place of Geology and History." The many editions through which these various writings have passed, and their ready sale on both sides of the Atlantic, testify to their popularity. In the English-speaking world his name became a household word, and a letter of introduction from him was a passport throughout Europe.

The phenomenal expansion of McGill University, as well as the character of his own scientific work, made him the recipient of honor after honor. In 1854 he was made a Fellow of the Geological Society; in 1862, a Fellow of the Royal Society; in 1881 a C. M. G.; in 1882 the first

President of the Royal Society of Canada. In 1884 he received the honor of Knighthood from Queen Victoria. He was a "man of quiet geniality, gentle and courtly in manner, but decided in opinion and firm in action. The pre-eminent note of his character was sincerity and singleness of purpose." In 1847 he married Margaret, daughter of George Mercer of Edinburgh. He had five children, the eldest being late George M. Dawson, C. M. G., the second son, William B. Dawson, D. Sc., Ottawa, Can. Dr. Rankine Dawson, the youngest of the three sons, is now practicing medicine in London, England. The two daughters are Mrs. J. B. Harrington, wife of the Professor of Chemistry at McGill University, and Mrs. Pope T. Atkin of Birkenhead, England.

Sir Wm. Dawson was a Presbyterian of an advanced type when his "Archaia" was published, in 1860, describing the evolutionary origin of the world as in agreement with the account in Genesis. But his non-acceptance of the evolutionary development of man left him among conservative theologians at the time of his death. He died at Montreal, on the 18th of November, 1899, in the eightieth year of his age, full of honors as of days, with the most distinguished record as a scientist of any Canadian, past or present. In no part of Canada has the career of Sir Wm. Dawson been more closely followed than in the Provinces by the sea. Here he was born; here he was inspired with the spirit of scientific research. His earliest educational and scientific efforts were made here; here were laid the foundations of his subsequent great achievements. And, while he left Pictou for wider fields of labor, he never forgot his native place. His life will continue to be an inspiration to many, as the stream of years flows on.

The following characteristic incident is well worth recording here: Over sixty years ago, a college student was appointed to survey a tract of "crown land" in eastern Nova Scotia,—a barren region about fifty miles in length and thirty in width, which at that time had within its bounds just twenty-six persons. The whole district was strewn with granite boulders; had no roads, and was traversable only on foot or horse back. There was no likelihood that the young surveyors' measurements would ever be tested, or his lines run over again, for the soil was poor, the timber small and unmarketable. But that student handled his chain and compass as under the eye of omniscience.

Some forty years afterward, gold was discovered there; the "leads" were vertical, and fortunes depended upon the accuracy of the student's work. Experts were sent by the Government to re-survey the whole territory. They could not find a single flaw in his work. Peter Grant, a Halifax merchant, a stock-holder in one of the mining companies said, that after all their tracing and computing the Government's most accurate surveyor gave at last the full meed of praise to the college student; and, in every instance pronounced his lines exact. That young student was none other than he who was afterwards the distinguished Sir William Dawson.

Rev. George Munro Grant, D. D., C. M. G., was one of Pictou's worthiest sons. The name Grant is one of the most celebrated in the annals of Scottish achievement, as well as in Canada. It is not necessary to prove this by any such method as a member of the Grant Clan is said to have taken to prove the antiquity of his family. The ambitious Grant referred to had a Bible with small print, and in one of the earlier chapters in Genesis discovered an indistinctness in one of the letters of which he took advantage and read it: "There were Grant's (giants) on the earth in those days." The clan which has given a President to the United States, one Principal to Edinburgh University, and another to Queen's University has no occasion to resort to such means to establish the worth of its blood.

PICTOU EDUCATIONISTS

George M. Grant was born at Stellarton, December 22, 1835. He was educated at Pictou Academy, West River Seminary, and Glasgow University. He soon became a striking figure at the University, and that, too, when James Bryce and a host of other great men were his fellow students.

On his return to Canada in 1860, he was ordained and placed in charge of the mission at River John. His energy led his parishioners to build a church for themselves, which they named St. George's Church, after him. In 1863, he was called to the pastorate of St. Matthew's Church, Halifax. Here he gave fourteen years of faithful and brilliant service. But such an active mind was not to be held within the limits of mere congregational work. Grant was too great for that, and ever took his part in the leading issues of the day; and in those days great issues were at stake;—Free schools, Union of the Provinces, and Church Union among the Presbyterians were questions threshed out and settled during those fourteen years. Into these struggles Grant flung himself with all the strength of his energetic nature.

A three months' trip, from Halifax to Victoria, was taken with Sir Sanford Fleming in 1872. At that time Western Canada was little known. An account of his journey was published, under the title, "From Ocean to Ocean," which revealed the marvelous resources of the West and the great future in store for Canada. Sir W. Robertson Nicoll, in the *British Weekly*, February, 1911, says, "Dr. Grant was the first author who understood the tremendous possibilities of Canada, and brought them home to a great public. He was an able and far-sighted man, a Canadian through and through, and one of the greatest of Canada's sons. He is destined to hold a permanent place in her history."

In 1877, he was appointed principal of Queen's University, to the interests of which he devoted himself with untiring zeal for a quarter of a century. His admirable educational equipment, his strong, keen intellect, his far-reaching vision, his commanding presence and voice, his great tenacity of purpose, would have gained for him eminence in any community or calling. In the diversity of his gifts, Grant was a Julius Caesar. Every public question claimed his attention; and he rendered signal service, not only to the Church, but to the public life of Canada. In 1889, he was Moderator of the General Assembly. He died in 1902.

It was naturally to be expected that Dr. Grant's alert mind would seek expression through literary channels. His successful advocacy of provincial federation doubtless prompted the optimistic views on Imperial unity which he expressed in his "Advantages of Imperial Federation." His equally broad views on the subject of comparative religion, are mirrored in his work on "The Religions of the World in Relation to Christianity." Not to mention his share in that monumental work, "Picturesque Canada," his "From Ocean to Ocean," was epoch making in its influence. It, more than any other one thing, perhaps, opened the eyes of Canadians to the wealth of their national heritage; stirred in them the pulsations of a new and broader patriotism, and prepared the way for the recent development of Canada. His work is being worthily carried on by his son and biographer, W. L. Grant, Prof. of Colonial and Canadian History, in Queen's University, Canada.

Rev. James Ross, D. D., LL. D., was a well-known educationist and scholar, and rendered distinguished service to the cause of education in Nova Scotia.

The life-work of a successful Christian educationist is one which might well inspire the most ambitious, as being one of the noblest and most beneficent careers open to human choice. Dr. Ross was a Christian educationist in the highest sense. He had the joy of unlocking the

COLLEGE PRESIDENTS

1 Donald Macrae, D.D.
2 A. Stanley Mackenzie, Ph.D.
3 John Forrest, D.D.
4 George M. Grant, D.D.
7 Clarence Mackinnon, D.D
5 James Ross, D.D.
6 Daniel M. Gordon, D.D.

gateways of knowledge to hundreds of young men whose influence is still felt throughout the land. He will be remembered as one of the "Fathers" of the Presbyterian Church. He was son of the late Rev. Duncan Ross, one of the two pioneer ministers of Pictou. He was born at West River, in 1811. He was ordained in 1835, succeeding his father as minister of the West River Church. Dr. Ross married a daughter of the late William Matheson, Esq., of West River; and it was through Dr. Ross' zeal in the interest of higher education that Mr. Matheson was led to donate the sum of $35,000 to that cause in connection with the Presbyterian Church.

In 1848 he was called to take charge of the West River Seminary. In 1864 he was appointed Principal of Dalhousie College. Whatever he undertook, he performed with conscientious fidelity, sparing neither time nor strength. For forty years he served the Church in its educational sphere, in West River, Truro, and Halifax; and thus left a deep impress upon the educational life of his time. His last illness was brief. On Monday evening, March eighth, while engaged in secret prayer before retiring to rest, he was stricken with paralysis, and died at noon the following Monday, March 15, 1886. His was a splendid life, unselfish in all its aims and purposes. Dr. Ross was unsparing in his efforts to advance the interests of his fellow citizens and of humanity in general, exercising withal, a high degree of power and influence for the moral good and uplift of his native Province. In the language of Socrates, regarding a well-spent life, it may truly be said of his: "For noble is the prize, and the hope is great."

Rev. Daniel M. Gordon, D. D., LL. D., was born in Pictou, 1845. He entered Glasgow University when only fourteen; graduated, Master of Arts at eighteen, and Bachelor of Divinity at twenty-one. Returning to Canada, he entered the Presbyterian ministry, and was settled at Truro, Winnipeg, St. Andrew's Church, Ottawa, and

St. Andrew's Church, Halifax. From this last ministry he was appointed to the Chair of Systematic Theology in the Presbyterian College, Halifax. On the death of Principal Grant he was elevated to the Presidency of Queen's University where he has been eminently successful. He was Moderator of General Assembly in 1896. His son, the Rev. A. M. Gordon, B. D., is assistant to Rev. Dr. Herridge, Ottawa.

Rev. Donald Macrae, M. A., (Aberdeen) D.D., (Queen's) was born at Hopewell, 1834, where his father, Rev. John Macrae, was minister. He graduated in Arts and Theology from the University of Aberdeen, and was ordained by the Presbytery of Edinburgh, in 1856. Dr. Macrae was a notable figure in the work of the Church in Canada, and held an eminent place as a preacher, being a most energetic worker. As minister in charge of his father's former congregation at Hopewell, N. S., as pastor in St. John's, Newfoundland, and in St. John, N. B.; as leader in connection with home mission work in the Presbytery of St. John; and later, as Principal of Morrin College, Quebec, he did most excellent and effective work, never grudging time or strength in the service of the Church or in the interests of the cause of righteousness in the land. He was the sixth Moderator of the General Assembly, held in Montreal, in 1880. He died at the home of his son, Rev. A. O. MacRae, Ph. D., Calgary, Alta., November 24, 1909. Another son, Rev. D. N. MacRae, Ph. D., is minister in Mitchell, Ontario.

Rev. John Forrest, D. D., LL.D., was born in New Glasgow, 1842. He is a son of the late Alexander Forrest, M. D. He was educated at the Presbyterian College, Truro and Halifax, and was ordained and inducted into the ministerial charge of St. John's Church, Halifax, in 1866. He succeeded Principal Ross at Dalhousie College. The growth and prosperity of Dalhousie during his presidency is sufficient evidence of his wise administration.

PICTOU EDUCATIONISTS

Dr. Forrest, for many years, has been a leader in the courts of the Presbyterian Church. At the General Assembly of 1910, he was elected Moderator. He retired from the Principalship of Dalhousie in 1911, having well earned the right to a period of rest in the evening of his life.

A. Stanley Mackenzie, Ph. D., F. R. S. C., born at Pictou in 1865, was appointed to the presidency of Dalhousie University on the retirement of Dr. Forrest. He took his preparatory course at Pictou Academy; in 1885 he graduated with high honors from Dalhousie University. He received his Ph. D., degree from Johns Hopkins University, and later studied in Germany and England. After graduating he was appointed tutor of Mathematics, and in 1905 Prof. of Physics.

Rev. Clarence Mackinnon, M. A., D. D., was born at Hopewell, N. S., in 1868. He is a son of the late Rev. John Mackinnon, a minister of the village for many years. His mother was Margaret Tait of Edinburgh. He received his degree of M. A., from Edinburgh University in 1889; his degree of B. D., from the New College, Edinburgh, 1896. He has ministered to congregations in Middle Stewiacke, N. S.; Park St. Church, Halifax; St. Andrew's Church, Sydney, and Westminister Church, Winnipeg. Since 1909 he has been the esteemed Principal of the Presbyterian College, Halifax, and Prof. of Systematic Theology. He is a very popular and effective preacher and lecturer.

The story of Messrs. McKenzie, Bayne, McGregor and Purves, the first of Nova Scotian students to take a postgraduate course in Germany, is one of peculiar interest to all. They crossed the Atlantic together in 1874. John J. McKenzie, the first mentioned, was Professor of Physics in Dalhousie College, Halifax, when he died, in the thirty-second year of his age. To go back to his earlier years, he was born at Green Hill, Pictou County, in 1847. He took his arts course at Halifax, winning the master's degree in

1872. Two years later he went to Germany with his fellow-students; and, after a distinguished course in the University of Leipsic, received the honorable distinction, Doctor of Philosophy in 1877. On his return from Germany, he was appointed to the Chair of Physics in Dalhousie College, which he occupied less than two years, when he was stricken down in the prime of his young manhood.

In addition to the regular work of the College, he delivered a series of popular lectures on scientific subjects before the citizens of Halifax, and was an active promoter of the Technical Institute. His devotion to science was the immediate cause of his death, which took place, February 2, 1879. Dr. Bayne, who was his constant companion for nearly half his life, was with him the night he died. He was buried, amid the regrets of students and friends, at his old home, Green Hill. In his death Nova Scotia lost an accomplished student of Science and a splendid specimen of manhood.

Herbert A. Bayne, his life-long friend, was a son of Rev. James Bayne D. D., Pictou. He was born in 1846, and graduated from Dalhousie College in 1871. For several years he was principal of Pictou Academy. In 1874 he went to Germany to take a post-graduate course in Chemistry, first at Leipsic University. He took his degree at Heidelburg. Here he studied under the eminent chemist, Bunsen; and received his degree *cum multa laude*, in 1876. On his return to Nova Scotia, he was appointed Principal of the High School, Halifax. Resigning from this position, he was appointed Professor of Chemistry in the Royal Military College, Kingston, Ont., where he endeared himself to faculty and students by his many manly qualities. Ill-health compelled him to resign, and he died in Pictou, September 18, 1886, in the fortieth year of his age.

Archibald Purves never became a professor, but would not doubtless have done so had he lived, for he was highly skilled in many languages. When J. J. McKenzie and Herbert A. Bayne, decided to go to Germany to study, he thought it might be good for him to go also. McKenzie and Bayne were well grounded in German with the assistance of General Oscar Malmross, at that time American Consul in Pictou. He was a German by birth, and well educated. The three fellow students went to Leipsic first. Purves afterwards went to Edinburgh, and spent some time there. He feared he could not become a fluent enough speaker for the ministry, and decided to study languages. He continued his studies in Edinburgh during the winters, and in Germany in summer time. It was at the latter place that he had an attack of pleurisy. Before he was convalescent he gave up his room to a student who had engaged it for the new term, and went to another boarding house. He caught cold in moving, and "lung fever" as the Germans call it, set in. He went to Leipsic to consult a doctor whom he knew. He was ordered to Davos in the Alps, a resort for those with weak lungs. There he lingered during the winter, and died in March, 1878, while his brother, Mr. David H. Purves, was on his way to be with him at the end. His brother bought a lot in the cemetery, and buried him in Davos.

A noteworthy coincidence in this connection was J. Gordon McGregor's strong desire to accompany the three to Leipsic. When he first crossed the Atlantic, as a Gilchrist Scholar, he was hardly expected to survive the voyage. His heart action was so weak that he was compelled to rest for a year with friends in Edinburgh. He recovered, and afterwards had a distinguished and brilliant career; as a graduate student in Great Britain and in Germany; as Professor of Physics in Dalhousie, succeeding his fellow-student, Dr. McKenzie, and as successor to Professor Tait, in the chair of Natural Philosophy at Edinburgh.

Professor McGregor was born in Halifax, and was the son of a well-known Presbyterian clergyman, Rev. P. G.

McGregor, D. D. He took his arts course in Dalhousie, where he earned a first class in every subject of his course, and where he afterwards taught for twenty-two years, closing his career by giving twelve years of eminent service to the Edinburgh University. The end came to him with startling suddeness. On the morning of May 21, 1913, he arose, to all appearances in his ordinary health. He had his bath, and returned to his room to dress. There he was taken suddenly ill; called in his son, and died almost immediately afterwards. Thus ended the chequered career of this quartette of students who crossed the Atlantic together to pursue their studies abroad.

It is distressing to think of these hard-working and promising young men thus falling by the way prematurely,— McKenzie from inhaling gas during an experiment; Bayne from cancer of the stomach, Purves from rapid consumption and McGregor from heart failure. It is interesting to conjecture what they might have accomplished had their lives been spared, for they were all men of fine ability, ambition and manhood.

The following list, though far from complete, gives the names of some of those who have been leaders in the educational life of Canada, as well as, of those who now uphold the prestige of their native County.

BAYNE, HERBERT A., Heidelberg, (Ph. D., 1876), F.R.S.C.
    Professor of Chemistry, Royal Military College, Kingston, Can. Died 1886.

CAMERON, JAMES S., M.Sc., McGill University.
    A member of the staff of the Technical Institute, Montreal. His home was Stellarton.

CAMPBELL, DONALD F., M.A., Ph.D.
    Son of George and Ellen (Gunn) Cameron; born in 1867; Educated Dal. Univ., (B.A., 1890, and Harvard Univ., Ph.D., 1898), married Miss Lou R. Bates, Davidson, Conn., 1906; Instructor in mathematics, Lawrence Science School of Harvard Univ.,

FOUR STUDENTS

ARCHIBALD PURVES   J. GORDON MCGREGOR, PH. D.

J. J. MCKENZIE, PH. D.   H. A. BAYNE, PH. D.

1897-1901; Prof. of mathematics and head of the Mathematical Department in the Armour Institute of Technology, Chicago, Ill., since 1903; Author of a text-book on mathematics, extensively used in the Colleges.

CAMPBELL, WILLIAM R., A.M., Dal. Univ., 1887.
Principal Truro Academy, 1887-1907. Inspector of Schools for Colchester Co., since 1907. In 1908 he was appointed lecturer in English in the Agricultural College, Truro, N. S. The Campbell Bros. were born at East River, St. Mary's, Pictou Co.

CREIGHTON, JAMES E., Ph.D., LL.D.
Born West River, 1861; attended Pictou Academy two years; taught schools for three years, was graduated from Dalhousie College in 1887; pursued post graduate studies in Cornell University and in Germany; married Miss Katherine F. McLean, in 1892. He is now professor of Logic and Metaphysics in Cornell University; editor of The Philosophical Review, and American editor of the Kant-Studien. Published a monograph on the "Will and its Functions," and "An Introductory Logic," 3d edition 1910 (Macmillan and Co.). Contributor of many papers to philosophical journals; received the degree of A. B., at Dalhousie, in 1887, that of Ph.D., from Cornell in 1892, LL.D., from Queen's Univ., in 1903, and Dal. Univ., 1914. Brother of William O. Creighton, West River.

CREIGHTON, GRAHAM, B. A., Dal. Univ., 1904.
Born at West River; Inspector of Schools for Halifax Co.

CONNOLLY, CORNELIUS J., Ph.D., (Munich).
Professor of Biology, St. Francis Xavier's College, Antigonish.

CUMMING, MELVILLE, B.A., B.S.A.
Principal, Agricultural College, Truro. The college was formerly opened in 1905. Principal Cumming is a native of Pictou County, a graduate of Dal. Univ., and of the Agricultural College, Guelph, Ont. He is a son of Rev. Thos. Cumming, D.D.

DAWSON, A. S.
Chief Engineer of the Department of Natural Resources, Calgary, Alberta; a native of Pictou, grand nephew of Sir William Dawson.

DAWSON, GEORGE MERCER, C.M.G., LL.D., F.R.S.
Mr. Dawson was born in Pictou in 1849. He was the eldest son of Sir William Dawson, the well known Principal of McGill

Univ. He took a course in the Royal School of Mines, London, where he not only graduated with honors but took the Duke of Cornwall scholarship and the Edward Forbes prize. Returning to Canada, he began original researches in geology. In 1873 he was appointed geologist and botanist of the British North American Boundary Commission; and his report is one of the classics of Canadian geology. In 1875, he was appointed to the staff of the Canadian Geological Survey; and entered on a remarkable career of exploration of northwestern North America. In 1891 he became a fellow of the Royal Society of England. During the same year received the Bigsby medal for eminent researches in geology. In 1892 he was decorated with the order of Companion of St. Michael and St. George. In 1893, he was elected President of the Royal Society of Canada, and in 1895 Director of the Geological Survey.

It falls to few men to have so many high honors and grave responsibilities thrust on them in so short a life; the succession is probably without parallel in Canada's history; yet it is the common judgment that the honors were fully merited, the responsibilities borne in such manner as to add renown to the country and the Crown. Dr. Dawson's career was a credit to Canada, and an elequent testimony to the wisdom of the nation in recognizing and utilizing the talents of her sons. He died in 1901, in his 52d year, after an illness of but a few hours.

DAWSON, WILLIAM BELL, D.Sc., F.R.S.C.

The second son of Sir Wm. Dawson—was born in Pictou, 1854. Mr. Dawson is a graduate of McGill Univ., in Arts and Engineering. In 1875, he won the Degree of Bachelor of Applied Science, with certificate of special merit in Engineering, which is the highest distinction in that course of study. In November, 1875 he studied in Paris—the highest School of Engineering in France, and one of the first in Europe. The course of study extends over three years. He passed as the first of his class, in 1878. On returning to Canada, Mr. Dawson entered upon professional business in Montreal. In 1881 he undertook a survey of a part of the Gold Fields in Nova Scotia; was next in the employ of the Dominion Bridge Company, the most important of his designs being the Cantilever Bridge over the St. John River. For nine years he was assistant engineer on the Canada Pacific Railway. Since 1893 he has been Supt. of the Survey of Tides and Currents, Department of Marine, Canada. Both of Dr. Dawson's sons inherited much of the intellectual power and industry of their distinguished father.

PICTOU EDUCATIONISTS

FINLAYSON, JOHN N., M.Sc., McGill Univ.
: Was born at Merigomish. He was educated at Pictou Academy and the School of Applied Science, McGill Univ.; and took his degree in 1908. He was appointed Professor of Civil Engineering, Dal. Univ., Halifax, 1913.

FRASER, ALEXANDER D., M.A. (Dal.) Ph.D., (Johns Hopkins).
: Graduated from Dal. Univ., in 1910, with High Honors in classics, and took a post graduate course at Johns Hopkins and Harvard. Substituting in classics at Pictou and Halifax Academies. He is the son of the late Rev. J. W. Fraser of Scotsburn.

FRASER, JAMES W., M.Sc., McGill Univ., 1901.
: Was born Bridgeville, 1874; married Miss Annie L. McGillivray; instructor Electrical Engineering McGill Univ., 1899-1901; Assistant Chief Engineer Southern Power Co., Charlotte, N. C., since 1905; Contributor to the Electrical Reviews.

FRASER, WILLIAM.
: Studied in Dal. College. For forty years teacher in Scotsburn District. Among the clergymen taught by him were John McMillan, George Murray, Kenneth McKay, John Murray, James Murray and James Fitzpatrick. Other well known teachers were Alexander Grant, Roderick McLean, Alexander Ross and Norman Logan.

FRASER, WILLIAM A., Poet and Novelist.
: Born and educated in Pictou County; spent his youth in New York and Boston. When quite young he went to India where he remained seven years; had five years' experience in the Canadian Northwest; some of his tales are connected with these Eastern and Western Lands. He has written many short stories, these appearing in the leading American and English Magazines. The following is a list of his publications in book form:—"The Eye of a God," "Mooswa and Others of the Boundaries," "The Outcasts," "Brave Hearts," "Thirteen Men," "The Lone Furrow," (1907); wrote a national song entitled "Canada, God and Our Land." He is a master of the short story, and is sometimes called "The Canadian Kipling." He resides at Georgetown, Ont.

FRASER, WILLIAM P., M.A.
: Professor in Biology, McDonald College, St. Anne's, Que. Mr. Fraser was born at French River. He was a former member of the Pictou Academy Staff.

FRASER, WILLIAM R., Ph.D., (Johns Hopkins).
Formerly Lecturer in Classics, McGill Univ., was born at West River. He is now conducting a private school in Montreal. He was for many years a successful teacher of Classics in Pictou Academy.

HARRIS, GEORGE WILLIAM, Librarian, Cornell Univ.
Son of the late John F. Harris, and nephew of a former Sheriff of the County. He graduated from Cornell University in 1873; and has ever since that time been connected with the library of the University, becoming head librarian in 1890. He is a recognized authority on bibliographical matters, being a life member of the Bibliographical Society of London, and of the American Library Society. He has contributed many articles to library journals, and is editor of the Library Bulletin of Cornell University. He was born in Pictou town, in 1849, and received his preparatory education at Pictou Academy.

HEPBURN, WILLIAM MURRAY, M.A., Dal. Univ., (1895.)
Chief Librarian—Purdue Univ., La Fayette, Ind.

JOHNSON, ALLEN C., Ph.D., (Johns Hopkins).
Assistant Professor in Classics, Princeton, N. J. Some time tutor in classics (Dal).

JOHNSTONE, J. H. L., B.Sc., (Dal.).
Born at Pictou, 1891. Graduated from Dalhousie University in 1911 with High Honors in Mathematics and Physics. Appointed Instructor in Physics, Dal. Univ., 1912.

KENNEDY, WILLIAM T.
Principal of Halifax Academy. Died 1907. The Presbyterian Witness says of him,—"Mr. Kennedy was born at Sunny Brae, of good Highland Stock. He was the stamp of a man we should like to see at the head of our institutions of learning; genuinely Christian, rigorously correct in life and work, never flinching from the path of duty. As a teacher, his merits have been recognized all over the country."

LOGAN, JOHN D., M.A., (Dal., 1894), Ph.D., Harvard (1896).
Is a well known educationist and man-of-letters. He was born in the Town of Pictou; educated at the Dal. Univ., where he graduated with High Honors in philosophy in 1893. Subsequently he studied at Harvard Univ. For some years he was head of the Dept. of Philosophy in the Univ., of South Dakota;

PICTOU EDUCATIONISTS

from 1908-1910 he was literary and musical critic of the Toronto Sunday World. Since then he has been on the editorial staff of the Toronto News. He is author of a number of books and of articles on Philosophy, Literature and Art. Author: "Preludes, Sonnets and other Verses," "Songs of the Makers of Canada," with an introductory critical essay on Canadian poetry.

McBAIN, ALEXANDER ROSS, B.A., (Dal.) M.A., McGill Univ.

Professor in the Protestant High School, Montreal, Can.

McCOLL, RODERICK.

Is a son of the late Jeffrey McColl, of New Glasgow; born there, 1866. Graduated from the Royal Military College, Kingston, 1886; from 1904 to 1913 was Provincial Engineer for the Province, with headquarters at Halifax, N. S. His brother Archibald McColl is Secretary and Chief Accountant for the Nova Scotia Steel Works, New Glasgow.

McCULLOCH, MICHAEL, Educationist.

A son of Dr. McCulloch, came to Pictou with his father at about three years of age. He was one of the first class which passed through the Academy. In 1824 he was appointed his father's successor, teaching Classics and Mathematics. After the institution closed he taught a private school in Pictou and was afterwards Principal of the Yarmouth Academy. He died in his eighty-third year. Mr. McCulloch was a man of strong powers of mind and accurate scholarship.

McCULLOCH, THOMAS, Professor in Dalhousie University.

Was a son of Dr. McCulloch of the Academy, and was appointed to aid Prof. Ross in the Classical and Philosophical Departments in the West River and Truro Seminaries. When Dalhousie College was reorganized, in 1863, he was transferred from Truro to Halifax to form a part of the Dalhousie Faculty. Both sons of Dr. McCulloch spent their lives in the work of higher education, and were thus worthy sons of a worthy sire.

MACDONALD, ARTHUR C., C. E.

Is a member of the firm MacDonald and Gibbs, with offices at London, England and Chili, South America. The Chilian Northern Railway, which runs through the Chilian Desert, was built by him. It is 430 miles long, and cost $15,000,000. He also built the Bolivia Railway. This road is 823 ft., above the sea level and is said to be one of the highest points ever reached by a railway. Mr. MacDonald was born in the town of Pictou; is a younger brother of the late Charles D. MacDonald, Barrister, of Edmonton, and a cousin of E. M. Macdonald, M. P.

MacDonald, Alexander H., a veteran, San Francisco Educator.

Mr. MacDonald was for fifty-one years identified with the common schools of California, thirty-two of which he was Principal of the Lincoln Evening School, San Francisco. He was born at Sunny Brae, in 1830, and was a brother of Rev. F. R. MacDonald.

McDonald, Daniel.

Born at Barney's River; Educated at West River Seminary, appointed Inspector of Schools for Pictou County in 1869, retired in 1879. Died 1880, aged 71 years.

MacDonald, Donald F., M. Sc.

Son of John J. MacDonald, Merigomish. In 1905 he graduated from Washington Univ., Washington, D. C. He also took the degree of Mining Engineer and Master of Science from same university. He then did two years' work in the Graduate School of Geology in the Univ. of Chicago. From 1909 to 1910 he was in charge of the work in Geology at Tulane Univ., New Orleans. He is now on the U. S. Geological Survey, Washington, D. C.

McIntosh, Douglas, B.Sc.,(Dal.) D.Sc. Cornell, F.R.S.C.

Associate Prof. of Chemistry, McGill Univ., was born in New Glasgow. He is the author of several valuable papers on Chemical subjects, the results of long experimenting and original study, which have been published in the leading Chemical Journals of the day. He took his B. A. degree at Dalhousie, and also studied in Cornell and in Germany.

McIntosh, Henry Havelock.

Inspector of Schools for Lunenburg and Queens, is a native of Merigomish, and was educated at Pictou Academy and Dal. Univ.

MacKay, Alexander H., M.A., F.R.S.C., LL.D.

Supt. of Education of Nova Scotia, was born at Plainfield, a district which has contributed many able men to the intellectual life of Canada. He was educated at Pictou Academy, and Normal School, Truro; graduated from Dal. Univ., with distinction in Mathematics and Physics, 1873; B.Sc., with Honors

PICTOU EDUCATIONISTS

in Biology, in 1880, from the Univ. of Halifax. The Degree of LL.D., was conferred upon him by Dal. Univ., in 1892. He married Maud A., daughter of the late Dr. G. M. Johnstone, Pictou, 1882. He was Principal of Pictou Academy for sixteen years, (1873-1899); Halifax Academy (1889-1890); since then Supt. of Education for Nova Scotia. He organized the Summer School of Science for the Atlantic Provinces, and assisted in the founding of the Educational Review, St. John, N. B. He is a Governor of Dal. Univ., and was a delegate to the Conference on Education, London, England, 1907. Dr. MacKay is one of Canada's foremost Educationists and Scientists.

MacKay, Ebenezer, B.A.,(Dal.) Ph.D., (Johns Hopkins).

McLeod Professor of Chemistry Dal. Univ., graduated from Dal. Univ., in 1886, with first class honors in Experimental Physics and Chemistry and the Mackenzie Gold Medal, and from Johns Hopkins Univ., Ph.D., 1896; Special Studies at Harvard Univ.; Principal of New Glasgow High School for six years; McLeod Prof. of Chemistry and Mineralogy at Dal. Univ., since 1896. Prof. MacKay is a native of Plainfield, where he was born in 1864.

MacKay, Henry Martyn, B.A., (Dal.), M.Sc.

Professor of Civil Engineering, McGill Univ., is a brother of Prof. Ebenezer MacKay, and was born in 1868. Educated in Pictou Academy and Dal. Univ.; B.A., with honors in pure and applied Mathematics, 1888, and B.Sc., with Governor General's medal for highest general standing 1894; married, 1910, Lillian Norton Evans, Montreal; Mathematical Master, Pictou Academy, for five years; in 1908 was made Professor and head of the Civil Engineering Dept., McGill Univ., Montreal, where he is acknowledged to be a high authority in his profession.

MacKay, Ira Allan, B.A., LL.B.

Professor of Philosophy and Political Science, Univ., of Saskatchewan, Saskatoon, Sask., is the eldest son of Robert MacKay, Millsville; B.A., Dal. Univ., with honors in Philosophy, 1897; M.A., 1898; LL.B., 1905; Ph.D., Cornell Univ., 1901; called to Bar 1895; Successfully practiced his profession in Halifax and Winnipeg for several years. Since 1910 has been connected with the Univ., of Saskatchewan. Dr. MacKay was a well known scholar and an author of some note, publishing, "Canadian Nationality" in 1907.

MacKay, Kenneth G., M.Sc.
Was born at Scotsburn; educated at the Agricultural College, Guelph, Ont., and the Moody Institute, Chicago; graduated B.Sc., Toronto Univ., 1906, and M.Sc., Iowa State College, U. S. A., 1913. He is now assistant Dairy Commissioner for the Province of Saskatchewan with headquarters at Regina.

MacKay, Norman C., B.Sc., Toronto Univ., 1911.
Brother of Kenneth G. MacKay; Lecturer on Agriculture for the Ontario Government.

Maclellan, Robert, LL.D., Principal of Pictou Academy.
Is the second son of the late John Maclellan, Esq., of Durham. His early education was received at the Grammar School, Durham and at Pictou Academy. He entered Dal., College in 1870, and led his classes at the end of the term in Mathematics and English and divided honors in Classics; married Miss Martha M. Fraser. Took charge of the Preparatory Department of Pictou Academy, 1873; appointed English and Classical Master in 1877; Government Inspector of Schools for the Counties of Pictou and So. Colchester, 1883; called to the Principalship of Pictou Academy on the retirement of Dr. MacKay, 1889, in which position he is now completing his twenty-fifth year—one fourth of the whole lifetime of the Academy. In addition he taught Classics, as a colleague of Dr. MacKay, for six years.

In 1908, the Senate of Dal. Univ., conferred on him the honorary degree of LL.D. In presenting him Prof. Murray, Dean of the Senate said: "Pictou Academy has been singularly fortunate in having at its head a long line of men who have earned distinction both as teachers and leaders in the educational world, and among these our distinguished Alumnus, Robert Maclellan, holds a high and honorable place. In recognition of the high character of his work as a teacher and of the eminent success of his Principalship, I ask you, Mr. President in the name of the Senate of this University to confer the degree of Doctor of Laws, honoris causa, on Robert Maclellan."

Macleod, James D., B.A., (Dal.).
Professor of Mathematics, Western Canada College, Calgary, is the son of Mr. William Macleod, Scotsburn. He was educated at Pictou Academy and Dal. Univ., Halifax, where he won the North British Society Bursary. For two years he was Principal of the Public Schools of Westville, and for two years Mathematical Master at Pictou and Sydney Academies.

PICTOU EDUCATIONISTS

MACLEOD, JOHN W., M.A.
Professor of Mathematics, St. Francis Xavier's College Antigonish, was born at Scotsburn, educated at Pictou Academy, St. Francis Xavier's College and McGill Univ., Montreal. For four years he was Principal of the Public Schools of the town of Stellarton, and three years Prof. of Mathematics, St. Francis Xavier's College. A member of the engineering staff of The Halifax Ocean Terminals. A sister, Anna Elizabeth Macleod, graduated from Dal. Univ., in 1906 with "Great Distinction." For five years she was Principal of the Protestant Schools of Antigonish. She is married to Rev. A. A. Macleod, B. D., Trenton.

McLEOD, DONALD F.
Graduated from Cornell College of Civil Engineering in the class of 1907. He is a native of Middle River, and was for some time Principal of the Trenton Schools. He is now located in Florida.

McLEOD, FRANK THOMAS, B.A., (Dal.).
High School Teacher, Victoria, B. C.

McLEOD, JOHN W., B.A., Univ. of London, 1913.
Principal of the High School, New Glasgow, N. S.

MACKENZIE, WILLIAM B., Canadian Railway Service.
Born at Kenzieville, 1848; entered the Railway Service, 1872; since 1897 has been chief engineer of the Intercolonial Railway with offices at Moncton, N. B.

MACKENZIE, WILLIAM R., B.A., (Dal.), Ph.D., (Harvard).
Professor of English Literature in Washington Univ., St. Louis, Mo. His brother Thomas E. Mackenzie, B.A., is a mining engineer in Mexico; both are sons of Archibald Mackenzie, Esq., River John.

McKENZIE, JOHN JAMES, M.A., (Dal.), Ph.D., Univ. of Leipsic, 1877.
Died 1879. Professor of Physics, Dal. Univ.

McLEAN, HERBERT B., M.A., Ph.D., (McGill Univ.).
Professor in the Technical High School, Montreal. His brother W. B. McLean, B.Sc., is a consulting Engineer in Montreal. The McLean brothers are sons of James McLean, Postmaster, Pictou.

PICTONIANS AT HOME AND ABROAD

McKIMMIE, ANDERSON, B.A., (Princeton Univ.).
Assistant Professor in French, Mass. Agricultural College, Amherst, Mass., is a great grandson of the late Rev. Duncan Ross, of West River, and a grand nephew of the late Principal Ross of Dalhousie College.

MATHESON, HOWARD W., B.Sc., (Dal.), M.Sc., (McGill).
Was born at Lime Rock; received his Master's Degree at McGill Univ., and was awarded the Governor General's Medal for Graduate Research. In 1911 he accepted a position on the Chemical staff of the Du Port Powder Co., Wilmington, Del.

MATHESON, ROBERT, B.Sc., Ph.D., (Cornell).
Son of Walter Matheson, Lime Rock; he was Professor of Entomology in the State College of Agriculture, So. Dakota, 1907-1909; Provincial Entomologist, Agricultural College, Truro 1912-1913; appointed for Research Work, Cornell Univ., 1913.

MURRAY, DANIEL A., B.A., (Dal.) Ph.D., (Johns Hopkins).
Is the son of the late Angus Murray, Scotsburn, a community which has produced some of the best men in the Province. The family moved to Truro when Mr. Murray was a boy of six years. He graduated with honors from Dal., College in 1884; studied at Johns Hopkins, Berlin and Paris; married Alice M. Malloch, Hamilton, Ont., in 1906. Professor of Mathematics in the University of New York and Dalhousie; since 1907 has been Professor of Applied Mathematics in McGill Univ. He is the author of several Mathematical Text Books adopted by many colleges and High Schools, among them "Differential Equations," "Integral Calculus," "Plane Trigonometry," "Infinitesimal Calculus." President Schurman says of him: "He is a man of the highest abilities." He has two brothers practising medicine; Dr. H. V. Murray, Honolulu, and Dr. L. N. Murray, Halifax.

MURRAY, EBENEZER H., B.A., Ph.B., Univ. of Chicago.
Supt. of Schools, Montana, is a native of Plainfield, and a brother of Dr. D. Murray, Campbellton, N. B., and Murdoch Murray, General Secterary, Y. M. C. A., Hyde Park, Mass.

MURRAY, HOWARD, B.A., (Lond.) LL.D., (Toronto).
McLeod Professor of Classics, Dalhousie, Univ. Mr. Murray is a son of the late Dr. George Murray and was born at New Glasgow, 1859. Was Canadian Gilchrist Scholar in 1881, B.A., Univ. of London, England; studied in Edinburgh, Univ.; married, Janet, daughter of the late George Hattie, Halifax, 1890;

PICTOU EDUCATIONISTS

successively teacher in Guysboro Academy, New Glasgow High School and Halifax Academy; Professor of Classics in Dal. Univ., since 1894 and Dean of the College since 1901; He is the author of a book on "Classics, Their Use and Future Prospects." As a classical authority, his reputation stands high.

PATTERSON, GEORGE, D.D., LL.D.

Was born at Pictou, 1824, and died at his home in New Glasgow, 1897, in the seventy-fourth year of his age. He was educated at Pictou Academy and the U. P. Theological Hall, Edinburgh. On his return to Nova Scotia, in 1849, he was inducted minister, at Green Hill where he labored for twenty-seven years. He then resigned and moved to New Glasgow where he resided until his death. In the Presbyterian Church, Dr. Patterson was recognized as a man of prominence and usefulness. He was an authority in Ecclesiastical law, and procedure. Though not settled as a minister, in charge, for over twenty-one years, he went far and wide, supplying vacant churches, organizing Home Mission Stations, and at the same time taking a most lively interest in the Courts of the church. Probably there is no man now living who has traversed the Maritime Provinces as thoroughly, or known so much of the past and present of every section. Dr. Patterson was a devoted friend of Foreign Missions and of Public Education. He was one of the founders of the Widows and Orphans Fund and for many years its manager. He was a prolific writer; his Life of his grandfather, Dr. McGregor is a most readable biography. His Life of Dr. Geddie, and a companion volume on Matheson and his wife, and S. F. Johnston, are excellent missionary books. His history of Pictou Co., is a work which involved an immense amount of care and pains and is of the highest value in many respects. His work on the Trinity is an able discussion of a difficult theme. Highly noteworthy are his scientific and historical papers, read before various societies—papers that are of permanent value. His son, Hon. George Geddie Patterson, Judge of the County Court, resides in the old home in New Glasgow, N. S.

POOLE, HENRY S., M.A., Kings College, Windsor, D.Sc. London, F.R.S.

Was born at Stellarton, 1844; educated Kings College and Royal School of Mines, London, Eng.; Inspector of Coal Mines for Nova Scotia, 1872-1878; subsequently general Manager Acadia Coal Co., Stellarton, retiring in 1901. He is now a resident in England.

PICTONIANS AT HOME AND ABROAD

POTTINGER, DAVID.
Was for fifty years in the service of the Intercolonial Railway; was born in Pictou, in 1843; entered the Railway Service as clerk in 1863; chief Supt. of the Intercolonial from 1879-1892; General Manager Canadian Government Railways, 1892-1904; since then has been a member of the Railway Managing Board. Mr. Pottinger has had an honorable career and is a thoroughly practical railway man.

ROBINSON, CHARLES B., M.A., (Dal.).
Was the only son of C. B. Robinson of Pictou. He graduated at Dalhousie College in the class of 1892, winning the Univ. Medal, and taught the Science Departments for several years in the Academies of Kentville and Pictou. His bent as a naturalist was strong, and after having familiarized himself with the botany of Eastern Nova Scotia, Newfoundland and the Lower St. Lawrence, he spent some years at Cambridge Univ., England, one of the great botany schools of the world. Association with a party of field workers in Pictou County sent out by Columbia Univ., N. Y., led to his being invited to take up work at the Bronx Museum, New York, about ten years ago, subsequent to which he received an appointment, under the United States Government, to classify the flora of the Philippines. After two years spent in the Islands, he returned to New York leaving for Manila, in September, 1912. On the 21st of December, 1913, he was killed by natives of Amboyna Island, Malay Archipelago, where he had undertaken an expedition for the study of the flora of the Island. He was forty-one years of age and unmarried. He was a young man of fine natural ability and attained high rank as a botanist.

ROSS, WILLIAM H., B.Sc., (Dal.) Ph.D., (Chicago).
Was appointed to the position of Soil Chemistry in the U. S. Department of Agriculture, Washington, D. C. He is a native of River John, and a graduate of Dalhousie Univ., where he was nominated to the Science Research Scholarship in 1904. The line of work which he is taking up consists of an endeavor to find some economical method for the extraction of potash from feldspar. This compound is used as one of the principal constituents of artificial fertilizers, and is at present imported from Germany to a large extent. He is assistant editor of "Chemical Abstracts," one of the largest Scientific Journals published.

PICTOU EDUCATIONISTS

Ross, ALEXANDER, B.A., (Dal.) 1867.
: Was born at Scotsburn. Teacher and Educator; Principal of High School, Dalhousie, N. B. Retired and residing in Halifax.

STRAMBURG, HECTOR M., B.A., (Dal.) 1875.
: Principal of the High School, New Westminster, B. C., is a native of River John.

SULLIVAN, CHARLES, B.A., (Dal.) Ph.D., (Chicago), M.Sc., McGill.
: Assistant Professor Mathematics, McGill Univ., was born and educated in New Glasgow, and is assistant to Prof. D. A. Murray.

TAIT, WILLIAM D., B.A., (Dal.) Ph.D., (Harvard).
: Assistant Professor of Experimental Psychology, McGill Univ., was born at Hopewell, 1879, and is of Scottish origin. He won honors in Philosophy in Dalhousie, and pursued a thorough course of study at Harvard, receiving his degree in 1909. He married Mary Alice, daughter of the late Edward Maxwell, Halifax, 1909. Dr Tait, in his department, has carried on original research which has been highly commended by the Univ., authorities.

WILSON, JOHN
: Was born in New Glasgow in 1877. He early exhibited a talent for sculpture; studied under Bela Pratt and Henry Kitson of Boston, has executed several commissions very successfully, including Soldiers Monument at Brownfield, Me., Firemen's Monument at Forest Hills Cemetery, Boston. He conducts a school of sculpture at Boston.

A nation is rich indeed which has such men as those above named among its assets. For they were, first of all, men. One does not have to apologize for blots and stains in their lives, as an American must do for Poe, an Englishman for Byron, or a Scotsman for Burns. Pictou County is justly proud of having given birth to these moulders of thought. Through them, it has made a monumental contribution to the ultimate history of this still young nation—it has put something of the touch of sublimity into the morning of our national life. Canada occupies the latitude whence sprang the greatest nations of history; no better or more promising people than hers ever broke virgin sod; she has a high destiny to idealize and realize; these worthies of Pictou County are among the best of the first fruits; they afford a cheering assurance that our Dominion's destiny is to excel in all which makes a nation's truest life—purposeful culture, guided by sanctified conscience.

Chapter VIII

PICTONIANS IN FOREIGN FIELDS

THE Presbyterian Church in Nova Scotia was the first of all the British Colonies to establish a mission in a foreign land; and the Rev. John Geddie was its first missionary. To Mr. Geddie belongs the honor of originating such a mission. It was largely through his efforts that the Foreign Mission Board was organized. He went out from Pictou in 1846 to the New Hebrides, the chosen field of his labors. He was one year and seven months in reaching his destination. For twenty-four years he labored there. After his death a memorial tablet was erected on the island on which were engraved these significant words: "When he landed, in 1848, there were no Christians here; and when he left in 1872, there were no heathen." The story of the first foreign mission enterprise of the Presbyterians of Canada is of deep interest.

The pioneer missionary, Dr. Geddie, was born in the quiet old Scotch town of Banff, Scotland, on the 10th day of April, 1815. When about a year old his parents removed with him to Pictou, N. S. His father being a clockmaker, of small earnings, the young lad could not get much assistance from him. Like many of the world's best men, he had to work his own way. At twenty-two he was licensed to preach. He entertained the hope that the Presbyterian Church in Nova Scotia, of which he was a member, would found a foreign mission of her own, and send forth and support her own foreign missionary. But the Church was not ready. In 1838, he accepted a call to Cavendish and New London, Prince Edward Island, and was ordained there. Two years before this he had married Charlotte, daughter of Dr. Alexander McDonald, Antigonish, who proved a faithful companion and helper. He entered upon his work with ardor; but he did not forget his darling purpose while engrossed in his labors at Cavendish. His letters to the local papers and the Presbyterian Banner attracted attention and were read widely. He organized a missionary society in his own church, and induced other congregations to do the same in theirs. He won many of the people; the Presbytery of Prince Edward Island, and finally, the Synod of Nova Scotia to his views.

In July, 1843, the year of the disruption in Scotland, an overture was introduced for the first time in Synod to undertake foreign mission work. At the next meeting of Synod, held in Pictou, July 11, 1844, it was resolved by a vote of 20 to 14 to appoint a Board of Foreign Missions. The Board consisted of Revs. John Keir, R. S. Patterson, Robert Douglass, William McGregor, John Geddie, John C. Sinclair, James Bayne, James Waddell, John McCurdy and John I. Baxter. Several elders were added. The first meeting was held at the close of Synod in Pictou, John Keir, convenor, James Waddell, recording Secretary, and John Geddie, corresponding Secretary. A year later, Revs. David Roy and George Christie, with John W. Dawson, (afterward Sir John W., principal of McGill University) were added to the Board. Dr. Dawson was a life-long friend of Dr. Geddie and his mission.

The Board reported progress to the Synod of 1845. By a majority of one the Synod authorized them to select a field and appoint a missionary. The Board met September 24, 1845; and, after prayerful consideration, chose the South Sea Islands as their field, and Rev. John Geddie as their missionary. Thus, nearly seventy years ago, the foreign mission work of the Church first took definite shape. It will be easily seen that the year was a marked one in the history of Canadian Presbyterianism. With a Synod composed of only twenty ministers, fifteen elders and five-thousand members; a treasury which had only

PIONEER FOREIGN MISSIONARIES
1 John W. McKenzie, D.D. 3 John Geddie, D.D. 5 Mrs. John W. Matheson
2 Hugh A. Robertson, D.D. 4 John Morton, D.D. 6 Kenneth J. Grant, D.D.

PICTONIANS IN FOREIGN FIELDS

$1000, and a motion to send a missionary carried with the bare majority of one, they launched the enterprise! No wonder there was much apprehension as to its future. In all the succeeding years that historic act has given energy and courage to the Presbyterians of the Maritime Provinces, and inspired the rest of the country to imitate their example. That enterprise with its one missionary has developed into missions in Trinidad, Central India, Formosa, China and Korea. In 1845, the Church was able to raise a foreign mission fund of only $1000. Today, the Church is raising about $310,000 to sustain its missions, and has 146 missionaries in foreign fields.

The designation services of Mr. and Mrs. Geddie took place in Prince St. Church, Pictou, November 3, 1846. Soon afterwards they started for their field of labor. Think of traveling 113 miles by coach to Halifax! Think of 8 days tossing on the sea from Halifax to Boston! Think of one hundred and seventy days from Boston to Honolulu, when for three weeks their little brig battled for life with tremendous storms at the Cape, and then, the voyage from Honolulu to Samoa occupying 38 days! They had sailed over 19,000 miles. At Samoa, they were detained for eight months. There Dr. and Mrs. Geddie left their eldest child as they could not take it to live among cannibals. Already they had had a taste of trial and hardship in their family. Dr. Geddie had left behind him an aged and devoted mother. Did these things quell his ardor or hinder his efforts? On the contrary, they stimulated him to push forward to reach the place of his chosen life-work. On the thirteenth day of July, 1848, he sighted Aneityum. On the following day he first set foot on its soil.

The voyage, it will be seen, occupied one year and seven months. We can form no conception of the toil and weariness and danger involved in such a long, stormy, and dangerous voyage. Now, the New Hebrides can be reached from Pictou, in less than three months, in the enjoyment of comforts and luxuries, besides speed and safety, to which our first missionary was a complete stranger. He was just as truly the "Apostle of the New Hebrides" as Paul was the "Apostle of the Gentiles." Here Mr. Geddie began his work among a people of the lowest type. Before many years the entire system of heathenism gave way. Churches were built, schools established, children trained and godly homes erected. Aneityum became a centre from which light radiated to the other islands. It became a crown of glory in the history of missionary endeavor.

In 1865, Dr. Geddie with his wife paid a visit to Nova Scotia, their only visit. They were the first "returned missionaries" ever welcomed by the Presbyterian churches in Canada. Dr. Geddie told the story of his work with a simplicity and pathos that could not be surpassed. The people never tired of his thrilling tale. He returned and continued his labors for six other years, till, December 14, 1872, when, at Geelong, Australia, he passed to his reward, at the age of fifty-eight—the pioneer missionary of the Presbyterian Church in Canada—the founder of the first Canadian Mission to the heathen in a foreign land.

Nova Scotia has many heroes and heroines on her roll of honor. Among these, Dr. Geddie and his devoted wife deserve a foremost place. Mrs. Geddie is still living at Melbourne, Australia, retaining her faculties and her interest in the work. She may fittingly be called the mother of the Mission, for she rocked the cradle of the first-born Nova Scotia Mission. Mrs. Geddie has two daughters, wives of missionaries in the New Hebrides: Mrs. Neilson, wife of Rev. Thos. Neilson, of Tanna, whom she had taken with her, a child in arms, when she left Nova Scotia; and Mrs. MacDonald, wife of Rev. D. MacDonald of Efate. Her youngest daughter, Mrs. C. G. Harrington of Halifax, died recently.

PICTONIANS IN FOREIGN FIELDS

Rev. J. W. Matheson and his wife settled on Tanna, in 1858. Mr. Matheson was born at Rogers Hill, Pictou, 1832. He enjoyed the precious privilege of a pious ancestry. He began attending the grammar school at Durham, taught by Daniel McDonald, afterwards Inspector of schools for Pictou County, to prepare himself for the Seminary. After being accepted as a missionary to the New Hebrides, he was ordained in Prince St. Church, Pictou, November 22, 1856. Rev. James Watson, his pastor preached the sermon; Rev. George Walker offered the ordination prayer, Rev. James Bayne delivered the charge, and Rev. A. P. Miller addressed the people. The winter of 1857, he spent in Philadelphia, prosecuting medical studies.

Before his departure, Mr. Matheson married Mary Geddie Johnston, the second child of James Johnston of Pictou, and born in that town, October 1837. Her mother was a sister of the Rev. John Geddie. Mrs. Matheson was one of the loveliest of women, of deep personal piety and admirably fitted for mission work. Both she and her husband entered upon their work with great earnestness. They underwent great hardships, and encountered perils of the gravest character. They only labored four years in the field. Mrs. Matheson died at the early age of twenty-five, the eleventh of March, 1862, and Mr. Matheson a few months later, at thirty years of age. Dr. Paton said that Tanna was often described as the hardest Mission field in the heathen world, but the light which Mr. and Mrs. Matheson kindled there was never wholly extinguished.

The church in the Maritime Provinces, in 1872, sent forth three young men to fill the blanks made by death and by retirement. These were the Revs. James D. Murray, J. W. McKenzie and H. A. Robertson. Mr. Murray was born at Durham, Pictou Co., and took his literary and theological courses at Truro and Halifax. His first and only charge was in Antigonish, N. S. His heart was in mission work, and he was appointed as Dr. Geddie's successor in Aneityum. On account of his wife's blindness, he resigned in a few years and settled in Australia. Resigning this charge he went to Tennessee, U. S. A., where he was settled over a congregation for a time. Subsequently he returned again to Australia and was called to Moruya, where he labored with great diligence and success for sixteen years, until his death, July 13, 1913. Mr. Murray was sixty-eight years of age and leaves a widow and one son. He was a man of great spirit and beloved both in the home and foreign fields.

Rev. John W. McKenzie, D. D., and his wife were for a long time, honored missionaries in Efate. Mr. McKenzie is a native of Green Hill. Pictou Co., the fourth of a family of ten children. His father, Alexander McKenzie, was for many years an elder in Salem Church, Green Hill, under the ministry of the Rev. Geo. Patterson, D. D. From the time he was eight years old, Mr. McKenzie cherished the thought of becoming a missionary, though he never spoke of it until he offered himself to the Foreign Board. He was educated at New Glasgow, Dalhousie College, and the Theological College, Halifax. He also took a short course in Medicine. Previous to entering on his mission work, he married Miss Amanda Bruce of Musquodoboit, N. S. In January, 1913, Mr. McKenzie, retired after forty years of faithful and fruitful service in the mission field. His tactfulness has meant much to the whole mission and his saintly character has exercised a unique influence upon Europeans as well as natives.

Erromanga, where five missionaries were murdered, two of them devoured by the cannibals, is now a Christian Island. Rev. H. A. Robertson and his wife were appointed to Erromanga, the Martyr Isle, where their efforts have been crowned with abundant success. Mr. Robertson was born at Barney's

PICTONIANS IN FOREIGN FIELDS

River, Pictou, in 1841. When a young man, he entered the employ of R. McKenzie, Pictou. His health not being good, and having a desire to see these beautiful isles for himself, he took passage to the South Pacific in the Dayspring, 1863. When in Melbourne, Australia, he was appointed agent for the New Hebrides Cotton Co., of Glasgow. His work was to buy the material from the natives and ship it to Scotland. Though accepting the situation for only six months, he remained over four years. He was familiar with the missionaries and deeply interested in their work. In 1868 while still on Aneityum, the Church of Scotland, at home, invited him to be their first missionary. He accepted the invitation and returned to Nova Scotia where he took a course of training in Theology and Medicine.

In 1871 he was ordained as a foreign missionary by the Kirk Presbytery of Halifax, as their second missionary, Rev. Mr. Goodwill being the first. On the sixth of September he married Christina McNeill, daughter of John Dawson, Little Harbor, Pictou. They sailed from Halifax, October 24, and landed at Aneityum, May 1, 1872. He died May, 1914, en route home on a furlough. Rev. John Goodwill of Antigonish, was sent out by the Kirk to the New Hebrides in 1871. He spent some time on Santo and then resigned.

The second pioneer Pictonian in the mission field was the Rev. John Morton, D. D. To him belongs the credit of originating the Trinidad Mission, in the West Indies, in 1867. Mr. Morton was born at Stellarton, Pictou Co., December 20, 1839. His parents removed to Fraser's Mountain, near New Glasgow when he was quite young. The family, one of that good, old Scottish type of the Cotter's Saturday Night, the father an elder, belonged to Knox Free Church, New Glasgow, and afterwards to United Church. He went to Halifax in 1855, and entered the Free Church College, where he completed his course in 1861.

In the summer of that year he was licensed and ordained to the charge of Bridgewater, N. S., where he labored with marked success. Some years after his settlement a throat trouble compelled a rest. He decided to spend a few months in the tropics, and went to Trinidad. While there he became greatly impressed with the destitute spiritual condition of the Coolies. Returning home, he laid the matter before the Board, and they brought it before the Synod which met in New Glasgow, in 1867. So moved was the Synod by his appeal that on motion of Robert Murray, it was unanimously agreed to establish a mission in Trinidad. Mr. Morton offered his services to the Board. He was gladly accepted, and so became the first missionary of the Trinidad Mission. He and his family sailed for the West Indies, December 1, 1867.

Dr. Morton was a man of singular devotion. He served his Master with his whole heart. Next to his devotion was his remarkable tact and good judgment which were felt not only in the Mission, but in all the affairs of the Colony. Shortly after his ordination he married Sarah E., daughter of the late William Silver, Halifax. Mrs. Morton entered with her whole heart into the work of her husband, and was for him a fitting help-meet. She and her four children survive him. One of the sons, Rev. H. H. Morton is in charge of his father's field at Tunapuna; Rev. Arthur S. Morton, Ph.D., is substituting in Toronto University, in Church History; Dr. William C. Morton is assistant Professor af Anatomy in Leeds Medical University, England, and the only daughter is married to Rev. A. W. Thomson, Pictou.

Scarcely had Mr. Morton settled down to his work, when he began appealing for another missionary. In consequence of Mr. Morton's appeals, steps were taken by the Board to secure a second missionary. They sent a call addressed to the Rev. K. J. Grant of Merigomish. This call was gladly accepted, and Mr. (now Dr.) Grant was designated for the work, March 29, 1870. He reached Trinidad, with his wife and family, November 22, 1870. From the very commencement the missionaries gave special attention to the education of the young. In 1875 John A. Macdonald, Hopewell, was sent as a missionary teacher, serving two years. He was followed by Mr. A. Campbell, McLennan's Brook, in 1880.

Rev. Dr. Grant is a native of Pictou, born there in 1839. His first charge was at Merigomish, N. S. He retired from the Trinidad mission in 1907, after thirty-seven years of most faithful and devoted service. He is now engaged in mission work among the Coolies in Vancouver, B. C. Dr. Grant was first married to Miss Sarah Geddes, Yarmouth. His second wife was Miss Copeland of Merigomish, N. S. A son of his, Rev. George A. Grant, is pastor at Black River Bridge, N. B.; another son, G. Geddes Grant, born in Pictou, is a leading business man in Port of Spain, West Indies.

Rev. William L. Macrae was born at Abercrombie, Pictou Co., and was educated at Dalhousie College and Pine Hill. He began his work in Trinidad in 1886, and was located at Princestown. Here he labored most faithfully and successfully in missionary and educational work for nearly nineteen years, until his health failing him, he returned home. Since July 1905 he has been serving a congregation at Golden, B. C. Mr. Macrae was first married to Miss Elizabeth Creelman, Stewiacke, N. S. She died in 1889. His present wife was Miss Sadie Mitchell, Merigomish, N. S.

Rev. A. W. Thomson was appointed missionary to Couva in 1890. Mr. Thomson is a son of the late Rev. James Thomson, and was born at Durham, Pictou Co. Graduating from Dalhousie University in 1885, he took his theological course at Princeton Seminary. For twenty years Mr. Thomson labored with great energy and with conspicuous success in the mission field. Ill health compelled him to resign and return to Nova Scotia. He is now pastor of Knox Church, Pictou, inducted there in 1911. His brother, Rev. William McC. Thomson, is pastor of Greyfriars Church, Port of Spain, Trinidad.

Pictou has sent three of her sons to do missionary work in far off India. Rev. Charles M. Grant, D. D., was for three years a missionary in India. He was sent out in connection with the India Mission Committee of the church of Scotland. While settled as a pastor in Halifax, he resigned at the request of Dr. Norman McLeod to preach to the educated natives of Calcutta, where his lectures were attended by hundreds of English speaking natives. His promising career was arrested by a severe illness, whereupon he was ordered home. A year later he accepted a call to Glasgow, Scotland, and then to Dundee. The Rev. Dr. Grant is a Pictonian, a brother of the late Principal Grant. He retired from active service a few years ago and makes his home in Dundee.

Rev. Robert C. Murray was sent to India in 1885 by the Western section of the Church—St. Paul's Church, Montreal, undertaking his support. Mr. Murray was a son of Hugh Murray and was born in Cariboo, Pictou Co., educated in Arts and Theology at Queen's University, Ontario. He graduated in the spring of 1885. In the fall of that year he began his work in Ujjain the oldest city in India, with rare tact and zeal. A year later, Miss Charlotte Wilson, daughter of the late Charles Wilson, Pictou, joined him and they were married. In less than a year Mrs. Murray died and four months later Mr. Murray himself died suddenly of sun stroke. "Lovely and pleasant were they in their lives, and in death they were not divided." Kenneth G. MacKay, B. S. A., Toronto Univ., was sent by the Canadian Church, 1906 to Central India to instruct the natives in agricultural and industrial work. He resigned in 1912, and returned to Pictou, his native place. Rev. William R. McKay is stationed at

GROUP OF FOREIGN MISSIONARIES

1 A. W. Thomson
2 L. L. Young
3 W. R. McKay
4 W. L. Macrae
5 Robt. C. Murray
6 Mrs. Robt. C. Murray
7 George M. Ross
8 D. M. Cock

PICTONIANS IN FOREIGN FIELDS

Kongmoon, South China. Mr. McKay was first sent to Macao, in 1902, and was the first missionary located there. He devotes most of his time to educational work. He was born in Springville, Pictou Co., and is a son of Mr. Joseph McKay, an elder in the Springville Presbyterian Church. He graduated from Dalhousie College in 1896, taking a B. D. degree from Princeton Seminary, in 1901. For three years previous to his departure for China, he held a pastorate at Noel and Kennetcook. He married Miss Mary O'Brien, B. Sc., Noel, N. S. Knox Church, Regina, supports them.

Rev. George M. Ross, B. A., son of Alexander Ross, was born at Blue Mountain, Pictou, and studied theology at Pine Hill, where he graduated in 1901. He married, Minnie Robertson of Ontario. He was sent as a missionary to North Honan, China, in 1903, where he is now laboring. He is supported by St. John's Church, Toronto.

Rev. Luther L. Young is Pictou's representative in Korea. He went out in 1906 and is settled in Ham Heung. He was born at Millsville, Pictou Co., graduated from Dalhousie University in 1903, and three years later from Pine Hill. He is married to Catherine F. Mair, B. A., Campbelltown, N. B. The first Presbyterian Church, New Glasgow supports Mr. and Mrs. Young.

Rev. D. G. Cock, a descendant of Rev. Daniel Cock the first settled minister of Truro, was appointed missionary to Mhow, Central India. He was born in the West River Valley, and graduated from Pine Hill in 1899. Soon after, he was sent as an ordained missionary to Alaska where he spent three years. On the eve of his departure as missionary to India in 1902, he was married to a college class-mate, Miss Ella Maxwell, Halifax, N. S.

So far as known, none of Pictou's fair daughters have entered the ministerial or legal professions or ventured far into the fields of literature and science. They have devoted their lives to the humbler yet equally important spheres of the home and the school-room. The county has been the home of the very best type of capable and self-sacrificing mothers and wives. Much of its fame and influence is due to them. Many families have furnished teachers for the public schools—some families as many as half a dozen. For that matter, nearly every man in the professional lists in this book, at one time or another, taught school; and as the students from the Academy and College went out into the country districts to teach in the summer, they had much to do with making Pictou the literary and educational centre which it is.

A few Pictou women have studied medicine, and over a dozen have gone to be missionaries and teachers in foreign lands, and have been faithful and fruitful workers for the Master. The first to go was Miss Mary B. McKay, a daughter of Mr. James McKay, elder, Stellarton, N. S. She was sent by the Western section of the Church to Central India, in 1888. She was only a short time in the field when she was married to Rev. John Buchanan, M. D., of Ontario. Mrs. Buchanan is a graduate of Mt. Allison Ladies' College, Sackville, N. B., and of the Ladies' Medical College, Toronto. She is now living in Amkhut, Central India, where she and her husband are successfully engaged in missionary and medical work among the Bhils.

Mrs. Elizabeth M. Butler went to India as an officer of the Salvation Army, in 1898, but in a few years joined the Friend's Foreign Missionary Association of England with her husband, the late Edward J. Butler. Altogether she has given eighteen years of active service with Sohagpur as a centre. Mrs. Butler is a daughter of the late James McLaren, Wentworth Grant, Pictou Co.

Cariboo, Pictou Co., has sent two missionaries from the same house to labor in India—Misses Jemima and Mary McKenzie. In 1904, Jemima McKenzie was appointed, under the Women's Union Missionary Society of America,

MISSIONARIES IN THE FOREIGN FIELD

1 Jessie C. Fraser
2 Mrs. Elizabeth McL. Butler
3 Mrs. John N. Culver
4 Mrs. A. A. Smith
5 Mrs. John Buchanan
6 Jemima McKenzie
7 Mary S. Herdman
8 Bessie McCunn
9 Annie Young

to medical work in Cawnpore, India. Two years later she went to Fatephur where she had charge of a large hospital which she was largely instrumental in building, and of which she is now in full charge. In 1905, her sister, Mary McKenzie, was appointed to succeed her in Cawnpore where for nearly six years she engaged in Medical and Bible work. In 1911 she was married to Rev. A. A. Smith, Verschoyle, Ont. The two sisters are graduates of Dalhousie University and the Medical School, Halifax, and are highly esteemed both for their work and their personal qualities.

From the Millsville district, Pictou Co., three young women have given their lives to the cause of missions. Miss Annie Young, a sister of Rev. L. L. Young, was settled at Wan Chi, Central China, in 1897. She was educated at Pictou Academy and in the Christian Alliance Institute, New York City, under whose auspices she is now laboring. Miss Jennie Fraser, also of Millsville, sailed for India in 1898. She has charge of a mission station at Shantipur. Her sister, Agnes Fraser, (now Mrs. John N. Culver, a missionary from the U. S. A.), went to India in 1904 and is located in Dholka, India. They were both trained for missionary work in the Christian Alliance School, at Nyack, N. Y., and are working under its Board.

Miss Mary S. Herdman, daughter of the late Rev. Andrew Herdman, Pictou, is doing missionary and educational work in Dhar, Central India. She was first sent out to Northern India in 1903 by the Church of England, but for the last dozen years she has been under the control of the Canadian Church and is supported by the W. M. F. Society, Toronto. She helps in the Dispensary, and acts as Bible teacher to women.

Another clergyman's daughter, Miss Bessie McCunn, daughter of the late Rev. R. McCunn, River John, is laboring in Jhansi, India. She was first appointed as teacher to Princestown, Trinidad in 1900, and spent five years there. Afterwards she attended the Ewart Missionary Training School Toronto, and while there was appointed by the Women's Union Missionary Society, N. Y., to go to India. Her work includes Hospital and Zenana work, and the superintending of day and Sunday schools.

Miss Maud M. Rogers, daughter of Mr. B. D. Rogers, Stellarton, was sent out, in 1909, by the Canadian Church and is now laboring in Song Jin, Korea. She took a course in Domestic Science in Boston.

Priscilla McDonald, daughter of Mr. John McL. McDonald, Durham, Pictou, (now the wife of Rev. Willard S. Tedford) is in the mission field in Rayagadda, India. Mrs. Bessie A. Robb, wife of Rev. A. F. Robb, Korea, is a daughter of Rev. Robert Cumming, D. D., Westville, N. S. They were appointed to Wonsan in 1901, and are supported by St. Paul's Church, Fredericton, N. B. Miss Jenny Hazel Kirk, daughter of J. H. Kirk, East River St. Mary's, Pictou Co., was appointed by the Foreign Mission Board of the Maritime Synod to Wonsan, Korea. She sailed December 5, 1913, from Vancouver, B. C. A daughter of William Cameron, County Clerk, Pictou, Christina Cameron, was married to Rev. Fred Paton, son of Rev. John Paton, D. D., and was engaged in mission work with her husband in Malekula, New Hebrides. She died April, 1914.

It will thus be seen that Pictou County has made notable contributions to the cause of Missions. Great honor has fallen to her in sending forth such a noble band of men and women to publish the message of the King.

CHAPTER IX

THE PRESS AND PRINTERS OF PICTOU

THE first newspaper published in Canada was the Halifax Gazette. It was published by John Bushnell, a partner of Bartholomew Green. The first number appeared on Monday, March 25, 1752. Mr Green was a son of Bartholomew Green who printed the first newspaper in America—the Boston News Letter. He set up the first printing press in the Dominion of Canada, at Halifax, Nova Scotia. The printing press was thus one of New England's contributions to Nova Scotia. The Gazette has been published continuously ever since, and still makes its appearance regularly each week as the Nova Scotia Royal Gazette. It is in all probability the oldest newspaper published in America.

The first printing press in Pictou was what was known as the Weir Durham Press. It belonged to the Synod of the Presbyterian Church of Nova Scotia. Soon after that body was formed, in 1817, it resolved to take collections for the purchase of a printing press to be employed in giving religious intelligence to the people. After some progress in this, a lady in Britain, Mrs. Weir Durham, hearing of it made them a present of a press which thenceforward was known by her name. Synod placed it in the Academy at Pictou, and in the early days was stationed in the library. It was a small press and would scarcely print a larger sheet than foolscap. It was well constructed and very convenient for small jobs. When Dr. Geddie was leaving Nova Scotia to go to the South Seas he needed a printing press and this one having been, for sometime unused, but being still in good condition, the Synod gave it to him to be employed in his work. He took it to the South Seas and set it up in the island of Aneityum where it was used in the early stages of the mission, printing primers and such other small works, in the language of the natives. Some years later a larger press was sent out from Britain, and the old one was transferred to the new mission field of Rev. G. N. Gordon, in 1856, on Erromanga, where it was used for the same purpose as in the other mission field. What has since become of it is not known.

The first printing establishment properly, so called, in Pictou, was set up in 1827 by J. S. Cunnabell of Halifax and William Milne, a Scotchman, recently from Aberdeen. The former was a practical printer but the latter was not. The partnership was dissolved in a few months and for some years Mr. Milne was the sole owner. On leaving Pictou he went to Providence, R. I., where some of his sons followed their father's trade.

A prospectus was issued in August 1827, signed by William Milne & Co., giving notice of intention to publish a paper to be called the "Colonial Patriot," and requesting the support of all interested in local affairs and in sound principles and politics. After much discussion on the part of its promoters the name of "The Pictou Patriot" was thought to be most suitable. Dr. McCulloch suggested the name "Colonial Patriot," which was adopted, a name which was fully justified by its broad sympathies. Nearly four months later, on Friday morning. December 7, the first number was issued. It consisted of eight pages of three columns each, and measured ten inches by twelve. It was strong in its advocacy of the policy of the Academy. This was the first native newspaper outside of Halifax. Shelburne had had three before 1800, but these were transplanted from the American colonies and soon ceased publication. The principles of the paper and the vigor and independence of the editor soon brought it into public notice.

The Patriot sounded the first note of Responsible Government in the British North American colonies. Though opinions favorable to reform were widely current there was as yet no organ which openly avowed reformed sentiments. The Halifax papers were too near the center of things to speak with any insistence on the great questions at issue. It was in the country that the great body of reform sentiment existed and where, no doubt, grievances were most felt. And it was from that quarter that reform was first to find a voice in its behalf through that powerful agency of enlightenment, the press. Pictou had the honor of establishing that organ, the predecessor of the reformed Nova Scotian, which began as that carried on, the work of propagating those ideas of liberty, equality and justice in our Provincial Government, which at length prevailed by sheer force of their inherent truth. It required an editor with ideas and convictions to do this work. Such an one was found in Jotham Blanchard. He was a New Englander by birth and no doubt was familiar with the freedom under republican institutions in the country of his birth. Any such ideas which he may have possessed would not be lessened while under the influence of Dr. McCulloch. In Blanchard the times found the man to do work that sorely needed to be done. He brought to his task keen intelligence, literary skill and power of argument, great perseverance, and a great zeal which all too early consumed his powers of body and mind, and cut short a career which gave every promise of greatness. From the office of the Patriot was issued for a time a paper for youth called the Juvenile Entertainer. It is not known how long it was published, but it served a good purpose at a time when children's books were few.

 Among those trained in the Patriot office two deserve particular notice.—Alexander Lawson and John Stiles. Mr. Lawson was a native of New Glasgow, and was employed on the Patriot as an apprentice from its establishment to its discontinuance. He then went to Yarmouth where he established the Yarmouth Herald, the first successful venture in newspaper printing in the Western part of the Province. With the exception of a short interval he conducted it for forty seven years. It is one of the oldest papers in the Province, and is now conducted by his son J. Murray Lawson.

In the year 1831, Pictou's second paper made its appearance. It was called the Pictou Observer. In politics it was opposed to the reform movement, and antagonistic to Dr. McCulloch's policy for the Academy. It was published by William Gossip. Rev. K. J. McKenzie, a Scottish Kirkman, was its editor. The Observer was not a success financially, and after a time it was discontinued. It was resuscitated by Roderick McDonald, a native of Scotland, who had been teaching the lower branches in Pictou Academy. The second attempt to establish the Observer proved futile after a year's effort, for we read that in 1843 it was once more revived by Mr. McCoubray of St. Johns, Newfoundland, with Martin I. Wilkins, a prominent lawyer and legislator, as editor, but it again became defunct. In this office was trained Alpin Grant. Born a mile back of the town in 1848, he bought from Gossip and Coade the old Halifax Times and commenced the publication in its place, of the British Colonist which he conducted through its whole course. He was also for sometime Queen's printer, and amassed a small fortune by printing in Nova Scotia, which few other men have done.

The next paper published in Pictou was "The Bee," a weekly journal devoted to politics, literature and agriculture. It was conducted by James Dawson, father of the late Sir J. William Dawson who purchased the plant of the old Patriot. The first number appeared May 27, 1835. The general character of its contents was similar to that of its predecessors. In the spring of 1838 John Stiles issued a prospectus of a new paper to be called "The Mechanic and Farmer." Mr. Stiles was brought up near Pictou, his father who had come originally from Cornwallis, settled

GROUP OF MEN IN PUBLIC LIFE

1 Frederic Yorston
2 Peter M. Macdonald
3 William MacDonald
4 R M. MacGregor
5 Hon. J. W. Carmichael
6 Hon. Adam. C. Bell
7 David Pottinger
8 Robert McConnell
9 R. H. Mackay
10 John U. Ross

PRESS AND PRINTERS OF PICTOU

near Scotch Hill, where he had a mill. Mr. Dawson, thinking there was not room for two papers in Pictou, agreed to sell his establishment to Mr. Stiles; and the Bee was discontinued in the month of May of that year. The Mechanic and Farmer was immediately announced in its stead, and was first issued on May 23, 1838. Mr. Stiles made his paper a success financially, and gave great stimulus to farmers in the amount of information circulated on agricultural subjects. In 1842 a religious paper in connection with the Presbyterian Church of Nova Scotia was established in Pictou under the name, Presbyterian Banner. It was edited by the Rev. James Ross; printed by Mr. Stiles, and continued for a little over one year.

On October 4, 1843, "The Mechanic and Farmer" and "The Banner" were merged in "The Eastern Chronicle" which is still issued at New Glasgow. The plant was purchased from Mr. Stiles by the Rev. George Patterson and Mr. J. L. Geldert, and was conducted by them for some time. Mr. Stiles went to Washington and secured a good position in the Pension Office there, where he died some twenty years ago. Among those employed in the office may be mentioned Donald Gunn of Hopewell who afterward conducted a printing establishment in Boston; Edward M. Macdonald, afterwards M. P. for Lunenburg, a native of West River, who at the close of 1846 bought out the establishment, and in January 1847, took the management of the paper into his own hands. He continued to conduct the paper until appointed Queen's printer when he removed to Halifax and there established the Halifax Citizen with Hon. William Garvie. His brother, John D. Macdonald, who had been for sometime employed in the office, took charge of the Eastern Chronicle after his withdrawal.

Up to about the year 1868, newspaper publication in the county was confined to the town of Pictou. Then the

Eastern Chronicle was removed to New Glasgow, with Robert McConnell and W. B. Alley, the latter for thirty years proprietor Colchester Sun, of Truro, in charge. Mr. McConnell was a Pictou man and a veteran journalist. He edited the Eastern Chronicle for ten years; served on the editorial staff of the Halifax Morning Chronicle; was publisher of the Truro Guardian; then editor of the Moncton Transcript; for a time Editor-in-chief of the Montreal Herald. Returning to Halifax in 1892, he became the managing editor of the Morning Chronicle. Some years later he retired from active journalism and was appointed to a position in the Finance Department at Ottawa, which he held until his death in 1909. He was born at Meadowville, in 1842, and was educated at Durham Grammar school and the Normal school, Charlottetown. While in the latter place, he acquired a knowledge of printing, and became from that time a "newspaper man." He was prominently identified with the Presbyterian church and active in the Sunday school and Temperance cause. His second son, J. Miller McConnell, is financial editor on the Montreal Daily Star. He was born in New Glasgow in 1870 and gained his early experience in newspaper work on the Eastern Chronicle. In 1887 he joined the staff of the Montreal Herald and ten years later went to the Montreal Star with which he has ever since been connected.

Later on the Eastern Chronicle passed into the hands of Daniel Logan, now a prominent journalist in Hawaii. Mr. Logan is a Scotsburn boy. He began his newspaper career in the office of the Eastern Chronicle in 1867. In 1877 he became editor and proprietor. In 1884 he went to Honolulu where for more than a quarter of a century he has been engaged in journalism and literary work and has justly earned the title "Nestor of the Press." After Mr. Logan's departure the Eastern Chronicle passed into the hands of S. M. MacKenzie, who published it as a semi-weekly for a number of years. In 1881 he disposed of it to a company with James A. Fraser as editor and manager.

On November 2, 1858, the Colonial Standard was established in Pictou town in succession to the Observer as the organ of the Conservative party. It was printed on a new press and with new type. Hon. S. H. Holmes of Halifax, was its editor and proprietor for over 20 years. The Standard has had a chequered history. For a number of years it ceased publication, but is now issued from the "News" office.

In 1880 W. D. Stewart started the Plain Dealer in New Glasgow. He conducted it for two years as editor and proprietor. The Rev. E. Scott, D.D., while pastor of the United Church, New Glasgow, began the publication of the Maritime Presbyterian, a religious monthly devoted to the interests of the church. It continued for a number of years but was finally merged in the Presbyterian Record of which Dr. Scott is the editor. It was in 1881 that the Liberals of Pictou decided that they should have a mouth piece to replace the Eastern Chronicle and the Pictou News appeared. The News prospered for a few years and gained a wide circulation. C. D. Macdonald was the editorial writer until 1889. Then came the Trades Journal at Stellarton, now the Mining Record, conducted by Hon. R. Drummond.

Next to enter the field, in 1889, was the Enterprise of New Glasgow. It was printed for a time in the Standard office in Pictou by Mr. Albert Dennis who was then publisher of the Standard. In 1890 Allan P. Douglas joined the paper and is now editor and proprietor. From Westville the next report of a newspaper came. R. A. Macdonald there began in 1895 the publication of the Free Lance, as the organ of the Orangemen. It appeared as such for a year or two only, when it became the property of J. W. H. Sutherland.

Reverting to the town of Pictou, the year 1890 witnessed the destruction of the Standard's office building and plant by fire; and as the gentleman who then owned the News had little in common with the town and county he sold to the Standard the News plant, and the latter paper ceased publication. This left Pictou with but one paper, till in 1893 the Pictou Advocate was established with John D. Macdonald son of John D. Macdonald, senior, as proprietor. The New Glasgow News, a daily, was first published in the fall of 1912.

Of the other periodicals published in this county, the only ones worthy of special notice are the monthly organs of the different religious bodies. The Missionary Register, 1850 to 1857, was the first missionary paper published in the Lower Provinces. This was merged with a monthly magazine called the Christian Instructor and was edited by the Rev. George Patterson, 1855 to 1860. The Record of the Church of Scotland was commenced in January, 1854, and during the greater part of the time was published in the office of the Colonial Standard.

Many Pictonians have been connected with the press elsewhere and one of the best known was George Munro, who was born at West River, 1825. At the age of twelve he entered the office of the Observer, Pictou, to learn the printing business. He only served two years when he became a student in the New Glasgow schools. He attended Pictou Academy for three years and for some years taught school in the county. His reputation as a teacher led to his being appointed head master of the Free Church Academy, Halifax, in 1850, where he continued until 1856. In that year he removed to New York City where he soon became a successful publisher of popular books and periodicals. He was engaged in the publishing business for nearly forty years and became a millionaire.

The Munro Publishing house was known everywhere in the United States and Canada. In 1867, he began the publication of the Seaside Library which contained the best fiction, essays and history. It provided good and cheap reading for the masses and it is impossible to calculate the great educational value of those publications, for they reached millions of readers. Mr. Munro was a discriminating editor and a man of excellent literary judgment. He was a warm supporter of higher education. He never ceased to be interested in his native land, especially in its educational institutions. The main recipient of his bounty, was Dalhousie College, in which he endowed successively five Professorial chairs besides providing for scholarships and exhibitions, giving in all to the amount of nearly half a million dollars. While a teacher in the Free Church College, Halifax, he managed to complete the regular course in Theology although he never entered the ministry. Mr. Munro died April 24, 1896, in the seventy-eighth year of his age. His whole life was marked by industry and uprightness. Mrs. Munro was a sister of Rev. Dr. Forrest, Halifax.

His brother Norman L. Munro was also a successful publisher of books and papers in New York City. Mr. Munro was born at Millbrook, Pictou Co., April 8, 1844. He went to New York in 1866, and engaged in publishing business under the name of the Munro Publishing Co. He died on February 24, 1894.

W. E. Maclellan, Barrister, was for a number of years managing editor and chief editorial writer of the Winnipeg Free Press. From 1900 to 1905 he was Editor-in-chief, of the Morning Chronicle, Halifax, N. S. Mr. Maclellan was born at Durham, Pictou Co., 1855. He was educated at Pictou Academy and Dalhousie College, and received the degree of Bachelor of Laws from the University of Halifax. He was called to the Bar, 1880. For several years he was Inspector of schools for the District of Pictou and South Colchester. In 1909, he won a prize for the best essay on Immigration. He has written many short stories and literary articles for leading American publications. He entered the Dominion Public Service, as Post Office Inspector for Nova Scotia, in 1905. Maclellan was a brilliant editorial writer, and is today a frequent and valued contributor to the magazines and public press. He married Margaret J. Mackenzie of Pictou and is a brother of Principal Maclellan of the Pictou Academy.

The Rev. P. M. Macdonald, M. A., is on the editorial staff of the Westminster Company, Toronto and has written a number of stories, essays and poems for the magazines and the religious press. For several years he wrote for the "Presbyterian," Toronto, under the name of "Donal Bhain." Mr. Macdonald is a native of Pictou. He graduated from Dalhousie University, 1894; and from the Presbyterian College, Halifax, 1896. He was Pastor of St. Paul's Church, Truro, from 1896 to 1904; since then until 1913 Pastor of Cowan Avenue Church, Toronto. He married Miss Christina Logan of Pictou.

Frederic Yorston, B. A. (Dalhousie & Harvard) is the managing Editor of the Montreal Standard, a high-class weekly published in that city. Mr. Yorston was born in Pictou town and after a thorough course of study at home and abroad, entered Canadian Journalism, taking a position on Montreal Daily Star. When the Standard was started he took position of Managing Editor. He is now President of the Montreal Publishing Company. Alvin F. Macdonald, editor of the Morning Chronicle, Halifax; Thomas M. Fraser of the Free Press, Saskatoon, Sask., and Albert E. Crockett, B. L. of the Post-Express, Rochester, N. Y., are Hopewell boys. The editor of the Wesleyan, the organ of the Methodist Church published in Truro, N. S., is the Rev. D. W. Johnson, D. D., of River John.

In the history of the press in Pictou there is much in this brief review of which Pictonians may well be proud. No place outside of Halifax has so long maintained efficient newspapers, or displayed so much journalistic talent in the discussion of the public questions of the day. The press of Pictou has generally been on the side of morality and religion. The general character of the community may have been the cause of this, but it is equally true, that the press has had very much to do with the moulding and the making of the character of the people. Especially is this true at the beginning of her history. The press of those early days fulfilled its educative mission to an even greater extent than it does now, for it was then one of a few such agencies, while now it is merely one of many. The Patriot and its successors had much to do with the moulding of public opinion for popular rights and reform and for the final triumph of the Pictou Academy.

Chapter X

PICTOU IN POLITICS

THE first election in Pictou County was held in 1799. These were the days of irresponsible Government, when an autocratic Executive at Halifax governed the Province, as they saw fit, and generally without regard to the just claims of the outlying settlements. It was natural, therefore, that the Scotsmen of Pictou should be strong in protest against this form of government, and when the opportunity was formally offered them they expressed themselves as strongly opposed to it.

At this time, the counties of Pictou, Colchester and Halifax were one for Electoral purposes, and were designated "Halifax" County. Out of the four candidates allotted to the county of Halifax, Pictou returned two, W. Cottman Tonge, and Edward Mortimer in opposition to the ruling element at Halifax. Mr. Tonge is said to have been a man of great independence, and fearless in asserting the rights of the people. In 1806, Colchester and Pictou again overruled Halifax by electing Edward Mortimer and S. G. W. Archibald of Truro. Edward Mortimer was of Scottish descent. He settled in Pictou town where he became a prominent merchant and shipper. Because of his wealth and influence he was sometimes styled "the King of Pictou." For over twenty years he represented the people in the General Assembly of the Province. Political seed was apparently sown in a fruitful field, and the men of Pictou have ever since taken the deepest and most intelligent interest in public affairs. Through worthy representatives they have made their influence strongly felt on the floors of successive Parliaments and Legislature.

The outstanding question in Pictou's early politics, and the one which contributed to a greater degree than any other in causing party strife, was the unfortunate controversy, lasting more than twenty years, over Pictou Academy's claims for Government aid, on lines similar to that accorded to King's College, Windsor, which was the special care of the Council of Twelve. Edward Mortimer, George Smith and Jotham Blanchard were successively the men who championed the cause of the Academy. In its earlier stages, the quarrel was ecclesiastical, as well as political, and intense feelings were aroused. Jotham Blanchard was elected in 1830 to the Assembly at Halifax. This was the year of the "big election," concerning which many stories of strife, bloodshed, and even death are told. Hon. J. W. Carmichael describes the famous election of 1830, when "Kirk" and "Antiburgher" were the war cries. Elections were not held then as now in one day. That one occupied three weeks, commencing in Halifax, adjourning to Truro, and then to Pictou, a week in each, the excitement increasing as the contest proceeded. From Truro came accounts of bands of electors marching in from Stewiacke, Londonderry and Tatamagouche with pipes playing, flags flying, and forming in a body around Court House Square.

The battle rolled on to Pictou and when Highlander met Lowlander then came the tug of war. A regular plan of campaign was marked out. On Monday, the Kirk men took possession of the town and drove the Antiburghers before them like leaves before the blast. The Antiburgher leaders took counsel with one another and orders were issued. Messengers sped over hills and dales; and "Antiburghers to the rescue," was the cry. From East and West and Middle River came in the detachments, and revived the drooping spirits of their party. The college was guarded. A body-guard was stationed in Blanchard's House. On Wednesday night a fierce and possibly fatal contest was prevented, solely by the interposition of Dr. McCulloch, who placed himself between the contending

MEN IN PROFESSIONAL AND PUBLIC LIFE

1 Chas. E. Tanner
2 Evan Kennedy, M. D.
3 Graham Fraser
4 G. Forrest McKay
5 E. M. Macdonald, M. P.
6 Hon. A. M. MacKay
7 George Munro
8 Col. Henry Lippincott, M D.
9 Thomas Cantley
10 A. W. H. Lindsay, M. D.

parties just as their columns were coming into conflict; and prevailed on both to retire. And so passed away the week—a week eventful in the history of Pictou, and of Nova Scotia. It was decidedly the most exciting election ever held in the Province. The bitter feelings engendered in that strife have long passed away. There are now few, very few, remaining who can even call them to recollection.

Joseph Howe followed the polling to Pictou and reported the events there in the interest of his paper, the "Nova Scotian." Howe at that time was attached to the Party of Privilege and afterwards said that it was the impressions made upon him by Blanchard and the other Pictou reformers that turned his mind towards the popular side, as he expressed it, "those Pictou scribblers converted me."

Next came the agitation for Responsible Government, and Pictou was the centre of the movement. Jotham Blanchard was the first public man in the Province, by voice and pen to press for Responsible Government, as we have it today. This he did through the columns of the Colonial Patriot and before the Home Government in 1831 when he went across to plead for justice to Pictou Academy. In 1836 the district of Pictou was established as a separate county. By that act, it received two representatives for the County and one for the township of Pictou. The first election under the new plan took place that year, when by a compromise between the parties, George Smith, a Liberal and an upholder of responsible government, and John Holmes, a Tory and openly opposed to the new order of things, were chosen. After a contest Henry Hatton was elected to represent the township.

In 1838 Thomas Dickson succeeded George Smith, the latter being elevated to the Legislative Council. From 1840-1843 Holmes, Henry Blackadar, and Hatton were the representatives. The next four years, Holmes and George R. Young represented the County and Blackadar the township. From 1847-1851 the members were Young, Andrew Robertson and Blackadar. George R. Young was a member without portfolio of the first real Reform Government that came into power after the election of 1847. In 1851 the Liberals lost the County and for four years the representatives were Holmes, Robert Murray and Martin I. Wilkins.

Mr. Holmes was one of the earliest settlers on the East River of Pictou. He came from Scotland when only eleven years of age. By his industry, intelligence and public spirit he won the confidence of the people and for many years represented them in Parliament. In 1858, he was appointed a member of the Legislative Council and in 1867 to the Senate of Canada. He died in 1876, aged 87 years.

In 1855 Captain George McKenzie and A. C. McDonald were elected for the County and Wilkins again for the township. Mr. McDonald was the first son of the soil to win the confidence of the electors of Pictou. He represented the County in the Nova Scotia Legislature, in the Liberal interest, for eight years, and was Speaker of the House of Assembly before Confederation. Captain McKenzie was one of the old school politicians and a leading man in the county. For eight years he represented it in the Liberal interest. Mr. Wilkins, though not a native of the county, was long identified with it. He went against his party at Confederation and was elected in 1867 on the Liberal ticket, becoming Attorney General in Mr. Annand's Government. In 1859 the County was divided into two districts, Eastern and Western. From 1859 to 1863 Captain George McKenzie and James McDonald represented the Eastern district and A. C. McDonald and R. P. Grant, Western. From 1863 to 1867, the Eastern district was represented by James McDonald and James Fraser, (Downie), and the Western district by Alexander McKay and Donald Fraser.

PICTOU IN POLITICS

After confederation, in 1867, the Dominion Parliament was established and met at Ottawa, with one representative from Pictou County. An additional member in the Local House was at this time given to the county. Hiram Blanchard, a son of Pictou, who represented Inverness County from 1857 to 1867 was sworn in on July 4, 1867 as the first Premier of Nova Scotia after Confederation, holding the portfolio of Attorney General. He was without mandate from the people and his stay in office was brief, for at the general election which took place four months later, September 17, 1867, he was utterly defeated, only two seats being carried for the Government, his own, and Henry G. Pineo for Cumberland County. Mr. Blanchard was unseated at the election in 1867 and remained in private life until the general election, 1871, when he was again returned by Inverness and became leader of the opposition in the Provincial House until his death in 1874.

In 1867, Pictou elected to the Local House three Liberals — Dr. George Murray, R. S. Copeland and Martin I. Wilkins. In 1871, the pendulum swung back and Simon H. Holmes, Alexander McKay, and Hugh J. Cameron, were elected, and again in 1874. In 1878 Simon H. Holmes, Alexander McKay and Adam C. Bell, were chosen by the people. In 1878 Simon H. Holmes became the fourth Premier of the Province, being leader of the Government for four years. During his administration, several laws and measures of great benefit to the Province, were passed. In May, 1882, Mr. Holmes retired from politics to accept the office of Prothonotary for the Supreme Court at Halifax, which office he still holds.

Upon the retirement of Mr. Holmes, J. S. D. Thomson became Premier and Adam C. Bell, Provincial Secretary. In an appeal made to the country, three months later, the Government was defeated, although Mr. Bell, with Robert Hockin and Dr. C. H. Munro were elected for Pictou. In

1886, Bell and Munro were again elected with Jeffrey McColl, New Glasgow, the first Liberal elected in Pictou for nineteen years. Mr. Bell resigned in 1887, and ran for a seat in the Federal House, but was defeated. His place in the Legislature was taken by William Cameron, who was elected by acclamation, and again returned by popular vote in 1890 and 1894. From 1890 to 1894, Alexander Grant and James D. McGregor, with William Cameron, represented the county.

James D. McGregor, New Glasgow, entered public life in 1890, and served for four years in the House of Assembly. He was returned again in 1897. In 1900 he was an unsuccessful candidate for the Commons. In 1903 he was called to the Senate, and in 1910 succeeded another Pictonian, the Hon. D. C. Fraser, in the office of Lieutenant Governor of the Province. Mr. McGregor is a grandson of the Rev. Dr. McGregor, and senior partner in the firm of R. McGregor & Sons. He has long been prominent in Church and State. His elevation to the Governor's Chair was a well-deserved honor to a worthy citizen.

Matthew H. Fitzpatrick represented the County in the House of Assembly from 1897-1901. In 1901 George G. Patterson was elected along with E. M. Macdonald and C. E. Tanner, and became a member of the Murray Government, but failed of election, in 1906. Robert M. MacGregor, son of the Hon. James D. McGregor, was nominated in 1904 to succeed E. M. Macdonald in the Legislature. He was opposed by A. C. Bell, whom he defeated. He was elected again in 1906 with Charles E. Tanner. John M. Baillie represented county at Halifax from 1906- to 1911. In 1909, R. H. MacKay was elected when Mr. Tanner sought to regain his seat. In the election of 1911, Charles E. Tanner, Robert M. MacGregor and R. H. MacKay were chosen and are the present representatives. Mr. MacGregor is a member of the Murray Government, and Mr. Tanner Leader of the Opposition.

PICTOU IN POLITICS

Reverting to the Confederation period, the County chose as its first representatives to Ottawa, James W. Carmichael, a Liberal, and a man of much ability, who served from 1867 to 1872, and again from 1874 to 1878. Redistribution in 1872 gave Pictou the right to send two members to Ottawa, and James McDonald and Robert Doull, were elected on the Conservative ticket. In 1898 Mr. Carmichael was called to the Senate, but resigned in 1903 and died on May 1, 1903 in his eighty-fourth year.

Mr. Carmichael was the son of James Carmichael and Christian McKenzie, his wife, both natives of Canada, of Scotch descent. He was born at New Glasgow, Dec. 16, 1819. Educated at Pictou Academy, married 1851, to Maria, daughter of Duncan McColl, of Guysboro, N. S., (she died Dec. 1874). Mr. Carmichael was long one of the best and most prominent citizens of Pictou County. He was widely and honorably known throughout Canada, as a business man and as a public man. From 1874-1878, John A. Dawson, represented the county in the Dominion Parliament with Mr. Carmichael.

In 1878, with the return of Sir John A. Macdonald to power, James McDonald and Robert Doull, were once more successful. For many years, Mr. McDonald was in the political arena, As a young man, he showed great aptitude for political life and leadership. He afterwards became one of the most prominent politicians in Canada. Elected by his native county to the Local and Dominion Parliaments, he soon took a leading place as a public speaker and debater. That James McDonald's honor and ability was recognized by his contemporaries is evidenced by the numerous responsible positions which he held. He was Financial Secretary for Nova Scotia, Railway Commissioner in Nova Scotia, Imperial Commissioner in a crown difficulty in Jamaica and member of several national trade commissions.

In 1878 he became Minister of Justice in the Sir John A.

Macdonald's Government, and three years afterwards was appointed Chief Justice of the Supreme Court of Nova Scotia. His place in Parliament was taken by John McDougald, C.M.G., who was re-elected in 1882, 1886, 1890 and 1896, retiring in that year to accept the position of Commissioner of Customs for Canada, which he still holds. Robert Doull was the colleague of Hon. James McDonald from 1872 to 1874 and again from 1878 to 1882. In 1882, Charles H. Tupper, now Sir Charles H. Tupper of Victoria, B. C., came in and continued to represent the County until 1904.

Edward M. Macdonald, first appealed to the Electors in 1894 at the Provincial election but was unsuccessful. In 1896 he was a candidate for the Dominion Parliament with the same result. In 1897 he won the election to the House of Assembly, and again in 1900. He resigned to stand for the Dominion House but was again defeated by Adam C. Bell. He was, however, returned to the Legislature unopposed. In 1894, Charles E. Tanner was elected to the Legislature with Wm. Cameron and Alex. Grant. In 1897 he was defeated, but elected in 1901 and 1906. He resigned in 1908 to run for the Federal Seat against E. M. McDonald and was defeated. He sought re-election to the Assembly, but was defeated by R. H. McKay. He was re-elected in 1911. In the general election of 1896, Adam C. Bell was nominated in place of John McDougald and secured election as he did again in 1900. In 1904 Edward M. Macdonald was elected to a seat in the Dominion which he has since held, being re-elected in 1908 and 1911, having now represented the County continuously in Legislature and Parliament for eighteen years.

The first Pictonian in the Legislative Council, was the Hon. James Fraser, Drummond, of New Glasgow, who was was appointed in 1867. Mr. Fraser was a man of much force and character and was a leader in Church and State.

He died in 1884, at the advanced age of 82. The next was the Hon. John D. McLeod in 1887. He served as Liberal Leader in the Council. Another Pictonian, a native of Durham, Hon. W. D. R. Cameron of Sherbrooke, became a member of the Council in 1892. In 1864 he settled in Sherbrooke and held office of Registrar of Deeds, from 1869-1902. He died at Halifax April 7, 1914, aged 77 years.

The County of Pictou was represented in the Senate by the Hon. John Holmes, 1867 to 1876. The Hon. R. P. Grant, a native of Scotland, was appointed in 1887. The first Pictonian called to the Senate was, Thomas McKay, of Truro in 1881. Mr. McKay was born at Hopewell, Pictou Co., and was long engaged in mercantile pursuits in Truro, N. S. For seven years he represented the County of Colchester before he was called to the Senate. The next was Clarence Primrose of Pictou, followed by James W. Carmichael of New Glasgow, 1898; James D. McGregor in 1903 and Adam C. Bell, 1911, both of New Glasgow. Thomas Fraser, Rogers Hill, represented California in the Senate for several years. Mr. Primrose, was the son of late James Primrose, a native of Scotland. He was born at Pictou, Oct. 5, 1830. Educated at Pictou Academy and the Univ., of Edinburgh. Became the head of the firm Primrose Bros., Commission Merchants, Lumber and Shipping Agents.

Adam Carr Bell was born in Pictou on November 11, 1847, and was the son of Basil Bell and Mary Carr. The progenitors of the Bells were natives of Scotland, and the Carrs were from England. Basil Bell was a distinguished man of letters and taught in the Pictou Academy when Senator Bell was born, while on his mother's side, Adam Carr was the first man to mine coal for commercial purposes at the Albion Mines.

Mr. Bell received his education in the New Glasgow Schools, at Mount Allison University and at the Glasgow University, Scotland. Always a studious man of affairs and a strong, logical, graceful speaker with a fine presence and commanding appearance he was elected by the Conservative party for the local house in 1878. In 1886 he was elected for Pictou County at the head of the poll of six candidates, but in 1887 resigned his seat to contest the County as an independent Conservative for the House of Commons, but was defeated   For the next nine years he remained out of active politics, but was always interested in the public welfare, and was seen on the platform on several historic occasions.   He was the first Mayor of New Glasgow in 1876   In 1911 he was called to the Senate by the Borden Government.   His death following soon after his appointment was universally regretted.

Pictou has not only had men to represent her worthily on the floors of Parliament, but has sent out many of her sons to win political honors in other fields.   Among the latter may be mentioned Robert Marshall of St. John, New Brunswick.   In 1874 he was a candidate for the City of St. John, N. B., in the Provincial elections, but was defeated.   In 1876 he was returned for the Constituency and was elected for a second term.   He was a member of the Government for some years until his retirement from politics, in 1882.   He was born in Pictou County, April 27, 1832.   His grandfather, was Robert,—commonly called, "Deacon Marshall," who came from Dumfries, Scotland, to Pictou, in 1775, with the South of Scotland people, and settled at the Middle River, where he built the first barn in the county, and where the Presbytery of Pictou held its first meeting.

E. M. Macdonald, senior, son of the late George Macdonald, of West River, and a younger brother of the late A. C. McDonald, was elected the first Dominion member, in 1867, for the County of Lunenburg.   He was born at West River, in 1825, and was one of Joseph Howe's chief lieutenants.   He was made Collector of Customs for Halifax, in 1870 and died in 1874.   He was a brilliant writer and speaker. Dr. Alexander Cameron of Glengarry was for many years a representative for the County of Huntington, in the Local Legislature for Quebec.

Hon. Angus McGillivray, a native of Bailey's Brook, was first returned to Local Legislature for Antigonish in 1878, as a Liberal; and continued a member thereof, with but little interruption until his elevation to the Bench in 1902. He was Speaker of the Nova Scotia Assembly from 1883 to 1886, and a member of the Fielding and Murray Governments.

William A. Patterson of town of Pictou, represented the county of Colchester in the Local House from 1874 to 1886, and again in the Dominion House from 1891 to 1896. Guysboro County had a worthy representative in Halifax in James A. Fraser of McLellan's Brook from 1882 to 1890. He is now Editor of the Eastern Chronicle and Mayor of New Glasgow. D. C. Fraser, afterwards Hon. D. C. Fraser, represented the county of Guysboro for many years. From 1888 to 1891, he was leader of the Government in the Council, when he was elected to the Dominion Parliament from Guysboro. He continued to represent the County until 1904 when he became Judge of the Supreme Court of Nova Scotia and in 1906 was appointed Lieutenant Governor for the Province, which office he held until his death in 1910. He was one of the best known and most popular men in the public life of Canada.

In Ontario, Dr. Peter Macdonald, a native of Toney River, represented Center Huron from 1896 to 1904 in the Federal Parliament and was Deputy Speaker in the House of Commons from 1900 to 1904. A. E. Fraser of McLellan's Brook, represented the County of Cumberland in the House of Assembly from 1894 to 1902. The same county was also represented from 1901 to 1906 by Daniel McLeod, who was born near Hopewell.

In 1906 the people of King's County chose a man of

Pictou, Chas. A. Campbell, for their spokesman at Halifax. In 1911 the County of Cape Breton selected another, John C. Douglas, a Stellarton boy, to send to the Halifax Assembly, after having had as their Dominion Representative from 1908 to 1911, James W. Maddin of Westville.

In British Columbia, Pictou men have also come to the front. The records of that Province show that Robert Grant of Pictou was elected for Comox County in 1903 and 1907; Neil F. MacKay, a son of the late Alexander MacKay, M.P.P., of Pictou, represents Kaslo; and another, Wm. R. McLean, son of the late D. K. McLean of Pictou, represents Nelson. H. M. Tweedie, was born at Stellarton, son of the Rev. Mr. Tweedie, pastor of the Methodist Church. He represents Calgary Center in the Legislative Assembly of Alberta.

In Newfoundland, the memory of Hon. A. M. MacKay, a son of Pictou, who achieved distinction in telegraph work is still revered. His political career in Newfoundland, was in many respects unique. For nineteen years he was a member of the House of Assembly, and enjoyed the distinction of never having been defeated. For many years he was a leading member of the Legislative Council.

A Pictou man who has won distinction in distant Australia, is Hon. Simon Fraser, son of William Fraser, of Lorne, where he was born in 1834. He went to Australia as a young man and engaged in bridge and road construction. He became active in public affairs and was elected to the Assembly in 1874, representing the County of Rodney, Victoria, for nine years. In 1886 he became a member of the Council and 1901 he was elected to the Senate. Hon. Senator Fraser, has taken a deep interest in all the public and religious interests of the Colony. He resides at Melbourne, Victoria. Another Mr. Fraser, from Lorne, was Commissioner of Public Works in San Francisco, Cal., for some time. He was a brother of late John Fraser, postmaster, Stellarton.

PICTOU IN POLITICS

Pictou has every reason to be proud of the part her sons have played in the political life of the country. Summing up the list we find that she has given to the service of the State—two governors of Nova Scotia, a Minister of Justice for Canada, seven Senators, a Chief Justice of the Province, a Supreme Court Judge, Three County Court Judges, two Premiers of the Province, and four Legislative Councillors. The County has had a representative in every Provincial Ministry since 1875.

CHAPTER XI

PICTOU IN THE BUSINESS WORLD

THE influence of Pictou County in the development of the industrial and commercial life of Canada has been highly important. Her enterprising sons have held positions of responsibility throughout the length and breadth of the land; and her mariners have trod the quarter deck on every sea. Only a few facts and names however can be presented in this chapter.

Pictou County is fifty miles long and about twenty miles wide, and contains 719,000 acres. It has one of the finest harbors on the northern shore of the Province with three fine streams,—East, West and Middle rivers, flowing into it. Along the shore the land is low and level, but in the interior it is hilly and undulating with fine natural scenery. From Fraser's Mountain, Green Hill and Mt. Thom are to be seen ever-varying and most beautiful views of hill and dale, sea and land, field and forest.

When the first settlers arrived in Pictou the whole of the county was covered with timber of the finest quality. White pine was particularly plentiful and common, but oak, fir, maple and all kinds of wood were found of large size and in great abundance, and afforded a valuable source of income to the inhabitants; and the lumbering industry was then, as it has been of later years, extensive and prosperous. In 1774 the first cargo of square timber was shipped to Britain. In 1803, some 50 vessels were loaded in Pictou Town. The cutting, hewing, hauling, rafting and shipping of ton timber, became for some years the chief business of many of the people of Pictou. As the timber was cut and removed men turned their attention more and more to farming.

PICTONIANS AT HOME AND ABROAD

Pictou County has always been considered one of the best agricultural counties in the Province. With the exception of a few tracts of land here and there, the whole county is fit for cultivation. The first Agricultural Society in the Province was formed at West River, Jan. 1, 1817, with the Rev. Duncan Ross as President, Daniel Fraser, Treasurer, and John Bonnyman Secretary. They imported seed grain, agricultural implements and Ayrshire cattle. In 1818 they held a ploughing match on Mr. Mortimer's farm, near Pictou. Prizes were offered for the best acre of wheat, and for the man who could stump and plough the greatest quantity of new land. A similar society was organized on the East River in 1820.

Coal was first discovered in Pictou County in 1798. Word was sent to England that there was coal in abundance in Pictou; that it was found on the margin of the East River; that it was accessible to ships of light tonnage, and that the coal was of the best bituminous quality. A wealthy firm purchased the ground. This was the beginning of Pictou's coal industry. In 1827 the General Mining Association purchased the property, immediately commenced active development, and, before the end of the year, were producing coal on an extensive scale, using a steam engine for hoisting. Stellarton is the largest coal producing center in the County, and is a thriving business town.

The Acadia Coal Company of Stellarton is the direct successor of one of the oldest mining corporations of the County. That it survives until today, and possesses as it does one of the most modern and the most complete coal-handling equipments in the country, speaks volumes for the great value of the coal fields of Pictou. It is said that the thickest coal seam in the world is found here—38 feet in depth. This company owns the Acadia Coal Mine at Westville and the Vale Mine at Thorburn.

Fifty years ago a wilderness of scrubby birch and

hemlock covered the site on which the town of Westville now stands, with a population of over 5000. In the year 1854 prospectors began searching for coal, and discovered the outcrop of a seam on the north side of the town where the land slopes toward the Middle River. The Black Diamond Company was the first to commence operations, and was soon followed by the Acadia, and in 1868 by the Drummond. A railway was completed to Granton and later to Abercrombie, where there are wharves and all conveniences necessary for shipping coal. The works of the Vale Colliery at Thorburn were started in 1872. Thorburn is prettily situated and has a population of over 1200. A railroad six miles long leading from the colliery to New Glasgow is in operation. The total coal production in Pictou County for 1913 was 700,000 tons.

In looking at the thousands of miles of railways in Canada it may be interesting to note that the first steam engine erected in Nova Scotia was at the Albion Mines, Dec. 7, 1827, and that the first railway built in Canada, and one of the earliest on the continent, was by the General Mining Association from its works at Albion Mines, six miles, to the old Loading Ground near Abercrombie. It was begun in 1836 and opened in 1839. The rolling stock came out from England, in a sailing vessel. In this vessel there were the several parts of three engines, the names of which were the Samson, the Hercules and the Hybernia. The Samson was named for Scotland; the Hercules for England; and the Hybernia for Ireland. The Samson was the first one set up and the one that made the first trip.

In 1830 the first steamboat was seen in the Harbor of Pictou. The "Richard Smith" was put in operation by the same company. She was commanded by Capt. McKenzie. The first steamer to cross the Atlantic wholly by her own steam power was coaled in and sailed from Pictou Harbor in 1833.

PICTONIANS AT HOME AND ABROAD

The first attempt to smelt iron in Pictou County was made by the General Mining Association in 1828, the year after the Company had commenced operations in this field. Just previously, iron ore had been discovered near McLennan's Brook, a short distance from the company's colliery. The ore was sent to England for analysis and, a favorable report having been made by the company's chemists, a deeper interest was aroused in the latent possibilities of the country. In 1829 an attempt was made to manufacture pig iron. For this purpose a blast furnace was erected at Albion Mines, the first in Canada. Iron was smelted to the extent of about 50 tons. The ruins of this furnace were standing until 1855.

In 1872 the Hope Iron Works, afterwards the Nova Scotia Forge Company commenced operations in New Glasgow with a capital of $4000 with a view to manufacturing railway and marine forgings. Six years later, the works were removed to a larger site, upon the banks of the East River, in the present town of Trenton. As the enterprise prospered, the principal shareholders of the company decided to engage in the manufacture of steel, at the same time organizing for this purpose a new company called the Nova Scotia Steel Company with a capital of $160,000. The first steel ingots were made here in July, 1883, being the first produced in Canada on a commercial basis.

One of the chief difficulties encountered by the Company was that of obtaining suitable ore. In 1894, the well known Wabana iron ore deposits of Bell Island, Nfd., was acquired. This deposit now forms the chief source of ore supply for the furnaces of the Province. In 1900, after purchasing the coal and other properties of the General Mining Association in Cape Breton, the Nova Scotia Steel Company was reorganized, and assumed the present name of the Nova Scotia Steel and Coal Company. New Glasgow is the seat of the manufacturing departments,

TOWN OF PICTOU

PICTOU IN THE BUSINESS WORLD

finishing mills, forges and machine shops. The company's axle-shops are world famous. It is claimed that this branch of the New Glasgow plant has produced a greater number of axles per day than any other works in the Empire. There are said to be none of the same capacity on the continent of Europe. Fish-plates, tie-plates, track-spikes, nuts and bolts of the various standard sizes are produced.

Another important new enterprise is the Eastern Car Company for the manufacture of railway cars. It was formed in 1912, and is virtually a creation of the Steel Company. A splendid site has been secured for it on the east bank of the East River, adjoining the Nova Scotia Steel Company. The shops and plant when complete will be capable of an output of 30 cars per day, and about 9000 cars per working year.

In a survey of the vast consolidated interests of the Nova Scotia Steel Company and the Eastern Car Company, it is difficult to realize that if, 30 years ago, one had visited the upper corner of the Graham Shipyard, in the town of New Glasgow, one would have found there the parent of it all—a small forge, whose main product was the iron-knees which were used for the wooden ships then being built there. Let it be noted that this company owes its existence largely to two sons of the soil, Graham Fraser, and G. Forrest McKay of New Glasgow. They now, naturally, possess a fair share of this world's goods, but their greatest reward for perseverance and toil in comparative obscurity in early days, must be the gratification of seeing, in less than four decades, their little forge shop expand into what is one of the largest steel industries in Canada. These men, along with Thomas Cantley, the present capable General Manager, have done a great work for Pictou County and for all Canada.

The Town of Pictou was long the second in importance in the Province, and it still enjoys a peculiar character and charm of its own. It has good reason to be proud of its history and institutions, its men and its ships. The corner stone of the first house in Pictou was not laid until 1789, but once it started, the growth of the village into a town, was rapid. The first leading business man in the town was Edw. Mortimer, an Englishman who came to this country while yet a young man, without means, went into the timber and fish business, first representing a Halifax firm in Pictou and then for himself. He first located himself a little above Mortimer's Point, near Squire Patterson whose daughter he married. Here he put up a small building, intended both for a house and a store. Afterwards he removed to the Point near the Stone House, where he had his home and where he built two large wharves out to deep water. Here he amassed a small fortune. He died suddenly, in 1819, at the age of 52, and his estate dwindled to practically nothing. He built Norway House, one of the historic and interesting places in the town.

Beckels Wilson in "Nova Scotia" speaks of Norway House as the best house in Pictou, perhaps the best built private one in Nova Scotia, with its walls a foot and a half thick, fine fat timbers, plenty of honest freestone, and a great dry cellar and as sturdy today as the day he built it.

Other business men of the early days of Pictou were John Dawson, Thomas Davidson, George Smith, William Mortimer, John Patterson, Abram Patterson, Henry Hatton and James Dawson who was the first bookseller in the Province outside of Halifax. William Matheson, Rogers Hill, began on a small scale and afterwards moved to West River, where he did a large country trade. Robert McKay began business in River John soon after Ed. Mortimer's death, with whom he had been a clerk.

River John was at one time a prominent center for shipbuilding and business enterprise. The leading men were the McKenzies, the McLennans, the Henrys, and the Kitchins.

PICTOU IN THE BUSINESS WORLD

Business being now well established, a number of merchants combined to build a vessel to be a regular trader between Pictou and the Old Country. She was called the Enterprise and was built by Thos. Lowden, and launched in 1820. Captain Lowden may be considered the father of the ship building art in Pictou. He was a native of the South of Scotland and settled in Pictou town about 1788. In 1798 he launched the ship Harriet, which was, at that time, considered the largest and finest ship built in the Province. In 1825 came the terrible financial crisis in the mother country which for a time killed the shipping and timber business in Pictou. The day on which the intelligence came was long known as "Black Monday."

Of what may be called the second generation of Pictou's business men, the late James Primrose, was one of the most prominent. He was the father of the late Hon. Clarence Primrose, Senator, and of the late Howard Primrose, almost equally prominent in their generation. James Primrose, senior, was a son of the Scottish manse, and came to Nova Scotia in his youth without any pecuniary endowment. By means of untiring industry and scrupulous uprightness, characteristics which he has transmitted to all his descendants, he made his way rapidly to the front in business and finance. He constructed at the east end of the Town, the handsome dwelling familiarly known as "The Cottage," now occupied by his grandson James and his two sisters, Miss Primrose and Miss Rachael.

Associated for a time in business with Mr. Primrose was the late A. P. Ross, barrister, who early withdrew from the Bar to devote himself to commercial and industrial enterprises.

More or less contemporary with these were such other successful business men as the late James Purves, William Gordon, William H. Davies, Roderick McKenzie, John Crearer, J. D. B. Fraser, John Yorston, James Kitchin,

PICTONIANS AT HOME AND ABROAD

David McCulloch, John T. Ives, William Ives, James Ives, James Hislop, A. J. Patterson, Robert Doull, Daniel Hockin, Richard Tanner, James P. McLennan, David Fullerton, all of whom made their mark in business, and most of whom have left descendants prominent in the social and public life of the Province.

The history of New Glasgow dates back to about the year 1809. At that time there were not more than a dozen houses in the place. Today, it is a large industrial and business centre with a population of over 7000. The men who founded New Glasgow were James Carmichael, John McKay, Hon. James Fraser, James McGregor, Roderick McGregor, Alexander Fraser, John McKenzie, George McKenzie, Thomas Graham and John Cameron. New Glasgow was fortunate in its founders, for they were men possessing fine business ability and great force of character. They were not only interested in the commercial growth and progress of the town but in its moral and religious life. Most of the men were officers in the church; some of them took a deep interest in state matters; many were zealous advocates of temperance, and all of them staunch upholders of law and justice. The credit of selecting New Glasgow as a business centre for East Pictou belongs to James Carmichael who opened a store there about the year 1810.

In the early days of New Glasgow shipbuilding was the chief and only industry in the place. From 1840 to 1870 saw its palmiest days. Vessels of all sizes were built, numbers of which made successful voyages to all parts of the world, commanded by captains born and trained in the county. Prominent and foremost among the shipbuilders of New Glasgow was George McKenzie, who not only built the largest vessels of the day, but commanded several of them. He made New Glasgow noted as one of the shipbuilding centers of Nova Scotia, and probably did more than anyone else to make the town.

PICTOU IN THE BUSINESS WORLD

The opening of the Albion Mines Railway in 1839 gave a great impetus to the business life of New Glasgow. Consequently a large number of merchants started business there from that time to 1850, among whom were Alexander Douglas, John F. McDonald, James Fraser, Downie, William Fraser, Basil Bell, Thomas R. Fraser, Angus Chisholm, Thomas Fraser, George W. Underwood and John Cameron. Associated with these as prominent citizens were William Lippincott, Robert McGregor, John Miller, William Chisholm, David Marshall, Kenneth Forbes, and George McKay who exerted a large influence in the development of the town at a later period.

Among the early business men of Stellarton were James Mitchell, James Wentworth, Donald Gray, Alexander Grant and James Keith. In Merigomish, R. S. Copeland was for many years a leading shipbuilder. Later on David Patterson built ships in Merigomish Harbor. John Logan, tanner, the founder of the present community of Lyon's Brook, was a prominent business man in his day.

Many natives of the county have made a place for themselves outside of Pictou in the business and industrial world. Beginning with Newfoundland, the late Hon. A. M. Mackay was Manager of the Anglo-American Telegraph Company. He was born near Pictou in 1834 and died in 1905. From early life he was distinguished for his wonderful memory and had a positive genius for figures and mathematics. He began life first as a teacher, next as a telegrapher and was one of the first to read a message by sound. For nearly half a century he retained his position, putting the company on a successful basis and serving it with great fidelity. Like Cyrus Field he had a firm belief in the ultimate success of the laying of the Atlantic Cable, and he had a large share in bringing it to a successful completion. Judge Prowse of Newfoundland says no man can rob Mackay's memory of this undying honor.

PICTONIANS AT HOME AND ABROAD

Perhaps the oldest representatives Pictou has in Montreal and those who have made the greatest material success are: Mr. David H. Fraser and his brother, Wm. H. Fraser The Fraser brothers are sons of Hugh J. Fraser, whose home was on the West River near Durham. They are now voted among Montreal's millionaires.

Another successful business man is Archibald Ross of the firm of Ross & Greig, second son of the late David Ross of Saltsprings. Mr. Ross is a Mechanical Engineer and the firm acts as manufacturers' agents.

Mr. A. P. Willis, another Pictonian has made for himself a reputation and at the same time a fortune by putting musical instruments into thousands of Canadian homes. Mr. Willis was born near Millsville in 1845. In 1873 he migrated to Montreal where he engaged in the sewing machine business, and selling of pianos and organs. After 25 years of selling, Mr. Willis decided to manufacture; and the company's factory at Montreal turns out about 4000 pianos every year.

Mr. Alpine McLean, born near New Glasgow, was for many years a prominent business man in Boston engaged in the wholesale flour and feed business. He was a leader in the moral and religious work of the city. He died in 1913.

Hugh R. McGregor was born at Brookville, Pictou County 1859. When he was 12 years of age he moved to Providence, R. I. In 1877 he went to Brown and Sharpe to learn the machinist trade. In the third year of his apprenticeship he was appointed Assistant foreman of the building of Milling Machines, and in 1898 to the position of Mechanical Superintendent. The Brown & Sharpe Company employ over 5000 men and at the present time are manufacturing 39 different Milling machines. The names of many other Pictonians of influence and business enterprise might be added if the writer knew of their location and business.

TOWN OF NEW GLASGOW

PICTOU IN THE BUSINESS WORLD

The county has made an enviable record in the past; it is still to do great things in the future. Pictou of today and Pictou of yesterday! What a contrast: The change seems almost miraculous, from the forest primeval to the present verdancy of its hills and valleys, with their well-tilled fields. Upon every hand, now, are comfortable homes, pretty villages, towns laid out with care, handsome churches, modern school houses, fine academic buildings, intersecting railways, vast coal and iron industries, and a population of thirty-six thousand enterprising, progressive and intelligent people.

Now my task is done. It has been an arduous duty, yet a pleasant one. It has been an honor and a privilege to pay a tribute to these noble men and women who did so much for God and native land.

These resolute men and women, who in strict morality and with high ideals laid the foundations of the social fabric enjoyed by us today, were spiritual seers and heroes. They won for us our fame, our freedom and our fortune. Too many of us have never fully acquainted ourselves with their heroism and their achievements.

If every Pictonian were as well acquainted with the history of his native county as he should be, and as proud of it as he might well be, he would have a higher appreciation of the splendid moral and material heritage his forefathers left him, and would in common loyalty seek to honor their memory and emulate their virtues.

INDEX

Abercrombie 185,219
Academy, Pictou 135
Acadia Coal Company 218
Advocate, Pictou 198
Albion Mines . . . 56,219,220,226
America's Oldest Paper 191
Archibald, S. G. W. 5,203
Arrival of the Hector 7
Arrival of the Hope 1,3
Australia 180,214

Bailey's Brook 90
Barney's River 82
  History of Churches . . . 52,83
  Ministers born in 87
Baptist Church 56
Barristers 124-129
Bayne, H. A. 141,160
Bayne, Rev. James . . . 41,61,159
Bench and the Bar 123
Bell, Hon. A. C. 207,211
Bible Society 45
Big Election 204
Blackadar, Henry 205
Blaikie, Rev. A. 19,92
Blaikie, Chas. 19
Blair, Rev. D. B. 52,81,83
Blanchard, Hiram 125,207
Blanchard, Jotham . . 124,139,205
Blue Mountain
  History of Churches 81
  Ministers born in 85
Bridgeville 70,72
Burns Family 68-70

Cameron, Alexander 7,9,10
Cameron, Rev. Duncan 86
Cameron, Rev. John 78
Cameron, W. D. R. 10,211
Cameron, William 10,208
Campbell, Don. F. 162
Campbell, Rev. John 100
Cantley, Thomas 221
Cape John 99
Carmichael, James 224
Carmichael, Hon. J. W. 209
Cariboo 5,101,188
Census, first 39,58
Churchville 22,71
Church of England 55
Clark, William 19
Coal Discovered 218

Coal Production 219
Cock, Rev. Daniel 35,87
Cock, Rev. D. M. 187
College Presidents 149-159
Colonial Patriot 192,205
Colonial Standard 197
Cobequid Road 3
Council of Twelve 138
County of Pictou
  Population 2,7,39,58
  Size 217
Creighton, James E. 163
Cumming, Rev. Robert 79
Cumming, Rev. Thomas 77

Dalhousie College 147,199
Dawson, Sir William . 150-154,178,194
Dawson, Geo. M. 163
Dawson, W. B. 164
Dawson, James 194,222
Dawson, John 16,222
Dawson, John A. 209
Davidson, James 34
Descendants of John Grant . . . 31
Denominations 58
Dentists 122
Dickson, Thomas 124,205
Disruption of 1843 50
Dobson, Rev. J. R 63
Donnelly, Dr. Jas. 106
Doull, Robt. 209,210
Durham 21,22,45,92
"Dumfries Settlers" 14

Earltown 99
East River
  First Settlers 22
  History of Churches 70
  Ministers born in 71
East River St. Mary's
  History of Churches 83
  Ministers born in 86
Eastern Chronicle 195
Eastern Car Works 221
Education 149
Educationists, Pictou 149
Elders 37,61,62,71,75
Elliott, Rev. Chas. 55
Enterprise, The 197

Falconer, Rev. A. 11,61,78
Falconer, Prin. R. A. 11

PICTONIANS AT HOME AND ABROAD

Families in the Hector	8
Families in the Hope	3
Field, Cyrus	225
Ferrona	75
First	
Agricultural Society	218
Bible Society	45
Churches	38
Election	203
Missionary	177
Native Ministers	43
Premier	207
Printing Press	191
Presbytery	40
Railway	219
Sabbath School	34,35
Sacrament	39
Session	37
Steamboat	219
Theological School	42
Temperance Society	46
Fraser, Alexander	10
Fraser, Rev. A. L.	
Fraser, Rev. D. A.	47,48,81
Fraser, Hon. D. C.	127,213
Fraser, David H.	226
Fraser, Rev. D. S.	92
Fraser, Rev. H. W.	68
Fraser, Graham	221
Fraser, Hon. Jas.	210
Fraser, James A.	23,213
Fraser, J. D. B.	9,223
Fraser, Hon. J. O.	48
Fraser, Hon. Simon	214
Fraser, Thos. Senator	9
Fraser, Rev. William	83
Fraser, Dr. William	110
Fraser, William A.	165
Fraser, Wm. R.	166
Fitzpatrick, M. H.	208
Free Church	50,51
Free Church College	53
French River	87,89
Fogo, Hon. Jas	124,130
Forbes, Rev. J. F.	85
Forbes, Hon. J. G.	127
Foreign Missions	178
Foreign Missionaries	178-190
Forrest, Rev. John	158,199
Gairloch	49,79
Geddie, Rev. John	177-180
Geddie, Mrs. John	180
General Mining Association	218-220
Gordon, Rev. D. M.	157
Goodwill, Rev. John	183
Grant, Alexander, M. P. P.	210
Grant, Rev. Chas. M.	186
Grant, Rev. Geo. M.	154,156
Grant, Rev. Edward	93
Grant, Finlay	31
Grant, Rev. H. R.	67,68
Grant, James	24
Grant, Rev. K. J.	184
Grant, Rev. R. J.	73
Grant, Hon. R. P	211
Grant, Rev Wm.	73
Grant, Prof. W. R.	25,110
Granton	81,219
Green Hill	
History of Churches	91
Ministers born in	92
Gunn, Rev. S. C.	86
Hardwood Hill	100
Halifax Gazette	191
Harris, Dr. John	3,6,105
Harris, Matthew	2,3
Hector People	5,7,8
Herdman, Rev. A.	48,63
Holmes, Hon. John	23,205,206,211
Holmes, Hon. S. H.	23,128,207
Hope People	1,2,3
Hopewell	
History of Churches	74
Ministers born in	75
Howe, Hon. Joseph	139,205
Iron Industry	220
Johnson, Rev. D. W.	103
Journalists	193-200
Kennedy, William	2,3,6
Kirk Church	47,50,139
Law, Bonar	17
Lawson, Alexander	193
Lane, Franklin K.	70
Legal Profession, first	123
Lindsay, Dr. A. W. H.	112
Lippincott, Dr. Henry	112
Lippincott, Dr. J. A.	112
List of Lawyers	129
List of Physicians	106
List of Educationists	162
Little Harbor	
History of Churches	88
Ministers born in	89

INDEX

Log Churches 38
Logan, Daniel 196
Logan, John D. 166
Logan, John 225
Lorne Ministers 76
Lowden, Thomas 223
Lumber Industry 24,217
Lyon's Brook 34
Lyon, Rev. J. 2,34

Macdonald, C. D. 128
Macdonald, E. M. 9,212
Macdonald, E. M., M. P. . 129,208,210
Macdonald, Jas. A., Toronto . . 27
Macdonald, Rev. John A. . . . 72
Macdonald, Rev. P. M. . . . 134,200
Macdonald, Dr. Peter . . . 115,213
Macdonald, Rev. W. B. 89
MacGlashen, Rev. J. A. 89
MacGregor, R. M. 208
Mackenzie, A. Stanley . . . 159
Mackenzie, Rev. C. E. 64
Mackenzie, William 7,8,10
MacKay, A. H. 142,168
MacKay, Hon. A. M. 214,225
MacKay, Ebenezer 169
MacKay, H. M. 169
MacKay, Ira W. 169
MacKay, R. H. 208
Mackinnon, Rev. C. 53,159
Mackinnon, Rev. John . . . 75
Maclean, Rev. A. 59,75,79
Maclean, Dr. Duncan . . . 118
Maclean, Rev. James . . . 53,71
Maclellan, Anthony 18
Maclellan, W. E. 19,199
Maclellan, Robt. . . . 19,142,144,170
Macleod, Prof. J. W 171
MacNaughton, Rev. S. 79
Macrae, Rev. Donald . . . 71,74,158
Macrae, Rev. John 49,71
Macrae, Rev. W. L. 185
McDonald, A. C. 124,206
McDonald, Rev. F. R. . . . 74
McDonald, Hon. James 26,125,206,209
McCabe, James 1,3
McConnell, George 8
McConnell, Robt. 8,196
McCulloch, Rev. Thomas
  16,40,43,136,140,149,204
McCulloch, Prof. Thos. . . . 167
McCulloch, Rev. Wm. . . . 62
McCunn, Rev. Robt. 102
McDougall, John 210

McGillivray, Rev. Alexander . . 52
McGillivray, Rev. Angus . . . 43
McGillivray, Hon. A. . . . 128,213
McGregor, Hugh R. 226
McGregor, Rev. James 36,40,46,137,149
McGregor, Hon. J. D. . . . 9.208
McGregor, Prof. J. G. . . . 161
McGregor, Rev. P. G. . . . 67
McGregor, Rev. S. 71
McInnes, Hector 131,143
McIntosh, Douglas 168
McKay, Rev. Alex. 101
McKay, Donald, Elder . . . 25
McKay, G. Forrest 221
McKay, Rev. H. B. 101
McKay, Rev. J. McG. . . . 53,86
McKay, Roderick 9
McKay, Hon. Thos. 211
McKay, William 8
McKay, Rev. W. R. 186
McKenzie, Rev. Alex 78
McKenzie, Capt. Geo. . . 206,224
McKenzie, Dr. G. I. 118
McKenzie, J. J. 142,159
McKenzie, Rev. J. W. . . . 182
McKenzie, Rev. K. J. . . . 48,194
McKinlay, Rev. John . . . 41,137
McLean, Alpine 226
McLean, Rev. John 20,43
McLean, John S. 20
McLeod, Rev. Hugh 94
McLeod, Hon. J. D. . . . 128,211
McLeod, Rev. J. M. 18,92
McLennan's Brook 47,220
McLennan's Mountain
  History of Churches 81
  Ministers born in 83
McMillan, Rev. John 100
McMillan, Rev. Wm. 71
McNutt, Col. 3,6
McPhie, John 29
McPhie, Peter 31
Marshall, Robt., Deacon . . 17,37,212
Marshall, Robt. 212
Matheson, David 12,124
Matheson, Rev. J. W. . . . 181
Matheson, Mrs. J. W. . . . 181
Matheson, William . . 12,157,222
Medical Profession 105
Merigomish
  History of Churches 87
  Ministers born in 88
Methodist Church 56-67

230

PICTONIANS AT HOME AND ABROAD

Middle River	17
History of Churches	79
Ministers born in	80
Miller, Rev. E. D.	95
Missionaries, Women	188-190
Mitchell, Rev. John	41
Mortimer, Edward	203,222
Morton, Rev. John	183-184
Morton, Dr. J. S.	113
Munro, George	144,198
Munro, Norman L.	199
Murdoch, Rev. J. L.	43,44
Murray, Daniel A.	172
Murray, Dr. George	114,207
Murray, Hon. G. H.	83
Murray, Prof. Howard	172
Murray, Rev. Isaac	95
Murray, Rev. John	94
Murray, Rev. James	94
Murray, Rev. Jas. D.	181
Murray, Rev R. C.	186
Murray, Walter	8
News, Pictou	197
New Glasgow	
Founders of	224
History of Churches	65,67
Ministers born in	67-68
Shipbuilding	224
Business men	224,225
Nicoll, Sir W. R.	155
Norway House	222
Nova Scotia Steel Works	220-221
Observer, Pictou	194
Officials of 1775	6
Oldest Grave in County	18
Oldest Newspaper	191
Olding, Nicholas P.	123
Patrick, Rev. Wm.	42
Patterson, Rev. George	173,195,198
Patterson, Hon. Geo. G.	11,129,208
Patterson, John	7,11
Patterson, Robert	1,2,3
Patterson, Rev. R. S.	44,62
New Hebrides	177,179
Philadelphia Land Company	1,2
Physicians and Surgeons	105-106
Pictonians in the Pulpit	61
Pictonians in Foreign Fields	177
Pictonians in Medical Profession	105
Pictou Academy	135-147
Pictou Educationists	149
Pictou Press	191
Pictou in Politics	203
Pictou Town	
First settlers	1-3,7-8
History of Churches	61
Ministers born in	62-64
Shipbuilding	223
Business men	222,223
Pioneers of Pictou	1-31
Plainfield	96,168
Pollock, Rev. Allan	59,66
Pottinger, David	174
Presbyterianism	33,177
Presbyterian Church	177,178
Presbyterian College, Halifax	54
Presbytery, first	40
Press and Printers, Pictou	191
Primrose, Dr. Alex.	120
Primrose, Hon. C.	211,223
Primrose, Howard	223
Primrose, James	223
Politics	203
Railway, First	219
Religious History of County	33-60
Responsible Government	192,205
Richards, Joseph	20
River John	41,102
History of Churches	102
Ministers born in	103
Businessmen	222
Riverton	78
Robertson, Rev. H. A.	182
Robinson, C. B.	145,174
Roddick, Rev. Geo.	90,101
Rogers, Rev. A.	2,66,96
Rogers, John	1,2
Rogers Hill	49,94-95
Roman Catholic Church	54,90
Rosebery Lord	13
Ross, Rev. Alexander	62
Ross, A. P.	223
Ross, Archibald	226
Ross, Rev. Duncan	40,46,149,218
Ross, Rev. E.	91
Ross, Rev. James	47,52,156-157,195
Ross, Rev. G. M.	187
Ross, Rev. R. D.	73
Ross, Donald	30
Roy, Rev. David	46,65
Sabbath School, first	34-35
Saltsprings	49,59
History of Churches	97
Ministers born in	98

INDEX

Scotsburn	49,59
History of Churches	94
Ministers born in	94
Scotch Hill	100
Scottish Characteristics	33,149,203
Scott, Rev. E.	197
Shipbuilding	223,224
Sinclair, Rev. A. McL.	70,85
Six Mile Brook	98
Smith, George	205
Smith, William	19
Smith, Rev. W. H.	88
Socrates	157
South of Scotland People	14
Springville	23-25
History of Churches	70
Ministers born in	71
Stearns, Rev. D. M.	63
Stellarton	
History of Churches	76
Ministers born in	77
Coal industry	218
Business men	225
Stevenson, R. L.	105
Stewart, David	19
Stewart, Rev. John	50,66
Story of Four Students	159
Stiles, John	193,194
St. Johns, Nfd.	48,214,225
St. Pauls	25,49,73
Sunny Brae	
First settlers	28-31
History of Church	71
Ministers born in	73
Sutherland, Rev. A.	51,96,97
Sutherland, Rev. Geo.	67
Sutherland, Rev. M.	51,62
Sutherland's River	
History of Church	88
Ministers born in	89
Tait, W. D.	175
Tanner, Chas. E.	129,208
Teachers, Pictou Academy	142-146
Theological School, first in Canada	42
Thorburn	88,89,219
Tonge, W. C.	203
Townsend, Sir Chas.	125
Thomson, Rev. A. W.	185
Thomson, Rev. Jas.	53,90
Trenton	
History of Church	57,67
Nova Scotia Steel Works	220
Trinidad	183-185
"The Bee"	194
The Big Election	204
The Samson	219
Tupper, Sir C. H.	210
Union of Churches	
Union of 1817	42
Union of 1860	59
Union of 1875	60
Wabana Iron Ore	220
Walker, Rev. George	66
Waugh, Wellwood	15,17
West Branch River John	98
West River	
First settlers	15
History of Churches	90
Ministers born in	91
West River Seminary	21,52,53
Westville	218
History of Churches	79
Ministers born in	81
Coal centre	219
Willis, A. P.	226
Wilkins, Rev. L. M.	64
Wilkins, Hon. M. I.	124,194,206
Wilson, Beckels	222
Women Missionaries	188-190
Yarmouth Herald	193
Yorston, Frederic	200
Young, Rev. L. L.	187

www.ingramcontent.com/pod-product-compliance
Lightning Source LLC
Chambersburg PA
CBHW052102230426
43671CB00011B/1906